The Art of Voice Acting
second edition

CD Included

The Art of
Voice
Acting
second edition

The craft and business
of performing for voice-over

James R. Alburger

Focal Press
An Imprint of Elsevier

Boston Oxford Johannesburg Melbourne New Delhi Singapore

This book is printed on acid-free paper.

Library of Congress Cataloging-in-Publication Data

Alburger, James R., 1950-
  The art of voice acting : the craft and business of performing for voice-over / James R. Alburger—2nd. ed.
        p.   cm.
     Includes bibliographical references.
    ISBN 0-240-80479-1 (pbk. : alk.paper)
      1. Television announcing—Vocational guidance   2. Radio announcing—Vocational guidance. 3. Voice-overs. 4. Television advertising—Vocational guidance. I. Title: Voice acting. II. Title.

PN1992.8.A6 A42 2002
791.45'028'023—dc21

                                                                      2001058618

The publisher offers special discounts on bulk orders of this book.
For information, please contact:
Manager of Special Sales
Elsevier
200 Wheeler Road
Burlington, MA 01803
Tel: 781-313-4700
Fax: 781-313-4802

For information on all Focal Press publications available, contact our World Wide Web homepage at http://www.focalpress.com

10 9 8 7 6 5 4

Printed in the United States of America.

This second edition is dedicated to the many students who have taken my voice acting workshops, especially to those who have become good friends and who have chosen to continue working with me.
Thank you for allowing me to share my knowledge with you and for helping me to grow as a voice coach, voice actor, and professional speaker.

and

To Penny Abshire, my voice acting and seminar partner, Creative Director of The Commercial Clinic, good friend, and an incredibly talented voice actor and writer.
Thank you for everything!

Contents

A GOLDMINE OF VOICE-ACTING
RESOURCES AND REFERENCES ON CD-ROM

The CD included with this book contains a CD-ROM section with a PDF file of resources and references. The file named **aovapdf.pdf** contains dozens of names, addresses, and Internet links you can use to instantly access information and voice-over resources on-line. There are links for training, services, supplies, recording equipment, and access to literally hundreds of voice-over talent demos. You can copy the PDF file to your hard drive or open it directly from the CD. You may copy and share this file.

This file will not auto-run. To access the resource PDF file, you will need to load the CD into your computer's CD-ROM drive and access the CD from your file manager.

You will need *Adobe Acrobat Reader* installed on your computer in order to open the PDF resource file. *Acrobat Reader* is a cross-platform program that allows you to view Portable Document Files (PDF) on any computer (Mac or PC). The current version of *Acrobat Reader* can be downloaded for free from **www.adobe.com** or you can install version 5.0 from the *Acrobat* folder on the CD.

There are several files included on the CD:

1. The **readme.txt** file on the CD has important information about the files on the CD. Use any text editor or word processor to open this file. Read this file before running or installing the PDF file.

2. The file **aovapdf.exe** is a self-extracting/self-installing ZIP file that contains the **aovapdf.pdf** file. By clicking on the .exe file, you will be asked to UNZIP the file. Click OK to automatically install the **aovapdf.pdf** file into a new folder on your C: drive named *Art of Voice Acting Resources*. Once installed, you can run the PDF file from your computer at any time.

3. Clicking on the file **aovapdf.pdf** will start *Acrobat Reader* and run the resource PDF file from your CD drive. This file can be run from the CD or you can copy it to a folder on your computer. In most cases it will run faster if you copy the file to your computer's hard drive before opening.

4. In the folder *Acrobat*, you will find the installation files for Adobe *Acrobat Reader 5.0* if you don't already have it installed on your computer.

The **aovapdf.pdf** reference and resource file is fully indexed and categorized to make finding and accessing resources quick and easy. The *Art of Voice Acting Resources* PDF file is updated several times a year. Instructions for downloading the current version and for submitting sites for a free listing are included in the PDF file.

Enjoy.

Foreword
By Mel Hall

So, you'd like to be a voice actor. Great. Just walk up to a microphone and start recording all those wonderful characters and noises you hear in your head, right? Wrong.

Maybe you have the talent, maybe you don't. I'll tell you one encouraging thing — you don't have to have the perfect, mellifluous voice of the "traditional radio announcer" to become a successful voice actor. Announcers are seldom good voice actors. Good voice actors can always "do" an announcer. That's what voice acting is all about.

Then, what do you "have to have," you ask? OK, tattoo this word on your heart. BELIEVABILITY. You must be able to create "believability" in all the persons and characters you create with your voice. Some people are "naturals," others often struggle. One thing's for sure: It takes commitment, passion, training and practice to become believable, then successful.

Voice acting is an industry, peopled by some of the most charming "nuts and freaks" you'll ever meet. To be truly successful, you must let a conceptual understanding of the voice-acting syndrome sneak into your very being. It'll come; just be patient . . . and work.

The first thing I'd suggest is READ THIS BOOK. Then, read it again, and keep it handy because you'll never stop learning from it. As you begin to understand what voice acting is all about (the industry, the process, the session, the copy, your character), this book will become more valuable and clear to you as time goes on.

It's been my excitement and pleasure to be a writer-producer-director and performer in the voice-acting and film industries for over forty years. I first met the author, Jim Alburger, 35 years ago, when he was one of the immensely talented sound designers at legendary Bell Sound Studios in Hollywood. In my view, Jim has written THE definitive book on professional voice acting. If you want to be a successful voice actor, LEARN from Jim, TRAIN with him, and above all, READ THIS BOOK!

Go get 'em, tiger!

Mel Hall, Executive Producer-Director
Cinira Corporation

Preface
James R. Alburger

When I wrote the first edition of *The Art of Voice Acting* in 1998, I knew I would not be able to cover everything I wanted to. There simply wasn't enough room. At that time, I was an unknown as an author, a voice coach, and, to some extent, a voice actor. It's amazing how quickly things can change!

In just a few short years, this little book on voice acting has received rave reviews and has become one of the most popular books available on this subject. I now operate my own production company (The Commercial Clinic), producing and voicing commercials for companies around the world. With my partner, Penny Abshire, I continue to hold workshops for people interested in learning voice and acting techniques for improved communication, and we present seminars around the country.

Most books on voice-over will talk about interpretation, how to deliver phrases, how to analyze a script, and some actually teach "announcing." The authors of these other books are generally very talented and skilled voice-over artists in their own rights, and I recommend you purchase their books. But I strongly recommend you read this one first!

This book is different. I've broken down the essential tools and techniques of the voice actor, and show you exactly how you can use them, not just in voice-over, but in everything you do. I don't focus on how "I" did it — I give you instruction in how "you" can do it!

The tools and techniques in this book are just that — tools and techniques. Without understanding how to use them, they are little more than words on the page. But once you learn how to use a few of these tools, you'll discover that they can be used to improve relationships, get more customers, resolve problems, close more sales, make you a better actor, improve your public speaking, and so on, and so on . . .

This is not just a book about voice-over. This is a book about how you can bring your personal life experience to every message you present, and by using a few simple voice and acting techniques, communicate your message more effectively than you can imagine. I'll reveal one of the secrets for great voice acting right here: The situations of your life are your key. When you apply voice-acting techniques you are communicating on an emotional level with your audience. Your message has power and impact that would not be there otherwise. Everything in your life experience holds an emotion that can be used to make you more effective as a voice actor. And even if you never intend to stand in front of a microphone at a recording studio, you can still use what you learn here to become a more powerful communicator.

I like to use the phrase "orchestrate your message," because that is exactly what you are doing when you use these tools. Every situation is different and you may find that you can use a certain combination of these techniques to get the results you want more often than not. You won't use every tool all the time, and some of these tools may not work for you. That's fine. Find the tools and techniques that work for you, take them, and make them your own. It is, indeed, very similar to the way an orchestra conductor blends and balances the various instruments of the orchestra, adjusting the tempo and volume to create the perfect musical sound.

I've tried to include as much in this second edition as I possibly could. This book is considerably larger than the first edition. Chapters 9-12 have been expanded and include completely different scripts than those in the first edition. The section on character and animation voice work has been expanded with all new material. The addition of a CD with this edition gives you the opportunity to hear how the projects actually sounded. The CD includes several exercises that will give you a greater insight into the craft of voice acting. For those of you who are embarking on a career in voice-over, there are a number of voice-over demos that will give you some ideas and standards of quality to strive for. And, finally, there is a special CD-ROM section that includes a PDF file with literally thousands of Internet resources you can access directly from your computer.

Additional training material is under development, including a series of videos that will take you step-by-step through the process of becoming a successful voice actor. Visit my website at **www.voiceacting.com** for more information on this and other products.

Thank you for your interest in voice acting. My goal with this book, as it is with my workshops, seminars, and other products, is to provide you with the best possible training in this craft that I possibly can. I am available to answer your questions or to provide additional training. Should you ever need to reach me with questions or comments about this book, I can be contacted at the e-mail address below. If you would like to receive "The Art of Voice Acting e-mail Newsletter," send an e-mail with your name, city, and state to: **newsletter-request@voiceacting.com**. Include the word "subscribe" in the subject line (without the quotes).

Enjoy and stay in great voice!

James R. Alburger
bookmail@voiceacting.com

Introduction

"You should be doing commercials!"

"You've got a great voice!"

"You should be doing cartoons!"

If anyone has ever said any of these things to you — and you have, even for an instant, considered his or her suggestions — this may be just the book you need! If you simply enjoy making up funny character voices or sounds, or enjoy telling stories and jokes, this book will show you how to do it better and more effectively. If you need to make verbal presentations as part of your job, this book will definitely give you a new insight into reaching your audience. If you are involved in any line of work in which you need to communicate any sort of message to one or more people, this book will help you make your presentation more powerful and more memorable.

This is a book about acting and performing, but it's about a kind of acting where you are not on a stage in front of thousands of people. In fact, with this kind of acting you rarely, if ever, see your audience, or receive any applause for your performance. This is a kind of acting where you will create illusions and believable images in the mind of the audience — a listening audience who might never see you, but who may remember your performance for many years.

This is a book about acting and performing for voice-over! Even though the focus of this book is on developing your talent for working in the world of voice-over, the skills and techniques you will learn can be applied to any situation in which you want to reach and motivate an audience on an emotional level.

Voice-over!

These words alone can be inspiring or intimidating. They can conjure up visions of a world of celebrity and big money. True, that can happen, but as you will learn in the pages that follow, the business of voice-over is just that — a business. It is a business that can be lots of fun and it can be a business that is, at times, very hard work. And it can be both at the same time!

Voice-over is also an art! It is a craft with skills that must be developed. The voice-over performer is an actor who uses his or her voice to create a believable character. The business of voice-over might, more accurately, be called the business of voice acting. It is most definitely a part of show business.

I'll be perfectly honest with you right from the beginning. Working as a voice actor is not for everyone. It requires an investment of time, energy, persistence, and a little money to get started. And, perhaps, just a bit of luck. As the saying goes in show business: An overnight success is the result of 20 years of study and paying dues.

However — if you love to play, have the desire to learn some acting skills, can speak clearly, read well, don't mind the occasional odd working hours, don't take things too seriously, have a good attitude, and can motivate yourself to be in the right place at the right time — this business may be just right for you. In addition, as I mentioned earlier, the skills and techniques of voice acting can be applied to any situation where you want your audience to connect emotionally with the message you are delivering. These skills are not limited to just doing radio and TV commercials.

This book shows you the steps to take to learn the performing skills necessary to be successful in the voice-over business. It also has the information you need to get your demo tape produced and into the hands of those who will hire you. You will get a solid foundation that you can build on to achieve lasting success in the business of voice-over.

You *don't* have to be in Los Angeles, New York, or Chicago to get voice-over work. Work is available everywhere. You *do* need to have the right attitude, the right skills, and a high-quality, professional presentation of your talents, or the casting people won't even give you a second look (or listen). If you master the techniques available to you in this book, you will be able to present yourself like a pro — even if you have never done anything like this before.

I began my adventure through the world of sound and voice acting when I taught myself to edit music at the age of 12. Through my high school and college years I worked for several radio stations creating dozens of commercials as engineer, performer, writer, and director. I have also performed professionally for over four decades as a stage and close-up magician. I put my ideas about performing magic to music in my first book, *Get Your Act Together — Producing an Effective Magic Act to Music*, which became a standard in the magic community. However, it was when I worked as a recording engineer in Hollywood that I began to realize what voice acting was all about. In the nearly three decades since then, I have directed some of the top voice talent in the country, I have been honored as a recipient of several Emmy[1] Awards for sound design, and my production company, The Commercial Clinic (**www.commercialclinic.com**), has received numerous awards for creative commercial production. I teach voice-acting workshops and seminars, speak professionally on how to unlock the magic of your voice (**www.speakingmagic.com**) and the effective use of radio advertising, and operate my own business as a voice actor, sound designer, and performance consultant.

You will notice that I refer to the voice-over artist as voice talent, voice-over performer, or voice actor — never as "announcer." This is because that's exactly what you are — a performer (or actor) telling a story to communicate a message to an audience on an emotional level.

The term voice-over is somewhat misrepresentative of what the work actually entails. It tends to place the focus on the voice, when the real emphasis needs to be on the performance. *Announcers* read and often focus their energy on the sound of their voice, striving to achieve a certain "magical" resonance. Effective voice acting shifts the focus from the voice to the emotional content of the message. This requires knowledge, skill, and a love of performing. Focusing on your performance, instead of the sound of your voice, helps you become more conversational, more real and more believable.

This is why acting is such an important aspect of good voice-over work. Talking *to* your audience conversationally is much better than talking *at* them as an uninterested, detached speaker. The best communication closes the gap between the audience and the performer and frames the performance with a mood that the audience can connect with emotionally. Many people have "great pipes" or wonderfully resonant voices. But it takes much more than a good voice to be an effective communicator or voice actor. In fact, a good voice isn't even necessary — most people have a voice that is perfectly suitable for voice acting. What is necessary are the knowledge and skill to use your voice dramatically and effectively as part of a voice-over performance.

As with most businesses today, the business of voice-over is constantly evolving. The applications for voice-over work are growing every day and there are new trends that require new or modified performing techniques. This revised, second edition has been expanded to include more scripts and "tricks of the trade." Plus, I've added an entire section of Internet resources for the voice actor.

As you read the pages that follow, I promise that I will be straightforward and honest with you. You will find techniques and tricks of the trade that you will not find anywhere else. For those of you considering a move into the business of voice-over, you will learn what it takes to be successful in the business. For those of you who simply want to learn new ways to use your voice to communicate effectively, you will find a wealth of information within these pages.

I wish you much luck — and please let me know when you land your first national commercial, or land that big contract as a result of using these techniques.

Acknowledgments

This second edition of my book would not have been possible without generous support and help from so many people and companies who work in the world of voice-over every day. As you read through the pages of this edition, you will see names, website links, and other references to the many individuals who have supported my efforts with their contributions.

I would like to personally thank the following individuals for their inspiration, support, and for allowing me to share their thoughts and ideas with you:

Penny Abshire, Jon Beaupré, DB Cooper, William Dufris, Ward Franklin, Phil Ganyon, Bruce Hayward, Paul Heckman, Bob Jump, MJ Lallo, Deborah Lawrence, Pam & Vince Lubinski, John Matthew, Viktor Pavel, Dennis Reagan, Melissa Reizian Frank, Michael Reck, Joe Sally, Joni Wilson, and Nancy Wolfson.

The following companies have graciously allowed me to include scripts or other materials so that you might benefit from their work:

Penny Abshire (The Commercial Clinic); Kathleen Boettcher (Celine Publishing/Eesoo Productions); DB Cooper; Phil Ganyon (TGIF); Ross Huguet (One Stop Voice Shop); Bob Jump (Bob Jump Worldwide); "Shotgun" Tom Kelly (BLT Productions); Peter Kern (Kern Media, Inc.); MJ Lallo (MJ Productions); Marc Lyman (Flashpoint Studios); Kristin Marshall Napoleon (Marshall Marketing & Communications, Inc.); the NBC Television Network; NBC 7/39 (KNSD-TV, San Diego); Dick Orkin & Christine Coyle (DOCSI and Radio Ranch, Los Angeles); Elliot Rose (AM Advertising); Marshall Sylver (Sylver Enterprises); and Joni Wilson (Joni Wilson Voice).

---

[1] National Academy of Television Arts and Sciences, Southwestern Regional Emmy awarded for outstanding sound design for television promos and programs.

1

What Is Voice Acting?

We live in an age of information and communication. We are bombarded with messages of all types 24 hours a day. From 30-second commercials to hour-long infomercials; from documentary films, to video games; from telemarketing sales messages to corporate presentations; and thousands of others. Much of our time is spent assimilating and choosing to act or not act on the information we receive.

It is well known among marketing and communications specialists that there are only two ways to communicate to an audience: intellectually and emotionally. Of these, the most effective way to reach an audience is to connect on an emotional, often unconscious level. This frequently involves drawing the listener (or viewer) into a story or creating a dramatic or emotional scene that the listener can relate to. In short, effective voice-over performing is storytelling and requires acting skills. The voice-over performer, in fact, can be more accurately referred to as a voice actor.

The Voice Actor

Voice actors play a very important role in sales, marketing, and delivery of information. It is the voice actor's job to play a role that has been written into the script. To effectively play the role and thus sell the message, the performer must, among other things, be able to quickly determine who the intended audience is, what the key elements of the message are, and how to best communicate the message using nothing more than the spoken word. Chapters 4 through 8 will cover these subjects in detail. For the moment, you only need to know that this type of work requires more from you than simply reading words off a page.

The purpose of voice acting is to get "off the page" with your message. Make it real — connect with your audience — and make the message memorable. You can think of virtually any communication as voice acting!

Types of Voice-Over Work

When most people think of voice-over, they think of radio and TV commercials. These are only a small part of the business of voice-over. There is actually much more to it.

Let's begin with a simplified definition of voice-over. *Voice-over* can be defined as *any recording or performance of one or more unseen voices for the purpose of communicating a message.* The voice-over is the spoken part of a commercial, program, or other announcement that you hear, but do not see the person speaking. The message can be anything from a simple phone message to a television commercial, sales presentation, instructional video, movie trailer, feature film, or documentary narration. It may be nothing more than a single voice heard on the radio or over a stadium public address system. The production may include music, sound effects, video, computer animation, or multiple voices. In most cases, the message is selling something, providing information, or in some way motivating the listener to take some sort of action.

You hear voice-over messages many times every day, and you are probably not even aware of it. The following sections describe just some of the many types of voice-over work that require talented performers, like you.

RADIO

There are three basic categories of radio voice-over work:

1. **The radio DJ** — This is a specialized job that requires a unique set of skills. Most radio DJs are not considered to be voice actors.

2. **On-air promotion** — Most radio promos are produced in-house, using DJ and station production staff. Occasionally, outside talent will be used, but not often.

3. **Commercials** — Most commercials are produced outside the station by advertising agencies. However, many radio stations do produce local commercials for their clients. Again, most in-house productions use station staff, but when the need arises, they will use outside talent.

TELEVISION

Commercials, promotion, and programming all use voice-over talent in one way or another. Most television productions using voice-over talent are actually produced outside of the station. However, there are two main departments at a TV station where voice-over talent is used.

The Promotion Department handles all the station's on-air promotion — from the short "coming up next" VOCs (voice-over credits), to full :30 second promos. The Production Department often needs voice-over talent for locally produced commercials and in-house projects. Some TV stations have a separate unit solely for the production of commercials while other stations work with an advertising agency or outside production company. Two other departments that use voice-over talent are the News Department and the Sales Department. Voice-over in news is part of a reporter's job in reporting a story. The Sales Department usually uses staff announcers for their projects or works with talent booked through the Production Department. In-house presentations for current and prospective clients and station marketing as well as commercials for local clients are just a few of the types of projects produced by a TV station's Sales Department. Most TV stations have an established pool of voice-over talent on staff or readily available. Staff announcers may come to the station and record their tracks on a daily basis, or the copy may be faxed to the talent a few days before it is needed, and the announcer records it and ships the tape to the station for production. Alternatively, some projects may be recorded at a local recording studio. Some TV stations are equipped with the latest digital ISDN telephone technology that allows for a live, high-quality recording of a voice-over performer in another city, or across the country.

CORPORATE/INDUSTRIAL

There are literally thousands of locally produced audio and video presentations recorded each year for the business community. Here are just a few examples of corporate and/or industrial voice-over work:

- **Message-on-hold** — Those informative sales pitches you hear while waiting on hold.

- **In-store offers** — Usually these are part of the background music program played over a store's speaker system while you shop.

- **Sales and marketing presentations** — Video presentations that are designed to attract clients and promote vendors or products. Talent could be either on-camera or voice-over. You will often find these videos as ongoing product demos in stores like K-Mart and Home Depot or in shopping mall kiosks.

- **Convention and/or trade show presentations** — These are similar to sales and marketing presentations, but usually target potential buyers at a convention or trade show. Again, usually these are a video presentation.

- **Training and instructional tapes** — As the name implies, these tapes are designed to train personnel on anything from company policies and procedures, to the proper use of equipment. Most corporate presentations are rarely seen by the general public.

ANIMATION

This is a very specialized area of voice-over work. It's definitely not for everyone, and it is a challenging area to break into. Good animation voice-over performers usually can do a wide range of character voices and have years of acting experience. Most animation voice-over work is done in Los Angeles.

CD-ROM AND MULTIMEDIA

This market for voice-over talent developed as a result of the explosion of computer-based CD-ROM games and instructional software. Some software manufacturers produce audio tracks for these products entirely in-house, while others are produced by outside production companies.

AUDIO BOOKS AND MAGAZINES ON TAPE

These are recordings of books and magazines, and fall into two basic categories: commercial tapes for sale and books or magazines on tape for the visually impaired. Audio books of best-selling novels are often read by a celebrity to make the recording more marketable. However, there is a growing market for audio book projects that use unknown voice talent. Books and magazines on tape for the visually impaired may be produced locally by any number of service organizations or radio stations. The pay is usually minimal or nonexistent (you volunteer your talents).

Most reading services prefer their "readers" to deliver their copy in a somewhat flat tone. For example, there may be several people reading chapters from a book over a period of days. To maintain a degree of continuity in the "reading," the performers are generally asked to avoid putting much emotional spin or dramatic characterization into their reading. This type of work is excellent for improving reading skills and acquiring the stamina to speak for long periods of time, but limits your opportunities to develop characterization and emotional or dramatic delivery skills. Check your local white pages under Blind Aids and Services or contact your local PBS radio station and ask about any reading services they might provide.

Regardless of the type of voice-over work you do, there are several basic requirements:

1. A decent speaking voice.
2. Good reading skills.
3. An ability to act and take direction.
4. The willingness to spend the time necessary to market and promote your talent to get auditions so that you can get the work.

Breaking into the Business of Voice-Over

Most people think voice-over work is easy. You have probably even said to yourself after listening to a commercial, "I can do that!" For some people, it is easy. For most, though, voice-over work — just like theatrical acting — is an ongoing learning process. Even experienced professionals will tell you that voice-over work can be potentially more difficult than on-camera or on-stage work. After all, the advantages of props, scenery, and lighting are not available to the voice actor. The drama, comedy, or emotions of a message must be communicated solely through the spoken word. This often requires a tremendous amount of focus and concentration, plus an ability to make quick changes in mid-stream. Prior acting experience is an advantage, but these are skills you can pick up as you go, so don't let a lack of experience stop you. As long as you can use your imagination, you can do voice-over.

One of the greatest misconceptions is that you need a certain type of voice to do voice-over. You do not need a "good" voice, or "announcer" voice. You do need a voice that is easily understood. If your voice has a unique quality or sound, you can use that to your advantage, especially for animation work. But a unique voice quality can also become a limitation if that is the only thing you do. You may find you are better suited to one particular type of voice-over work — corporate/industrial, for example. If that's the case, you can focus on marketing yourself for that type of work. Still, you should consider other types of voice work when the call comes.

Variety is an important aspect of voice-over performing. By variety I mean being able to use your voice to convey a wide range of attitudes, personality, delivery, and emotions (that's why acting is so important). These are the characteristics of your voice presentation that will sell the message. And selling a message is what voice-over is all about.

Many people think that because they can do lots of impersonations or make up crazy character voices, they can do voice-over work. Vocal versatility is certainly valuable; however, success in the world of voice-over also takes focus, discipline, and an ability to act. When an advertiser wants to use a celebrity voice, they will either hire the celebrity, or use an impersonator who is well known and established.

Character voices are usually hired from an established pool of character voice talent — mostly in Los Angeles. These people are highly skilled actors who can create unique voice characterizations on demand and sustain the character voice over long periods of time. If you enjoy making up voices and have a talent for mimicking, this may be the place for you.

Auditions, either in person or via your demo tape, are the first step to getting work in this business. The toughest part of the business is breaking in and getting those first few jobs. Once your name gets around and you become established, the work almost seems to come to you. Remember, as with most businesses, voice-over work is a "numbers game." The more connections you can make, and the more you circulate your tape to the people who hire voice talent, the more work you will get. As for spending the time and energy necessary to get auditions, remember that voice-over work must be treated as a business if you are to succeed — and your degree of success will be directly proportional to the time you spend promoting yourself.

Just how do you break in and get yourself known as a voice actor? That's what the rest of this book is all about. The simple answer is: Get your voice recorded and get yourself known. The more complex answer is: Learn everything you can about acting, communication, and marketing. In this business, an old adage, "It's not what you know, but who you know," is very true. Getting work as a voice actor is largely a numbers game — a game of networking and making yourself known in the right circles. To be successful you cannot be shy. Let every person you meet know what you do! But you must also possess the skills that qualify you as a professional, and that is what this book is really about!

A career in voice-over can be lots of fun, and it can give you lots of time for other activities. Most recording sessions last from about 10 or 15 minutes to an hour. That's it! Once your voice is recorded, you're free to do whatever you want, or you're on your way to another session.

Enjoy!

Voice Acting in the Business Community

The principles of voice acting are powerful tools that can be used by business professionals and individuals alike, whether you are working from a script or simply having a conversation. In our seminars we refer to the human voice as "your most powerful business assistant." Most people truly do not understand how much more successful they could be if they applied some voice-acting techniques in their presentations, sales calls, or everyday life. The most successful business people use many of these tools, perhaps without even realizing it. Now you will be able to get results you never dreamed possible.

2

The Best-Kept Secret

Let's face it — if everyone were equally good at every job, there would be no need for résumés or auditions. Fortunately, in this world, every person has uniquely different talents, abilities, and levels of skill. It is this variety that makes the voice-over business a potentially profitable career for anyone willing to invest the time and effort.

Voice-over is probably one of the best-kept secrets around. The job can be loads of fun and very profitable, but it is not an easy business to break into. The competition is tough, and it is easy to become frustrated when just beginning.

Voice-over work is part of "Show Business." As such it has all the potential excitement, celebrity status, and opportunities as the other areas of Show Business, as well as the long periods of waiting, frustrations in getting "booked," and problems dealing with agents and producers.

The Pros and Cons of Voice Acting

You have probably heard most of the pros of voice-over work: big money, short hours, celebrity status (fame and fortune without anyone actually knowing who you are), and more. For some voice-over performers, these things are true but it takes a long time, and constantly being in the right place, to get there. In other words, they had to work at it. Most overnight successes are the result of many years of hard work and dedication to the craft. One voice-over coach I know suggests that it takes 15 years to become successful in voice-over. I disagree with that! Everyone defines "success" differently. Sure, if you define success as being in high demand and making the "big bucks," it might take 15 years to get there. But if you are doing voice-over because you really love it, and you wonder why you're not paying them to let you get in front of the mic, then success can be as soon as next week.

7

Like most of the performing arts, voice acting is a hurry-up-and-wait kind of business. By that I mean you will spend a lot of time waiting: waiting at auditions, waiting for a callback, and waiting in the lobby of a recording studio. Then, once you are in the studio, things happen very fast. Even then, you may still find yourself waiting in the studio as the producer works on copy changes. If you are lucky, you will get your copy early and have a chance to read through it a few times. Most often, you will not see the copy until you walk into the studio — and you may have only a few minutes to do your best work.

Producers assume that you know what you are doing and expect you to deliver your lines professionally. Direction (coaching) from the producer or director often comes very fast, so you must listen and pay attention. Sometimes, the producer or director completely changes the concept of the reading or makes major copy changes in the middle of an audition or session — and you need to be able to adapt quickly.

The session can be over before you know it! Most voice-over sessions last from ten minutes to an hour, depending on the project, how much copy there is, and, of course, the performer's ability to deliver what the producer wants. (Whether the producer actually knows what he or she wants is another issue — more about producers, writers, and directors later.) Auditions will usually last anywhere from five to ten minutes — just long enough for the producers to get an impression of what you can do as a voice performer.

Your job as a voice-over performer is to perform to the best of your abilities. When you are hired, either from your demo tape or after an audition, your voice has been chosen over many others as the one most desirable for the job. Unless there is a serious technical problem that requires your being called back, you will not get a second chance after leaving the studio.

Full-Time versus Part-Time

If you think voice-over work is for you, you may have a decision to make. Not right this minute, but soon. Do you want to do voice-over work as a full-time career, or as a part-time avocation? It may not be easy to decide!

Doing voice-over work on a full-time basis is unlike just about any other job you can imagine. You must be available on a moment's notice when you are called for an audition. In addition, you must constantly market yourself, even if you have an agent.

Full-time voice-over work may also mean joining a union, and even moving to a larger city — if that's where your destiny leads you. Los Angeles, New York, and many major cities are strong union towns for voice-over work, and you must be in the union to get well-paying jobs in these cities. Although the possibilities for nonunion work do exist in larger cities, it may require some additional effort to find it.

Smaller cities are a different story, however. The union for voice-over performers, AFTRA (the American Federation of Television and Radio Artists), is not as powerful in smaller towns and there is a much greater opportunity for freelance voice-over work than in bigger cities. On the other hand, major advertising agencies and big clients often use only union talent. So, if you want those jobs you may need to join the union local in your area. There are also many out-of-town ad agencies that do production in smaller cities, and most of them use union talent. Nonunion work is frequently limited to lower-budget commercials written and produced by the advertiser, corporate/industrial work, and some local radio and TV voice work. Unions are covered in more detail in Chapter 15.

OK — you have decided eating is still a pleasurable pastime, and you would rather not quit your day job just yet. So, how about doing voice-over work on a part-time basis? Good question!

Doing voice-over work part-time is quite possible, although you probably won't be doing the same kind of work as you would if you devoted more time to it. You will most likely do some corporate/industrial work and smaller projects for clients who have a minimal or nonexistent budget. Some of your work may be voluntary, barter, or you will do it just because you want the experience. The pay for nonunion freelance work is usually not terrific — but freelance work is a way of getting experience doing voice-over. You can gradually build up a client list and get tapes you can use later on when, or if, you decide to go full-time.

The biggest problem with doing voice-over work part-time is that you may find it difficult to deal with last-minute auditions or session calls. If you have a regular full-time job, you usually will need to arrange your voice-over work around it, unless you have a very understanding employer. If you are only working part-time, you most likely will find it easier to make the auditions and sessions. Voice-over work can be an ideal opportunity for the homemaker who is not working a 9 to 5 job and wants to do something creative, for a retired person with good performing skills, or for the self-employed individual who has a flexible schedule.

As a part-time performer, you can (and should) market your talent and get an agent. As your skills improve and you get more work, you may eventually join the union. If your agent knows you are only doing this part-time, he or she may be reluctant to send you out on many auditions. The image of a performer who is only available part-time is not one that agents particularly like. On the other hand, agents do understand that you need to eat, so they may be willing to work with you.

Doing voice-over work can be very satisfying, even if you only do an occasional session. Generally, the more you work, the more skilled you become — and the greater your skills, the more you can charge for your talent. The day may come when you decide to do voice-over full-time and go for the "big money" in Los Angeles, Chicago, New York, or some other major voice-over market. In the meantime, don't be in a hurry — make the best of every opportunity that comes along and create your own opportunities whenever possible. Networking — telling people you meet what you do — is extremely important. You never know when you might be in just the right place to land that important national spot that changes your entire life!

In the chapters that follow, you will learn the skills you need to become an accomplished voice-over performer. You will also learn how to prepare for your demo tape, and you will be guided step-by-step through the process of producing your demo. Once you know how to get your demo ready, you will learn some methods of marketing your talents.

3

Where to Start: Voice-Over Basics

When you stand in front of a microphone as voice talent, your job is to effectively communicate the message contained in the words written on the paper in front of you. You are a storyteller. You are an actor! The words in your script, by themselves, are nothing but ink on a page. As a voice actor, your job is to interpret those words in such a way as to effectively tell the story, bring the character to life, and meet the perceived needs of the producer or director.

The Voice-Over Performer as Actor and Salesperson

I use the words "perceived needs" because many producers or writers only have an idea in their head. The producer may think he knows what he wants, when, in reality, he hasn't got a clue as to the best way to deliver the message. You may find yourself in the enviable position of solving many of your producer's problems simply by performing the copy in a way that you feel effectively communicates the message. In other words, your acting abilities are the vital link between the writer and the audience.

YOUR ROLE AS A VOICE ACTOR

You are the actor playing the role of the character written in the script. Unlike stage performers, who may have several days, or weeks, to define and develop their characters, you may have only a few minutes. You must use your best acting skills to deliver your best interpretation of the copy. Your job is to breathe life into the script, making the thoughts of the writer become real. You need to be able to quickly grasp the important elements of the script, figure out who you are talking to, understand your character, find the key elements of the copy, and choose what you believe to be the most effective delivery for your lines. In most cases, the producer or director will be coaching you into the read that gets you as close as possible to his or her vision. Sometimes you will be on your own. Every script is written for a purpose and you must be able to find and give meaning to that purpose.

One mistake made by many beginning voice-over performers is that they get nervous when they approach the microphone. They are focused on their voice, not their performance. They fidget, stand stiff as a board, cross their arms, or put their hands behind their backs or in their pockets. It is impossible to perform effectively under those conditions.

What is needed is to get into the flow of the copy, breathe properly, relax, have fun, and let the performance take you where it needs to go. Discover your character and let that character come into you so that you can "become the character."

UNDERSTAND YOUR AUDIENCE

Every message has an intended (or target) audience. Once you understand who the audience is and your role in the copy, you will be on your way to knowing how to perform the copy for the most effective delivery. Figure out who you are talking to. Narrow it down to a single individual and relate to that person on an emotional level. This is the first step to creating an effective performance and a believable character.

Chapter 7, The Character in the Copy, goes into greater detail about analyzing the various kinds of copy and creating characters.

TAKING AIM TO HIT YOUR TARGET AUDIENCE

To hit any target, you must be skilled at using the proper tools, and you must take aim. If your aim is off, you stand the chance of missing your target, no matter how good you may be at using the tools. This book is all about learning how to use your voice effectively to develop a flawless aim.

In voice-over, or any verbal communication, the goal is to make a connection with our listener in such a way that he or she will understand the message and take some sort of action. In order to do that, we must present our message (take aim) in way that is appropriate for our audience, holds their attention, and results in some action on their part.

Regardless of the message, there are only two possible ways it can be communicated:

1) intellectually — dry data, statistics, details, information, etc.
2) emotionally — stories, relationships, feelings, descriptions, etc.

Of these two paths, the strongest and generally most effective connection will be achieved on an emotional level. Emotions are far more powerful and memorable than mere information (unless the information has a specific emotion attached to it), because when properly presented, a listener will become personally involved with the message, which will result in a longer-lasting memory of the event.

In the real worlds of advertising, corporate marketing, telephone messaging, and training videos, it is very easy for a writer to fall into the trap of communicating solely on an intellectual level. You know the kind of project I'm talking about: lots of information, plenty of specs, ample detail, long lists, and enough numbers to keep any accountant happy. The problem with this sort of message is that most people do not absorb large amounts of information easily when that is all they are presented with. The tendency is to "tune out" or lose interest.

The same is true of a message that is presented as a purely emotional experience. As "warm and fuzzy" as it might be, the message will likely miss its target simply because an emotional experience without meaning is of little value to most people, and can be uncomfortable for many.

The ideal communication is achieved when a message contains just the right blend of information (intellect) and positive feelings (emotion) to get the audience's attention, keep their attention, and leave them with something memorable. This blend will vary for each message and for each audience. Although creating this blend is the job of the copy writer, it is important that you understand the concept so that, as a voice actor, you will know how to add an emotional facet to a script that is top-heavy with information.

The best way to connect with an audience on an emotional level is to take careful aim.

A	= Attention	Get the listener's attention quickly by creating interest within the first few seconds.
I	= Information	Hold the listener's attention by presenting only enough information to keep them wanting more. Don't overdo it.
M	= Make it Memorable & Motivating	Motivate the listener by presenting the information in an interesting (often entertaining) manner that gets the listener emotionally involved with the message and leaves them with a strong memory and a sense or desire to take action.

WHAT TO LOOK FOR IN A SCRIPT — (CD track 2)

Here's an example of some of the things to look for in a script. This is copy for a single voice :15 TV promo. Dialogue copy has some additional requirements, but this will give you the idea. Read it through once to get a feel for the copy. Then listen to track 2 on the CD.

This is Yosemite. Before the traffic. Before the floods. Before it became a national disgrace. See what it takes for Yosemite to make a miraculous comeback so it won't be lost forever. "Yosemite: Treasure or Tragedy?" Tonight only at 5, only on NBC 7/39.

Now, read it a second and third time, looking for the following points. Finally, read it out loud for time, to see how close you can come to 15 seconds.

- Who is the audience this copy is trying to reach?

- How can you create interest within the first few words (get attention)?

- What is the single primary message in the copy (what are you selling, or what is the information)?

- What are the supporting statements for the primary message?

- What is your role (your character) in the copy?

- Why is your character telling this story?

- What does your character want or need from telling this story?

- What is the emotional hook in the copy (if any)?

- What sort of delivery do you think would be the most effective to create the strongest memory of the message — strong, hard-sell, happy, smiling, mellow, soft-sell, fast, slow?

- What is your attitude as the character in this spot — serious, comfortable, happy, sad, and so on?

- What visual images come into your mind as you read the copy?

OK, how did you answer the questions? This spot was a TV promo for a news feature series, so there are visuals that go with the copy. You would normally know that at the session and would most likely have access to a storyboard that would describe the visual action your words would play against. Sometimes, however, you will not have anything more than the words on the page. Here's an interpretation of this copy:

- The target audience is men and women who are concerned about the environment. The focus is primarily on adults who are outgoing, enjoy traveling or camping, and may have had the first-hand experience of traveling through the once pristine beauty of Yosemite. Specifically, you would choose to speak to only one person.

- The message is *not* what Yosemite once was. Rather, it is an offer to answer the question of what will happen in the future (the emotion of uncertainty). To have the question answered, the viewer must watch the program.

- The copy uses some emotionally charged words such as "traffic," "floods," "disgrace," and "miraculous." These words (along with the visuals) are intended to create a response in the audience. Each viewer's response to these words will be unique, but the intent is to create an impact in the viewer's mind as to how tragedies created by humans and nature affect beautiful places.

- The character here is telling the story of Yosemite, a once beautiful place that is now ravaged or threatened by people and nature. The character wants to convey the importance of caring for our environment. The first sentence is delivered with a sense of drama, seriousness and anticipation. Each of the following three sentences is delivered with a different attitude, all leading up to the question that is posed. To effectively deliver this copy, it is helpful to set a mental picture of each of the four scenes: a beautiful woodland park, traffic congestion, the aftermath of a flood, and the ugliness of a disaster area. The mental image changes at "miracle comeback" and shifts again to an appropriate image of a "paradise lost."

- The overall delivery is sincere, compassionate, and concerned, with a serious tone. The emphasis for each of the first four sentences is on the first word, to provide punctuation for the emotion that follows. A secondary emphasis is on the emotion word. The end of the copy is delivered in a more matter-of-fact manner, but still keeping the tone of compassion about the story.

All these answers combine to provide the information you need to effectively deliver the copy. The visual image is important because it sets a solid framework for your character and helps establish the attitude of the spot. As an actor, you need to know these things. Otherwise, you are just reading words on a page — and that's boring!

With experience, you can get a complete analysis in a matter of seconds, just from a single reading of the script. Trust your instincts and use what you have learned from your interpretation to give depth to your character and life to the copy. Above all, bring your unique personality into the copy and everything else will come naturally.

THE VOICE ACTOR AS A SALESPERSON

The message — or sell — is the most important part of all copy, and virtually all voice-over copy is selling something. Commercials usually sell products or services, or try to get an emotional response from the audience and motivate action; instructional tapes sell procedures; books on tape sell entertainment; and so on. Acting is the means by which any of these messages can be effectively communicated, the story told, and the listener motivated to take action. So, you are not only a performer, but you are also a salesperson. For the time you are in the recording studio, you are an employee of your client's business. In fact, you are the advertiser's number one salesperson and must present yourself as a qualified expert.

Your acting job may only last a few minutes in the studio, but that performance may be repeated thousands of times on radio or TV. Your voice may be heard by more people in a single minute than might walk through the front door of a business in an entire year. The credibility of the product or advertiser — and the success of an advertising campaign — may be directly related to the effectiveness and believability of your performance. Are you beginning to see there's more to this thing called voice-over than merely reading words on a page?

Getting the Skills You Need

The bottom line here is to get experience — as much as you can, wherever you can, any way you can! Take classes in acting, voice-over, and marketing. Get as much experience as you can reading stories out loud. Read to your children. Read to your spouse. Practice telling stories with lots of variety in your voice.

Analyze the characters in the stories you read. Take more classes. Ask the basic journalism five "Ws": who, what, when, where, and why. Read the same copy in different ways, at different speeds, and with different feelings or emotional attitudes — loud, soft, slow, fast, happy, sad, compassionate, angry. If possible, record yourself and listen to what you did to see where you might improve. Take some more classes. You can't take enough classes!

One of the best ways to acquire skills as a voice actor is to constantly be listening to what other voice-over performers are doing. Mimicking other performers can be a good start to learning some basic performing techniques. But to really get an understanding of communicating on an emotional level, listen to how they deliver the lines:

- How do they interpret the message?

- How do they reach you emotionally?

- How do they use inflection, intonation, pacing, and express feelings?

- Is their delivery conversational or screaming?

- What is your reaction?

In short, do they sound as if they are reading or do they sound natural and believable? Use what you learn from studying others and adapt that information to your own voice and style. One of the keys to successful voice acting is to "make the copy your own." This simply means that you bring to the performance something of yourself to give the character and copy truth and believability. That's good acting! Chapters 4 and 7 discuss techniques for doing this.

A TWIST OF A WORD

You will notice that the better commercials and voice-over work do not sound like someone doing voice-over work. They sound like your best friend talking to you — comfortable, friendly, and most of all, not "announcery." A good performer can make even bad copy sound reasonably good — and what can be done with good copy is truly amazing.

Create an emotional, visual image in the mind of the audience with a twist of a word. A slight change in the delivery of a word can change the entire meaning of a sentence. Speaking a word softly or with more intensity, or perhaps sustaining a vowel, making the delivery crisp, or taking the inflection up or down can all affect the meaning of a sentence and its emotional impact in the mind of the listener. These are skills that are acquired over time and are all basic acting techniques that help to create an emotional connection with the audience.

To be an effective voice performer you need to discover the qualities and characteristics of your voice that will make you different from all those other voices out there. Keep trying new techniques. Keep practicing and studying the work of others in the business. Find your unique qualities and perfect them. Learn how to make any piece of copy your own, and you will be in demand.

CLASSES

You can never take enough classes! There is always something new to be learned. Even if you leave a class with only one small piece of useful information, that small piece may someday pay big dividends. The same is true of books and articles. You will be amazed at where you can find a tip or trick that will help you create a believable performance.

There are three types of classes that are most valuable for the voice-over performer: acting, voice-over, and improvisation. Acting classes will give you opportunities to learn about directing, dramatic structure, comedic timing, stage presence, emotional delivery, and innumerable other fine points of performing. Voice-over classes will give you opportunities to practice your skills on-mic and get some coaching. Improvisation in voice work is most common with dialogue or multiple voice copy. This type of training helps improve your spontaneity and ability to adapt quickly. You will also learn skills that can be applied to character development and copy interpretation. Take some classes! I promise you will learn a lot, and you might actually have fun. Here are some of the places you can find classes:

- Community theater groups are constantly in need of volunteers. Even if you are working on a crew, you will be able to study what goes on in the theater. Watch what the director does, and learn how the actors become their characters. Don't forget that voice acting is theater of the mind — without props, scenery, or lighting.

- Most community colleges offer continuing education classes, often in the evenings or on weekends. Tuition is usually reasonable and the skills you can learn will pay off later on. Suitable courses can also be found in most college theater arts curriculums.

- The Learning Annex has classes in many cities across the country and offers a variety of classes in voice-over, acting, comedy, improvisation, and other subjects that can give you opportunities to acquire the skills you need. Visit **www.learningannex.com** or check your local adult or continuing education office for classes offered in your area.

- Many cities have private acting and voice-over courses. They are usually not advertised in the phone book, so they may be somewhat difficult to locate. Check the classifieds of the local subscription and free newspapers in your area. You can also call the drama department at high schools and colleges for any referrals they might be able to make.

- For voice-over classes, try calling some of the recording studios in your area. Many recording studios work with voice-over performers every day and can offer some valuable insights or give you some good leads. Some studios offer classes or do the production work for a class offered by someone else. Or they might be able to simply point you in the right direction by suggesting local workshops or refer you to a local talent agent who might be able to give you some direction.

A WORD OF CAUTION

Larger cities, such as Los Angeles and New York, have many voice-over workshops and classes available. Most are reputable and valuable resources. Be careful, though, because some classes are little more than scams designed to take your money. Usually the scam classes will provide you with "teaser" information. They tell you just enough to get you excited — usually conveniently underplaying the negatives of the business. Then they tell you they will produce and market your demo for a fee — usually $500 to $1,500. You may even be required to take their class if you want them to produce your demo. Demo fees are usually in addition to the fees you pay for the class, although some will include a demo as part of their overpriced tuition. You may get a demo from these classes, but the quality may be poor, and their promises of marketing the tape or sending it out to agents are usually worthless.

Many legitimate classes will also offer their services to assist with your demo. The difference is that you will not be pressured into buying their services and the demo will not be a condition of taking the class. An honest voice-over instructor will not encourage you to do a demo until you are ready. When they do assist with your demo, the production quality is generally high. Regardless of who you hire to produce your demo, be sure to check them out. Get copies of some demos they have done and get a list of former clients. If they are legitimate, they will be happy to help you. Some will even give you a free consultation.

Be aware that it is highly unlikely that any demo producer will be able to guarantee that your demo will be heard. No matter what they tell you, you will be much better off making the calls to the agents yourself to get your demo out there. Do not rely on someone else to do it for you. See Chapter 13, Your Demo Tape, for more about demos.

4

Taking Care
of Your Voice

As a voice actor, the tool of your trade — the instrument for your performance — is your voice. Just as any other craftsperson must know how to care for the tools of his or her trade, you must know how to care for your voice. So, with that in mind, this chapter includes some simple exercises and tips, most of which you will probably find helpful, others merely interesting, and some perhaps totally weird.

Be Easy on Yourself

My first recommendation as you begin studying the craft of voice-over is for you to record yourself reading copy every chance you get. I guarantee that you will most likely not care for the way you sound, and what you hear may surprise you. There is a good reason why most people are uncomfortable listening to their recorded voice. When you speak, you are not actually hearing your own voice in the same way others do. Much of what you hear is actually resonance of vibrations from your vocal cords traveling through your body and bones to your inner ear. When other people hear you, they don't get the advantage of that nice resonance. The way your voice sounds to other people is what you hear when your voice is played back from a tape recorder.

I suggest you get a portable cassette recorder — one that you can use wherever you are to record your voice. Some are made with a built-in microphone, while others need a mic that plugs in. A small micro cassette recorder can be used, but the quality is usually not very good. You can also use your home stereo cassette machine if it has a mic input jack — check the owner's manual. In this age of digital audio, there are new recording devices coming out every day. Mini-Disc recorders provide very high-quality recordings, but may require an external mic, and some digital handheld voice recorders now have very high quality and long recording time. Another option is to use the sound recording capabilities of a computer if you have the proper hardware and software.

With the proper equipment, you can even use a VCR. Radio Shack has inexpensive microphone mixers that can be hooked up to most audio and videocassette recorders. Be sure to properly connect a microphone to the equipment's line input. Videocassette recorders need a video source in order to properly record audio. So, if you use a VCR, make sure it has a mode that allows you to record a picture along with your audio. A basic tip: A typical microphone connector for consumer equipment is one-quarter inch. The RCA connectors on the back of most stereo equipment are for line-level inputs or outputs and won't work for a microphone — you need a microphone mixer with a line-level output to connect to the RCA line-level input of the recorder. If you have any questions about the type of connector you have, or how to hook it up, any stereo store salesperson can help you.

Practice reading out loud the newspaper, magazine ads, and pages from a novel — anything that tells a story. Record yourself reading a few short paragraphs with different styles of delivery and different emotions. Create different characters and read the copy with their attitudes. Change the pitch of your voice — make your voice louder or softer — and vary the dynamics of pacing, rhythm, and emotion. Practice looking for, and emphasizing, the key elements of the copy. Now, go back and read the same copy again — this time, read with an entirely different attitude, emotion, and character.

By now you are probably listening to other voice-over work at every opportunity. How do you compare? Try to adapt your style to imitate the delivery of someone you have heard on a national radio or TV commercial. Don't try to be that other performer, but rather imitate the techniques and adapt them to your style. If you are still looking for your style, the exercises in this chapter will help you find it.

Listen to your tapes to evaluate what you are doing, but don't be too hard on yourself. Don't be concerned about what your voice sounds like. Focus on what it feels like as you work on your reading. Listen to where you are breathing and if your delivery indicates an understanding of the copy. Listen for your pace, rhythm, and overall believability. Be as objective as you can and make notes about the things you hear that you would like to correct. Practice the exercises and techniques in this book that apply. Recording and listening to yourself can be an enjoyable process and a great learning experience that helps give you an awareness of what you are doing with your voice.

One other tip: If you have a video camera, you might want to videotape yourself as you work on your vocal delivery. One of my students uses video every chance he gets. It may sound odd, but studying your physical movement can make a big difference in the way you sound.

Exercising Your Voice

Two things are essential when exercising your voice: (1) a deep breath with good breath control and (2) making a sound. Your vocal cords are muscles, and as with all other muscles in your body, proper exercise and maintenance will provide greater endurance and stronger performance. The vocal cord muscles are little more than flaps that vibrate as air passes over them. Sound is created by a conscious thought that tightens the vocal folds enabling them to resonate as air passes by. Overexertion and stress can cause the vocal cords to tighten too much, resulting in hoarseness and an impaired speaking ability. A sore throat, cold, flu, or other illness can also injure these muscles. If injured, your vocal cords will heal more rapidly if they are allowed to stay relaxed.

The manner in which we speak — how we breathe and use our vocal and facial muscles — can often be traced to our childhood. Cultural and regional speech patterns have a major influence on how we speak, as do family attitudes and speaking habits and the way in which our parents spoke to us. From the time we first began to talk, we developed speaking habits and attitudes that remain with us today. We became comfortable with these habits because they worked for us as we learned to communicate with others. Some of these habits might include a regional accent, rapid speech, slurred speech, not thinking thoughts through before speaking, a lack of confidence in our ability to communicate, and improper breathing. These and many other speech habits can be corrected through exercise and technique.

Changing a habit will take approximately 21 days and at least 200 or more repetitions. For most people, it takes about seven days of repetition of a new behavior pattern before the subconscious mind begins to accept the change. It takes another 14 days, more or less, for a new habit pattern to become established in the mind. This time frame is true for changing just about any habit and will vary from person to person. As much as we might wish otherwise, it does take a concentrated effort and constant awareness to achieve the desired results.

Discover which of the exercises in this chapter are most helpful and do them on a regular basis, setting aside a specific time each day for your voice exercises. A daily workout is especially important if you are correcting breath control or a specific speaking habit.

Correcting Speech Problems and Habits

As you do these exercises, it is very important for you to observe what is happening with your voice, diaphragm, body, and facial muscles. Awareness of what is happening physically is vital to improving your ability to experience yourself as you work on changing a habit. Self-awareness helps you discover and correct problems with your speech. Without it, you will not be able to recognize the characteristics you need to work on. As you develop skills for self-awareness, you will also be developing instincts for delivery and interpretation that will be of tremendous benefit during a performance.

It is often helpful to have another set of ears listening to you as you work on correcting a problem or speaking habit. A speech therapist or voice coach can be invaluable to improving your speaking voice. You can also get constructive criticism designed to improve your communication skills from acting classes and workshops.

There are many common speech problems that can be corrected by simple exercise and technique. However, all these problems have an underlying cause that requires self-awareness to correct them. Cicely Berry, in her book *Voice and the Actor* (1973)[1] discusses the human voice and methods to improve a vocal performance in great detail. She also explains some of the following common speech problems and how to correct them.

UNCLEAR DICTION OR LACK OF SPEECH CLARITY

Usually, unclear diction or lack of speech clarity is the result of not carrying a thought through into words. A lack of focus on the part of the performer or an incomplete character development can affect diction. This problem can be heard in the voice as a lack of clarity or understanding, often communicated through inappropriate inflection or attitude.

To correct this problem, work on getting a clear understanding of each thought before you speak. Then, speak more slowly than what might feel comfortable to you. Speaking slowly forces you to stay focused on what you are saying.

Stuttering can be classified in this problem area. Although the actual cause of stuttering is still not known, research has shown that it may have different causes in different people and is generally a developmental disorder. Even though research has found three genes that appear to cause stuttering, there is no evidence that all stutterers have these genes or that stuttering is an inherited trait.

There are two traditional therapies to correct stuttering. The first is *stuttering modification therapy,* focusing on reducing fears and anxieties about talking. It can be done with a self-therapy book or with a speech pathologist. The second is *fluency shaping*. This therapy teaches the stutterer to talk all over again by beginning with extremely slow, fluent speech and gradually increasing the speaking rate until speech sounds normal. This therapy is normally done at a speech clinic.[2]

OVEREMPHASIS, EXPLOSIVE CONSONANTS, AND OVERENUNCIATION

The source of overemphasis or overenunciation usually derives from the actor's insecurity or lack of trust in his or her ability to communicate. As a result, the tendency is to push too hard to make sense and start to explain. The moment you begin to overemphasize, you lose the sense.

To correct this problem, don't worry about the listener understanding what you are saying. Stay focused on your thought and just tell the story. Don't explain it, just tell it. It may help to soften the tone of your voice and slow down, or simply to focus on talking to a single person. If you find yourself overemphasizing, you may be trying too hard to achieve good articulation.

Sibilance, the overemphasis of the "s" sound, is often caused by not differentiating between the "s," "sh," and "z" sounds. It can also be the result of dental problems, loose dentures, or missing teeth. Minor sibilance problems can be corrected in the studio with a "de-esser," but serious problems can only be corrected with the help of a speech therapist or perhaps a good dentist.

LOSING, OR DROPPING, THE ENDS OF WORDS

A habit common to many people who are just starting in voice-over and acting is to simply not pronounce the ends of words. Words ending in "b," "d," "g," "p," "t," and "ing" are especially vulnerable.

The cause of this problem is simply not thinking through to the end of a thought. The brain is rushing from one thought to another without giving any thought an opportunity to be completed. This is usually due to a lack of trust in one's abilities, but can also be the result of a lack of focus or concentration.

One way to correct this problem is to force yourself to slow down — speaking each word clearly and concisely as you talk. Think each thought through completely before speaking, then speak slowly and clearly, making sure that the end of each word is spoken clearly. You may find this difficult at first, but stick with it and results will come. Awareness of this problem is critical to being able to correct it.

LACK OF MOBILITY IN THE FACE, JAW, AND LIPS

A person speaking with lack of mobility is one who speaks with only minimal movement of the mouth and face. This can be useful for certain types of characterizations, but is generally viewed as a performance problem. Lack of mobility can be due in part to insecurity or a reluctance to communicate; however, it can also be a habit.

To correct this problem, work on the facial stretching exercises. Practice reading out loud in front of a mirror. Watch your face as you speak and notice how much movement there is in your jaw, lips, forehead, and face. Work on exaggerating facial expressions as you speak. Raise your eyebrows, furrow your brow, put a smile on your face, or frown. Stretch your facial muscles. Go beyond what feels comfortable.

CLIPPED VOWELS

Many people think in a very logical sequence. Logical thinking can result in a speech pattern in which all parts of a word are treated equally. This often results in a monotone delivery with vowels being dropped or clipped. There is little emotion attached to the words being spoken even though an emotional concept may be the subject.

Vowels add character, emotion, and life to words. To correct the problem of monotony, search for the emotion in the words being spoken and commit to the feeling you get. Find the place in your body where you feel that emotion and speak from that center. Listen to your voice as you speak and strive to include emotional content and a variety of inflections in every sentence. For someone who is in the habit of speaking rapidly or in a monotone, this problem can be a challenge to overcome, but the rewards are well worth the effort. Once again, slowing down as you speak can help you overcome this problem.

BREATHINESS AND DEVOICING CONSONANTS

Breathiness is the result of exhaling too quickly, or exhaling before starting to speak. Improper breath control, resulting from nervousness or an anxiety to please, is the ultimate cause. Consonants and ends of words are often dropped, or unspoken, and breaths are taken at awkward or inappropriate places within a sentence.

To correct this problem, work on breathing from your diaphragm. Take a good breath before speaking and maintain a supporting column of air as you speak. Also, be careful not to rush, and think each thought through completely.

EXCESSIVE RESONANCE OR AN OVEREMOTIONAL QUALITY

This problem arises from an internal involvement with an emotion. It is usually the result of becoming more wrapped up in the emotion than understanding the reason for the emotion.

Correcting this problem may involve developing the skill of looking at things a bit more objectively. People who exhibit this problem are generally reactive and live life from an emotional center. For them life is drama. Work on looking at situations from a different angle. Try to be more objective and less reactive. When you feel yourself beginning to react, acknowledge the feeling and remind yourself to step back a bit from your emotional response.

ACCENT REDUCTION OR MINIMIZATION

Many people feel their natural accent or dialect is a problem when doing voice-over. This can certainly be true if you are unable to adapt your style of vocal delivery. In some cases, an accent or dialect can be used to your advantage to create a distinctive style for your performance, when you create a character, or when you are working in only a certain region. However, if you want to be well received on a broad geographic level, you will need to develop the skill to modify your delivery style to one that is expected, and accepted, by the general population. In the U.S., most people have come to expect a certain "sound" for a voice-over performance. A noticeable accent that does not "fit" within the expected sound may not be as effective as a more generic delivery style. Keep in mind, however, that different regions of a country may respond better when hearing a message in their regional accent. If you want to do voice-over, and have a foreign accent, or thick regional accent, you have two choices: 1) develop your acting skills to a high degree and create a niche for the sound of your voice, or 2) learn how to adapt your voice to create characters with an accent different from yours, and that includes the "expected" generic accent.

Many famous actors have learned how to either use their accent to enhance their performance image, or have learned how to adapt their voice to create uniquely believable characters: Sean Connery, Mel Gibson, Patrick Stewart, Nicole Kidman, Meryl Streep, and Tracy Ullman to mention only a few. Mel Gibson has a thick native Australian accent, yet he can play a very believable American. Tracy Ullman has a native British accent, yet she creates dozens of characters from around the world. And Meryl Streep has developed a reputation for creating incredibly authentic and believable foreign accents, even though she is American.

When we first learn to speak, we imitate and mimic those around us as we develop our speaking skills. The mannerisms and vocal stylings that we adopt become the habit pattern for our speaking. Over the years, we become very comfortable with our speaking patterns to the point where it can be difficult to modify them. However, if you have lived in different regions or countries, you may have noticed that your speaking patterns begin to take on the characteristics of that region.

Accent reduction or minimization is, in essence, a process of learning new habit patterns for speaking. For most adults, it is impossible to eliminate completely their native accent. However, reducing the accent or modifying the way words are formed is certainly possible. There are many good books and audio programs designed to help people speak with a more "natural" American, regional, or foreign accent. An Internet search for "accent reduction" will result in a wealth of resources.

The process of re-training your speaking habits can be lengthy, and may involve working with a dialect coach or speech pathologist. Contact your local University Speech Department for recommendations of a licensed speech pathologist, or look into an English as a Second Language (ESL) program in your area. The time and energy required can be more than most people are willing to invest. But a basic level of accent reduction or modification can be achieved if you simply listen to someone with the desired accent, study the sound of their speech, mimic the sound of their words, and practice the speaking pattern until it feels comfortable. This is essentially how actors do it.

In the United States, most voice-over talent perform with a standard American accent. Regional inflections, dialects, and tonalities are, for the most part, absent unless required for a character in the script. Although this has become the generally accepted sound for American voice-over, it does not mean that someone who speaks with an accent or dialect cannot be successful. The most successful voice actors are those who are versatile with their speaking voice and who possess the ability to create a variety of believable characters. If you have an accent (foreign or domestic) there are several things you can do to make yourself more marketable as a voice actor:

1. Refine your accent and learn how to use it to your advantage. Although you may be able to create a unique performing style, you may find that you are limited in the types of projects you can do if you focus only on improving your native accent.

2. Learn how to adapt your speaking voice to mimic other accents for the purpose of creating believable characters. Learn to do this well and you can develop the ability to create any character on demand.

3. Work with a diction coach or study methods of modifying your speech patterns. All of these will require some time and effort on your part, but the results will be well worth it.

Voice and Body Exercises — (CD track 3)

A variety of methods to use to care for your voice are covered later in this chapter. But first, let's begin with some ways to create a relaxed body and mind. That will be followed by a variety of exercises designed to tune your voice and exercise the muscles of your face. When doing breathing or relaxation exercises, it is important for you to breathe correctly. Most of us were never taught how to breathe as children — we just did it. As a result, many of us have developed bad breathing habits. See the All About Breathing section in Chapter 5 for breathing techniques and exercises to help you become comfortable breathing from your diaphragm.

You will find it much easier to get into the flow of a script if you are in a relaxed and alert state of mind. This makes it easier for you to concentrate on your performance. The exercises that follow will help you relax and serve to redirect your nervous energy to productive energy that you can use effectively as you perform.

These relaxation exercises will be most effective when you allow yourself to take slow and deep breaths. Take your time with these and allow yourself to feel and experience the changes that take place within your body. Try to spend at least a few minutes a day with each of these exercises.

EXERCISE 1: RELAX YOUR MIND

This exercise is best done while sitting in a quiet place. Begin by allowing a very slow, deep breath through your nose. This is the basic breathing technique used for vocal awareness described in Chapter 5. Expand your diaphragm to bring in as much air as you can, then expand your chest to completely fill your lungs. Hold your breath for a few seconds, then slowly exhale through your mouth — breathe out all the air. As you do this, think calm thoughts, or simply repeat the word "relax" silently to yourself. Take your time. Do this about ten times and you will find that your body becomes quite relaxed, and your mind will be much sharper and focused. You may even find yourself becoming slightly dizzy. This is normal and is a result of the increased oxygen going to your brain.

If you are nervous going into an audition or session, this exercise is an excellent way to convert your nervous energy into productive energy. Do this in your car before entering the studio.

EXERCISE 2: RELAX YOUR BODY

The deep breathing exercise for relaxing your mind will also help to relax your body. But you may still experience some tension in certain parts of your body. An excellent way to release tension is to combine breathing with stretching. There are several steps to this stretching exercise, so take it slow and if you feel any pain, stop immediately.

Begin by standing with your feet about shoulder width. Close your eyes and breathe deeply from your diaphragm, inhaling and exhaling through your nose. Extend your arms over your head, stretching to reach the ceiling. Stretch all the way through the fingers. Now, slowly bend forward at the waist, lowering your arms as you stretch your back. Try to touch the floor if you can. If you need to bend you knees, go ahead. The idea here is to stretch the muscles in your arms, shoulders, back, and legs. When you feel a good stretch, begin to slowly straighten your body, allowing each vertebra to straighten one at a time as you go. Don't forget to keep breathing.

Now that you are once again standing, with your arms still over your head, slowly bend at the waist, leaning to the left, reaching for a distant object with both arms. You should feel a good stretch along the right side of your body. Slowly straighten and repeat with a lean to the right, then straighten.

Next, lower your arms so they are directly in front of you. Rotate your body to the left, turning at the waist and keeping your feet pointing forward. Allow your hips to follow. Slowly bend at the waist as you stretch your arms out in front of you. Keep your head up and your back as straight as you can. Now, rotate forward and repeat the stretch as you reach in front of you. Finally, turn to the other side and stretch in that direction before slowly returning to an upright position.

EXERCISE 3: RELAX YOUR NECK

A relaxed neck helps keep the vocal cords and throat relaxed. Begin by relaxing your entire body with the technique described in Exercise 1. If you want to close your eyes for this one, feel free. As with Exercise 1, I do not recommend doing this while driving.

This exercise should be done very slowly and it can be done sitting or standing. Do *not* do this if you have a neck injury. If, at any time, you feel any pain in your neck, stop immediately. There may be a neck injury present that your doctor should know about. Begin by sitting or standing up straight. Slowly tilt your head forward until your chin is almost resting on your chest. Allow your head to fall forward, slightly stretching your neck muscles. Slowly rotate your head to the left in a circle until your left ear is over your left shoulder; then move your head back and to the right. Inhale as you move your head back. Begin to exhale as you continue moving your head around until your chin returns to its starting point. Keep breathing. Now rotate your head in the opposite direction. This exercise will help loosen your neck and throat muscles, which will help keep you relaxed.

EXERCISE 4: RELAX YOUR ARMS

This exercise helps remind you to keep your body moving and converts locked-up nervous energy into productive energy you can use. When you are in a session, it often can be helpful to simply loosen up your body, especially if you have been standing in front of the mic for a long time. Remember that moving your body is a very important part of getting into the flow of the script. Loosen your arms and upper body by letting your arms hang loosely at your side and gently shake them out. You can do this before or after any of the other exercises. This relaxation technique works quickly and can be done inconspicuously. You can also expand your shake out to include your entire upper body.

EXERCISE 5: RELAX YOUR FACE

A relaxed face allows you to be more flexible in creating a character. You can use your facial muscles to add sparkle and depth to your delivery. Your face is one of the best tools you have as a voice actor.

To relax your face, begin by relaxing your body. Then, scrunch up your face as tight as you can and hold it that way for a count of ten. Relax and stretch your face by opening your eyes as wide as you can. Open your mouth wide and stretch your cheeks and lips by moving them while opening and closing your jaw. You can also use your fingers to help stretch your cheeks and forehead. The process of stretching increases blood flow to your face and gives a feeling of invigoration.

EXERCISE 6: RELAX YOUR TONGUE

This may sound odd, but your tongue can get tense too. A simple stretching exercise can relax your tongue, and also helps relax the muscles at the back of your mouth. You may want to do this exercise in private.

Begin by sticking out your tongue as far as you can, stretching it toward your chin. Hold for a count of five, then stretch toward your right cheek. Do the same toward your left cheek and finally up toward your nose.

Another tongue stretch that also helps open up the throat is to gently grasp your extended tongue with your fingers. You might want to use a tissue or towel to keep your fingers dry. Begin with a deep breath and gently stretch your tongue forward as you slowly exhale and vocalize a "HAAA" sound, much like the sigh you make when yawning. In fact, this exercise may very well make you feel like yawning. If so, good. Yawning helps open your throat.

EXERCISE 7: HORSE LIPS

Take a long deep breath and slowly release air through your lips to relax them. Let your lips "flutter" as your breath passes over them. This is a good exercise to do alone in your car on your way to a session. By forcing the air out of one side of your mouth or the other, you can also include your cheeks as part of this exercise.

EXERCISE 8: YAWNING

There is a good chance that all this stretching will result is a big yawn. If that happens, enjoy it. Yawning is a good thing. It stretches your throat, relaxing it and opening it up. More important, yawning helps you take in more air, increasing the flow of oxygen to your brain, improving your mental abilities. It also helps lower the pitch of your voice and improves resonance.

To increase the feeling of relaxation, vocalize your yawn with a low pitch "HAAA" sound, concentrating on opening the back of your throat. It is also important that you allow yourself to experience what happens to your body as you yawn.

EXERCISE 9: THE CORK (OR PENCIL)

You will probably find this a little odd at first, but the results will most likely amaze you. Trust me, this one may seem weird, but it works! If a cork is too large or awkward for this exercise, you will find it much easier with a pencil. Using a cork will be a tougher workout, and it may also be a bit messier.

Get a wine bottle cork — save the wine for later, or have it first (your choice). Now, find a few good paragraphs in a book or newspaper. Before doing anything with the cork (or pencil), begin by recording yourself reading the copy out loud. Stop the recorder. Now place the cork in your mouth horizontally so that it is about one-quarter inch behind your front teeth. If you use a pencil, place it lengthwise between your teeth so you are gently biting it in two places. Don't bite hard enough to break the pencil, and don't place the pencil too far back — it should be positioned near the front of your mouth. Now read the same paragraphs out loud several times. Speak very slowly and distinctly, emphasizing every vowel, consonant, and syllable of each word. Don't cheat and be careful not to drop the ends of words. In a very short time your jaw and tongue will begin to get tired.

After you have spent a few minutes exercising your mouth, remove the cork, turn the recorder back on, and read the copy one more time. Stop the tape and play back both recordings. You will notice a remarkable difference in the sound of your voice. The *after* version will be much crisper and easier to listen to.

The cork (or pencil) is a good exercise you can do any time you feel the need to work on your articulation or enunciation. You can even do this in your car, singing to the radio, or reading street signs aloud as you drive to an audition or session. Although a pencil is a suitable substitute for a cork, using a cork will give you quicker results simply because it forces you to work your muscles harder.

EXERCISE 10: THE SWEEP

Vocal range is important for achieving emotional attitudes and dynamics in your performance. By vocal range, I am referring to the range from your lowest note to your highest note. Start this exercise by taking a deep breath, holding it in, and releasing slowly with a vocalized yawn. This will help to relax you. Now fill your lungs with another deep breath and release it slowly, this time making the lowest note you can with a "HAAAA" sound. Gradually increase the pitch of your voice, sweeping from low to high. It may help to start by holding your hands near your stomach and gradually raise your hands as you raise the pitch of your voice.

Probably, you will find one or two spots where your voice breaks or "cracks." This is normal and simply reveals those parts of your voice range that arc not often used. Over time, as you practice this exercise, your vocal range will improve. This is also a good breathing exercise to help you with breath control. If your recordings reveal that you take breaths in mid-sentence or that the volume (overall loudness) of your voice fluctuates, this exercise will help. Practicing this regularly will improve your lung capacity and speaking power, as well as vocal range.

An extremely valuable aspect of this exercise is that for every note along your sweep, you have a place at which you can create a unique voice. This concept is called *voice placement*, and it is something you should become familiar with. You will find that as you create characters for your voice-over work, each character will have certain traits that are distinctly different from other character voices you create. It is this versatility in being able to create a unique voice at different places along your vocal range that will help create a demand for your voice-acting talent. Chapter 11, Character & Animation Copy, discusses voice placement in greater detail.

EXERCISE 11: ENUNCIATION EXERCISES

The following phrases are from a small but excellent book titled *Broadcast Voice Exercises* by Jon Beaupré (1994).[3]

To improve diction and enunciation, repeat the phrases that follow. Speak each syllable clearly and precisely, stretching your lips and cheeks as you read. Make sure all sounds are being heard, and don't cheat on the ends of words. Watch yourself in a mirror as you do these exercises. Listen to yourself carefully and be aware of what you are feeling physically and emotionally. Do the exercises slowly and deliberately making sure that each consonant and vowel is spoken clearly and distinctly. Remember that consistent repetition is necessary to achieve any lasting change. For an extra challenge, try these with the cork or pencil.

Specific Letter Sounds — do each four times, then reverse for four more. Make a clear distinction between the sounds of each letter.

Gudda-Budda (Budda-Gudda)
[Emphasize the "B" and "G" sounds.]
Peachy-Weachy (Weachy-Peachy)
[Emphasize the "P" and "W" sounds.]
Peachy-Neachy (Neachy-Peachy)
[Emphasize the "P" and "N" sounds.]
Peachy-Leachy (Leachy-Peachy)
[Emphasize the "P" and "L" sounds.]
Fea-Sma (Sma-Fea) [pronounce as FEH-SMA]
[Emphasize the difference between the "EH" and "AH" sounds.]
Lip-Sips (Sip-Lips)
[Make the "P" sound clear and don't drop the "S" after lips or sips.]
TTT-DDD (Tee Tee Tee, Dee Dee Dee)
[Emphasize the difference between the "T" sound and the "D" sound.]
PPP-BBB (Puh Puh Puh, Buh Buh Buh)
[The "PUH" sound should be more breathy and have less vocalizing than the "BUH" sound.]
KKK-GGG (Kuh Kuh Kuh, Guh Guh Guh)
[Emphasize the difference between the "K" and "G." Notice where the sounds originate in your mouth and throat.]

Short Phrases — make sure every syllable is spoken clearly and that the ends of words are crisp and clear.

Flippantly simpering statistics, the specifically Spartan strategic spatial statistics of incalculable value

[This one works on "SP" and "ST" combinations. Make sure each letter is clear.]

She stood on the steps
Of Burgess's Fish Sauce Shop
Inexplicably mimicking him hiccuping
And amicably welcoming him in.

[Make each word clear — "Fish Sauce Shop" should be three distinctly different words and should not be run together. Once you've mastered this, try speeding up your pace.]

TONGUE TWISTERS

Tongue twisters are a great way to loosen up the muscles in your face and mouth. Go for proper enunciation first, making sure all letters are heard and each word is clear. Speak each tongue twister slowly at first, then pick up speed. Don't cheat on the end of words. For an extra challenge, practice these using your cork. You will find that after working these with your cork, they will be a bit easier to do.

I slit a sheet; a sheet I slit, upon the slitted sheet I sit.

A proper cup of coffee in a copper coffee pot.

A big black bug bit a big black bear, and the big black bear bled blood.

The sixth sick sheik's sixth sheep's sick.

Better buy the bigger rubber baby buggy bumpers.

Licorice Swiss wrist watch.

Tom told Ted today to take two tablets tomorrow.

The bloke's back brake block broke.

Most Dr. Seuss books can provide additional tongue twisters, and can be lots of fun to read out loud in a variety of styles. Some excellent tongue twisters can be found in *Fox in Sox* and *Oh, Say Can You Say* (1979). Another good book of tongue twisters is *You Said a Mouthful* by Roger Karshner (1993). Most major booksellers, both retail and on-line, can help you find a variety of other tongue twister books.

In 1984, while at a dinner party with people from 12 countries representing more than 15 languages, Michael Reck, of Germany, began collecting tongue twisters. Since then, he has compiled the largest collection of tongue twisters to be found anywhere — "The 1st International Collection of Tongue Twisters" at **www.uebersetzung.at/twister/en.htm**. You'll find more than 2000 tongue twisters in 87 different languages. If you think the English tongue twisters are challenging, try some of the other languages (assuming, of course, you can read them!).

Tips and Suggestions for Maintaining Your Voice

Keeping your voice in good condition is vital to keeping your performing abilities at their peak. Some of the following tips may seem obvious, and you may already be aware of others. Some of the tips here were taken from the private files of some top professional voice actors. None of them is intended to be a recommendation or endorsement of any product, and as with any remedy, if you are unsure please consult your doctor.

TIP 1: SEEK GOOD TRAINING

A good performer never stops learning. Take classes in acting and voice-over. Even classes in improvisation and singing can be helpful. Learn the skills you need to become the best you can be. Study other performers. Watch, listen, and learn from television and radio commercials. Observe the trends. Practice what you learn to become an expert on the techniques. Rehearse regularly to polish your performing skills. Take more classes.

TIP 2: NO COFFEE, SOFT DRINKS, SMOKING, ALCOHOL, OR DRUGS

Coffee contains ingredients that tend to impair voice performance. Although the heat from the coffee might feel good, the caffeine can cause constriction of your sinuses or throat. Coffee is also a diuretic. The same is true for some soft drinks. Soft drinks also contain sugar that can cause your mouth to dry out.

Smoking is a sure-fire way to dry out your mouth quickly. Smoking over a long period of time will have the effect of lowering your voice by damaging your vocal cords, and the other potential risks are not worth it. Besides, in this age of digital audio, if the pitch of your voice needs to be changed, the engineer can do that electronically.

Alcohol and drugs both can have a serious effect on your performance. You cannot present yourself as a professional if you are under their influence. Using alcohol and drugs can have a serious negative influence on your career as a voice actor. Word can spread quickly among talent agents, studios, and producers affecting your future bookings. I have seen sessions cancelled because the talent arrived at the studio "under the influence."

TIP 3: KEEP WATER NEARBY

Keep a bottle of room temperature water with you whenever you are doing voice work. Water is great for keeping the mouth moist and keeping you hydrated. You can tell when your mouth is getting dry because you will start to hear little clicking noises that drive engineers crazy.

As your mouth dries out, tiny saliva bubbles begin to form, and as you speak, the bubbles are popping. Swishing water around in your mouth from time to time will greatly reduce the dreaded "dry mouth" and helps reduce "mouth clicking." Your water should be at room temperature because cold liquids may constrict your throat. Here are some interesting statistics about water, hydration, and the human body:

1. It is estimated that up to 50% of the world population is chronically dehydrated.
2. It is estimated that in 37% of Americans, the thirst mechanism is so weak that it is often mistaken for hunger.
3. Mild dehydration can slow down the human metabolism up to 3%.
4. One glass of water shuts down midnight hunger pangs for almost 100% of dieters studied in a University of Washington study.
5. Lack of water is the #1 trigger of daytime fatigue.
6. Preliminary research indicates that drinking 8-10 glasses of water a day could significantly ease back and joint pain for up to 80% of sufferers.
7. A drop of 2% in body water can trigger fuzzy short-term memory,

trouble with basic math, and difficulty focusing on a computer screen or a printed page.

8. Drinking 5 or more glasses of water daily may decrease the risk of colon cancer by 45%, plus it may slash the risk of breast cancer by 79% and reduce the likelihood of bladder cancer by up to 50%.

It actually takes about 45 minutes for a drink of water to achieve proper hydration, so you may want to start drinking water well before you leave for a session.

TIP 4: HAVE SOME JUICE

Some juices can be helpful in keeping your mouth moist and your throat clear. Any of the Ocean Spray brand juices do a good job of cleansing your mouth. A slice of lemon in a glass of water can also help. Grapefruit juice, without pulp, can help strip away mucus and cleanse the mouth. Any juice you use to help clear your mouth and throat should be a clear juice that contains no pulp. Be careful of fruit juices that leave your throat "cloudy" or that leave a residue in your mouth. Orange juice, grape juice, carrot juice, and others can be a problem for many people.

TIP 5: THE GREEN APPLE THEORY

This is a good trick for helping reduce "dry mouth." Taking a bite of a Granny Smith or Pippin green apple tends to help cut through mucous buildup in the mouth and clear the throat. Lip smacks and mouth noise are the nemesis of the voice actor, and a green apple can help with this problem. This only works with green apples. Red apples may taste good, but they don't produce the same effect.

TIP 6: AVOID DAIRY PRODUCTS

Dairy products, such as milk and cheese, can cause the sinuses to congest. Milk will also coat the inside of the mouth, affecting your ability to speak clearly. Stay away from milk and cheese products when you know you are going to be doing voice-over work.

TIP 7: CLEARING YOUR THROAT

When you need to clear your throat, do it gently with a mild cough rather than a hard, raspy throat clearing, which can actually hurt your vocal cords. Try humming from your throat, gradually progressing into a cough.

The vibration from humming often helps break up phlegm in your throat. Always be sure to vocalize and put air across your vocal cords whenever you cough. Building up saliva in your mouth and swallowing before a mild cough is also beneficial. Be careful of loud yelling or screaming and even speaking in a harsh, throaty whisper. These can also hurt your vocal cords.

TIP 8: AVOID EATING BEFORE A SESSION

Eating a full meal before a session can leave you feeling sluggish and often leaves your mouth in a less-than-ideal condition for performing. If you do need to eat, have something light and be sure to rinse your mouth with water before performing. Avoid foods that you know will cause digestive problems. I know of one voice actor who had to avoid eating anything for several hours before a session. Even the smallest amount of food resulted in her saliva glands working overtime, causing her speaking to be very "slurpy."

TIP 9: AVOID ANYTHING THAT CAN DRY OUT YOUR THROAT

Air conditioning can be very drying for your throat. Be careful not to let cold, dry air be drawn directly over your vocal cords. Smoke and dust can also dry out your throat.

TIP 10: BE AWARE OF YOURSELF AND YOUR ENVIRONMENT

Get plenty of rest and stay in good physical condition. If you are on medication (especially antihistamines), be sure to increase your intake of fluids. If you suspect any problems with your voice, see your doctor immediately. Be aware of dust, smoke, fumes, pollen, and anything in your environment that may affect your voice. You can also have reactions to food that will affect your voice. If you have allergies, you need to know how they will affect your performance, and what you can do about them. An Internet search for "allergies" will reveal resources with lots of information you can use.

TIP 11: USE A THROAT LOZENGE TO HELP KEEP
YOUR MOUTH MOIST

Allowing a throat lozenge or cough drop to slowly dissolve in your mouth can help keep your throat and mouth moist. However, most lozenges are like hard candy and contain sugar that can actually dry your mouth. Exceptions to this are Ricola Pearls natural mountain herbal sugar-free throat lozenges and breath mints and Grether's Red Current or Black Current Pastiles lozenges. These are soft lozenges and contain ingredients which are soothing to the vocal folds. The best time to use a lozenge is about 30 minutes before a session. Do not hold the lozenge in your mouth when speaking — it may affect your performance.

TIP 12: DON'T USE SPRAYS OR LOZENGES TO COVER UP THROAT PAIN

Covering up throat pain will not improve your performance and may even result in serious damage to your vocal cords. If you feel you cannot perform effectively, the proper thing to do would be to advise your agent or client as soon as possible so that alternative plans can be made. The worst thing you can do is to go to a session when you are ill. If you must attend a session when your voice is not in top form, be careful not to overexert yourself or do anything that might injure your vocal cords. Some lozenges and throat sprays like "Entertainer's Secret" and "Singer's Relief" can help keep your throat lubricated.

TIP 13: LEARN TO BREATHE FROM THE DIAPHRAGM

Proper breathing technique is essential for good voice acting. Practice breathing slowly from your diaphragm rather than from your chest. Standing and sitting with good posture will help with your breathing. See All About Breathing in Chapter 5.

TIP 14: PRACTICE CREATING VISUAL MENTAL PICTURES

Visual images will help you express different emotional attitudes through your voice. Close your eyes and visualize the scene taking place in the copy or visualize what your character might look like. Lock the image in your imagination and use it as a tool to help feel and experience whatever it is that you need to express in the copy. Visualization will also help create a sense of believability as you read your lines. Don't worry if you can't visualize in "pictures," However you use your imagination is how you visualize. Some people visualize in colors, some in sounds, some in images. Use whatever works for you.

TIP 15: KEEP YOUR SINUSES CLEAR

Clogged or stuffy sinuses can seriously affect your performance. They can be appropriate at times, if they are consistent with a character, or if they are part of a style that becomes something identified with you. Usually, however, stuffy sinuses are a problem.

Many performers use a decongestant to clear their sinuses. Nasal sprays tend to work more quickly than tablets or capsules. Be careful when using medications to clear your sinuses. Although they will do the job, they can also dry your mouth and can have other side effects. Even over-the-counter decongestants are drugs and should be used in moderation.

When used over a period of time, the body can build up an immunity to the active ingredient in decongestants, making it necessary to use more to achieve the desired results. Once the medication is stopped, sinus congestion can return and may actually be worse than before. Also, some decongestants can make you drowsy, which can be a problem if you are working long hours.

An alternative to decongestants is a saline nasal rinse, technically known as Buffered Hypertonic Saline Nasal Irrigation[4]. Rinsing the nasal passage with a mixture of warm saline solution is a proven method for treating sinus problems, colds, allergies, and post-nasal drip and for counteracting the effects of environmental pollution.

There are a variety of ways to administer the nasal wash, including a syringe, bulb, and water pik. However, one of the easiest to use, and most effective, is a Neti[TM] Pot. This is a small lead-free ceramic porcelain pot with a spout on one end. Although the nasal wash can be done using only a saline solution, some studies have shown that the addition of baking soda (bicarbonate) helps move mucus out of the nose faster and helps the nose membrane work better.

The following recipe for a saline nasal wash can be an effective method of clearing stuffy sinuses.

THE BUFFERED HYPERTONIC SALINE NASAL IRRIGATION
(Otherwise known as: Rinsing the nose with salt water)

The Benefits:
- Rinsing the nose with this salt water and baking soda solution washes out crusts and other debris and helps the mucous membrane in your nose function properly.
- Salty water pulls fluid out of swollen membranes. Washing the inside of the nose decongests it and improves air flow. It will help keep your sinus passages clear and open and make breathing easier.

The Recipe[4]:
- Carefully clean and rinse a one-quart glass jar. Use the Neti Pot to fill the clean jar with 16 ounces of bottled water (the Neti Pot holds about 8 ounces). DO NOT use tap water because it contains many chemicals and undesirable contaminants. It is not necessary to boil the water.
- Add one slightly rounded teaspoon of noniodized salt such as kosher salt. DO NOT use regular table salt because it has unwanted additives. Kosher salt can be found at the grocery store.

- Add half a rounded teaspoon of baking soda (pure bicarbonate).
- If the mixture is too strong, use less salt. A properly mixed solution should not burn or irritate the sinus membrane.

Instructions[5]:
- Pour half the mixture into the Neti Pot or a small bowl. If you prefer the solution to be slightly warm, place the bowl in a microwave oven for a few seconds. Before using, be sure the water is warm, NOT hot.
- If you use a syringe, bulb, or water pik, do not put the used syringe or bulb back into the storage container because this will contaminate the mixture.
- Stand over the sink or in the shower so that you are looking directly down, then rotate your head to one side so one nostril is directly above the other. The forehead should be level with the chin, or slightly higher.
- Gently insert the spout of the Neti Pot into the upper nostril so it forms a comfortable seal. Keep your mouth open as the solution enters the upper nostril and drains out the lower. If using a bulb or water pik, gently pour or squirt the mixture into your nose. Aim toward the back of your head, NOT the top of your head. If your forehead is higher than your chin, the solution will drain into your mouth. If you get some on the solution in your mouth, spit it out. It will not hurt you if some is swallowed.
- After rinsing both sides, exhale vigorously through both nostrils while holding your head over the sink. Do not pinch your nostrils.
- If you use a nasal steroid such as Flonase, Vancenase, Beconase, or Nasacort, you should always use this mixture first. Steroid sprays work best and will reach deeper into the nose and sinuses when applied to nasal membranes that have been cleaned and decongested with this salt water and soda solution.
- You can put this mixture into a small spray container, such as a decongestant nasal spray bottle. This is a good way to use the mixture with children. Squirt the solution many times into each side of the nose.

The Neti Pot is inexpensive, easy to use, and perhaps the best way to apply a nasal wash. You can obtain yours by contacting the Himalayan Institute at their address, Web site, or by phone at:

Himalayan Institute	Toll-free: (800) 822-4547
RR1 Box 400	Direct: (717) 253-5551
Honesdale, PA 18432-9706	Fax: (717) 253-9087
	web: **www.himalayaninstitute.org**

TIP 16: IF YOU HAVE A COLD

You know what a cold can do to your voice and sinuses. If you feel a cold coming on, you should do whatever you can to minimize its effects. Different precautions work for different people. For some, taking Alka Seltzer changes their blood chemistry and helps to minimize the effects of a cold. For others, decongestants and nasal sprays at the first signs of a cold help ease its onset. Lozenges and cough drops can ease the symptoms of a cold or sore throat, but be aware that covering up the soreness may give you a false sense of security and that your vocal cords can be more easily injured in this condition.

The common cold is a viral infection characterized by inflammation of the mucous membranes lining the upper respiratory passages. Coughing, sneezing, headache, and a general feeling of "being drained" are often symptoms of the common cold. In theory, there are more than 200 strains of rhinovirus that can enter the nasal cavity through the nose, mouth, or eyes. Once in the nasal cavity, the virus replicates and attacks the body. Most cold remedies rely on treating the symptoms of a cold to help you "feel better" while your body's immune system attempts to repair the damage.

Gel Tech, LLC markets a homeopathic cold remedy called Zicam that has been shown in clinical studies to reduce the duration and severity of the common cold. According to Gel Tech's Website (**www.zicam.com**), Zicam's active ingredient is Zincum Gluconicum contained in Zinullose™, a unique patented ionic emulsification formula. I'm not quite sure exactly what that is, but I do know it works for me, and several of the people I've recommended Zicam to have told me it has reduced the severity of their colds.

If you have a cold and need to perform, it will be up to you to decide if you are fit for the job. Many performers find that they can temporarily offset the effects of a cold by drinking hot tea with honey and lemon. The heat soothes the throat and helps loosen things up. Honey is a natural sweetener and does not tend to dry the mouth as sugar does. Lemon juice cuts through the mucus, thus helping clear the throat. The only problem with this mixture is that tea contains caffeine, which may constrict or dry the throat.

You can't prevent a cold, but if you can find a way to minimize its affects, you will be able to perform better when you do have a cold.

TIP 17: LARYNGITIS AND COLD REMEDIES

There can be many causes of laryngitis, but the end result is that you temporarily lose your voice. Frequently this is the result of a cold or flu infection that has moved into the throat and settled in your larynx. When this happens to a voice-over performer, it usually means a few days out of work.

The best thing to do with laryngitis is nothing. That is, *don't* talk and get lots of sleep! Your vocal cords have become inflamed and need to heal. They will heal faster if they are not used. Also, the remedy of drinking hot tea with honey and lemon juice will often make you feel better.

A classic bar remedy (I'll give the nonalcoholic version here) is a mix of hot water, Collins mix, and fine bar sugar. This is similar to hot tea, lemon juice, and honey with the benefit of no caffeine. The idea is to create a hot lemonade that can be sipped slowly. Many performers have reported this mixture actually helped to restore their voice.

Another remedy that is said to be effective is to create a mixture of honey, ground garlic cloves, and fresh lemon juice. This doesn't taste very good, but many have reported a quicker recovery from laryngitis after taking this remedy. Garlic is known to strengthen the immune system, which may be a factor in its effectiveness.

Similar to hot tea with honey and lemon is a remedy popular in the eastern United States. This was given to me by one of my voice students and seems to work quite well. Boil some water and pour the boiling water into a coffee cup. Add 1 teaspoon of honey and 1 teaspoon of apple cider vinegar. The mixture actually tastes like lemon tea, but with the benefit of having no caffeine. Slowly sip the drink allowing it to warm and soothe your throat.

Another cold and sore throat remedy that seems to do the job for many people is this rather tasty recipe: 1 can of regular Dr. Pepper (not diet), 1 fresh lemon, 1 cinnamon stick. Pour Dr. Pepper into a mug and add 1 slice (circle) of lemon. Heat in microwave to preferred temperature. Remove and add one cinnamon stick. Relax and sip slowly.

TIP 18: ILLNESS

The best thing you can do if you have a cold or laryngitis or just feel ill is to rest and take care of yourself. If you become ill, you should let your agent, or whoever cast you, know immediately and try to reschedule. However, there are times when you must perform to the best of your abilities, even when ill. These can be difficult sessions, and the sound of your voice may not be up to your usual standards. In situations such as this, be careful not to force yourself to the point of causing pain or undue stress on your voice. In some cases, it is possible to cause permanent damage to your vocal cords.

If you are ill, use your good judgment to decide if you are capable of performing. Talent agents and producers are generally very understanding in cases of illness.

TIP 19: RELAX, AVOID STRESS, AND HAVE FUN

Use the exercises in this chapter to stay relaxed before and during auditions or sessions.

Working as a voice-over performer can be like getting paid to play. The more you enjoy what you do, the easier it will be for you to give a believable performance. If you begin to get stressed during a session, practice some of the relaxation exercises in this chapter. Above all, keep breathing.

TIP 20: THE VOICE-OVER SURVIVAL KIT

Being prepared for the unexpected just makes good sense. Sooner or later you may find yourself at a session where you are recording in a very strange environment, or the studio may be out of pencils or not have a pencil sharpener, the water may be turned off, or any number of other situations might occur.

Enter the Voice-over Survival Kit! You can purchase a small bag or pouch to hold the following items and keep it with you whenever you go to a session. Feel free to add other things you might need, but these are the essentials.

A bottle of water
At least one pencil with a good eraser (mechanical pencils are always
    sharp)
A white-out pen
Throat lozenges
A green apple (to cut mouth noise)
A wine bottle cork (for articulation warm-up)
Decongestant spray
Travel pack of facial tissue

[1] Berry, Cicely. *Voice and the Actor*. New York: Macmillan, 1973.

[2] Kehoe, Thomas David. *Stuttering: Science, Therapy and Practice*. Boulder: Casa Futura
    Technologies, 1997.

[3] Beaupré, Jon. *Broadcast Voice Exercises*. Los Angeles: Broadcast Voice Books, 1994.

[4] Buffered Hypertonic Saline Nasal Irrigation recipe provided in part by John H. Taylor, M.D.,
    Inc., and Patrick G. McCallion, M.D., La Mesa, CA.

[5] Neti Pot instructions provided by the Himalayan Institute.

5

Techniques

A technique is something you might think of as homework — there are always new techniques to study and learn. The application or use of any technique is something that becomes very personal over a period of time as the process of the technique evolves into something that is uniquely yours.

A voice-over technique is really nothing more than a skill that allows you to become a better performer. Sure, you can do voice-over without learning any skills, or you may already have an innate ability with many of them. However, having an understanding of basic acting and voice-over techniques gives you the knowledge necessary to work efficiently under the pressure of a recording session — and to make your performance more real and believable.

As a voice actor, your job is to give life to the words written by the copywriter. The writer had a vision — a sound in mind — when writing the script. You must make the words real and believable. Technique is the foundation for your performance. It is the structure on which your character, attitude, and delivery are built. Technique must be completely unconscious. The moment you begin thinking about technique, the illusion is broken and the moment is lost.

As you begin to study and learn the techniques that follow, you will find yourself thinking about what you are doing. However, as you gain experience and become more comfortable, your technique will become automatic, and you will be able to adapt quickly to changes without having to think. Voice exercises can help you develop and perfect your acting techniques. Chapter 6, Taking Care of Your Voice, includes many exercises, tips, and suggestions for improving your voice and developing your skills.

Style

It is interesting to note that using the voice is the only art form in which an individual style may be developed out of an inability to do something. It may be an inability to form certain sounds, or it may be a cultural affectation of your speaking pattern (an accent or dialect) that results in a quality uniquely your own.

One person's vocal style might emphasize lower frequencies, creating an image of strength and power. Someone else may not be able to reach those low tones, and his or her style might be based on a somewhat warped sense of humor expressed through attitude as he or she speaks. Each of us has developed a unique vocal style for speaking in our everyday lives.

Your fundamental speaking style is a reflection of how you perceive yourself. And your style may change from moment to moment as you move from one situation to another. When you are confident of what you are doing, you might speak with determination and solidarity. But when your insecurities take over, your voice might become weak, breathy and filled with emotion.

Your style as a voice actor comes first from knowing who you are, and then expands on that by adding what you know about human nature, personality, character development, and acting. Chapters 6 and 7 cover these aspects of voice acting in detail.

Developing your style as a voice actor is an ongoing process. You start with your voice as it is now, and as you master new acting and performing skills your style will begin to develop. The tools you use to learn new skills are called *techniques*.

The Road to Proficiency

Acquiring a skill, and becoming good at that skill, is called *competency*. Becoming an expert with the skill is called *proficiency*. You must first be competent before you can become proficient. Sorry, but it just doesn't work the other way around.

BECOMING COMPETENT

Your degree of competency with any skill actually falls into the following four distinct levels. Each person works through these levels at his or her own pace and with varying degrees of success.

LEVEL #1: *Unconscious Incompetence.* At this level you are not even aware that you don't know how to do something. You have absolutely no skill for the task at hand.

LEVEL #2: *Conscious Incompetence.* You become aware that there is something you don't know or understand, and you begin to take steps to learn what you need to know.

LEVEL #3: *Conscious Competence.* You have acquired the basic skills necessary to accomplish the task. However, you must consciously think about what you are doing at each step of the process.

LEVEL #4: *Unconscious Competence.* When you reach this level, you have mastered the skills necessary to accomplish the task without thinking about what you are doing.

THREE STAGES TO PROFICIENCY

There are three stages to acquiring a proficient level of skill to become an expert that must be worked through regardless of the skill that is being learned. Playing the piano, building a table, or performing in a recording studio all require the same three stages of learning and perfecting the skills needed to achieve the end result.

STAGE #1: *Understand the underlying mechanics.* Every skill requires an understanding of certain basic mechanical techniques that must be learned before any level of expertise is possible. In the craft of voice acting, some of these mechanics include: breath control, pacing, timing, rhythm, inflection, and effective use of the microphone.

STAGE #2: *Understand the theory and principles that are the foundation for using the skill effectively.* In voice acting, these principles include script analysis, character development, audience psychology, and marketing.

STAGE #3: *Apply the knowledge learned in the first two stages and continually improve on the level of skill being achieved (practice and rehearsal).* For the voice actor, this means constantly studying acting techniques, taking classes and workshops, studying performances by other voice actors (listening to commercials, etc.), following the trends of the business, and working with what you learn to find the techniques that work best for you.

Three Steps to Creating a Successful Performance

In all areas of performing, there are three steps to creating an effective performance; the end result of any task can be considered as a performance. For example, when building a table, you are performing a series of tasks required to result in a finished table. Your degree of proficiency (expertise) at performing the various tasks will determine how sturdy your table is and what it looks like when you are finished.

The following three basic steps to performing any task are necessary in the business of voice acting as well:

1. Practice — learning the skills and techniques

2. Rehearsal — perfecting and improving techniques and skills

3. Performance — the end result of learning and perfecting

The steps must be done in that order. You, no doubt, have heard the phrase "practice makes perfect." Well, guess what! It's a misnomer. Even *perfect* practice may not make perfect, because it is possible to practice mistakes without realizing it — only to discover too late that the end result is ineffective — and you may not understand why.

PRACTICE

Practice is the process of learning what is needed to achieve the desired result — acquiring the skills and applying the basic mechanics and techniques to achieve proficiency. In voice-over work, the practice phase begins with the initial read-through; having any questions answered by the producer; doing a character analysis; doing a script analysis; working on timing, pacing, and delivery; locking in the correct pronunciation of complicated words; and possibly even recording a few takes to determine how the performance is developing. To discover problems in the copy or character, and correct them, practice is an essential step in voice-over.

If problems are not corrected quickly, they will need to be addressed later during the rehearsal phase. In the real world of voice-over, there are two aspects to the practice phase. The first is when you are practicing on your own to learn basic skills and techniques, and the second is the initial practice read-through at a session. Personal practice should be a life-long quest of learning new skills and techniques. The practice phase at a recording session generally lasts only a few minutes.

REHEARSAL AND PERFORMANCE

Rehearsal begins once all the details of the performance are worked out. The character's attitude, voice, delivery and timing are set during practice. You have committed to your choices of attitude, character, vocal texture, and so on. Rehearsal in voice-over work begins as tracks are recorded. The choices you have committed to are polished, tweaked, tuned and perfected. Every rehearsal (read as: recorded take) has the potential of being used as the final performance, either in whole or in part.

The process of perfecting the performance progresses through a series of takes. Each take is subject to refinement by direction from the producer, director, or engineer. Once an aspect of the performance is set, it should be rehearsed in the same manner, as much as possible, until adjusted or modified by the director. When the delivery on a line is set, don't vary it too much in the following takes. Set the tone of the delivery in your mind so that you can duplicate it in the takes that follow as you polish the rest of the copy.

Eventually, every line of copy will be set to the liking of the producer. In some cases, a producer may actually have the voice actor work line-by-line, getting just the right timing and delivery on one line before moving on to the next line. Later, the engineer will assemble each line's best take to create the final track.

Theatrical actors practice their lines as they work on their blocking and staging. The director gives them some basic instruction, but for the most part, actors are in the practice phase as long as they are working with a script and learning what they are doing and where they need to be at any point in time during a scene. By the time they are ready to put down their scripts, they are at a point where they know what they are doing on stage — and rehearsal begins.

As they rehearse, the director makes adjustments and polishes the performance. Finally, there is a dress rehearsal where all the ingredients of the show — music, scenery, props, lighting, special effects, actors, and so on — are brought together. The dress rehearsal is normally the final rehearsal before opening night and usually is considered to be the first complete performance. There is no such thing as a dress practice! Some theatrical directors even consider the entire run of a show as a series of rehearsals with an audience present.

Never assume you have perfected a technique. There will always be something new, more, or different that you can learn to expand your knowledge. There will always be new techniques for you to try and use. There will always be a different way you can approach a character or piece of copy. There will always be new trends in performance style that require learning new techniques. To be an effective and versatile voice actor, you need to be aware of the trends and willing to learn new techniques.

All About Breathing

To do any voice-over work, it is essential that you know how to breathe. Proper breathing provides support for your voice and allows for emotional expression. It allows you to speak softly or with power, and to switch between the two styles instantly. Proper breathing is what makes possible the subtleties of communicating a broad range of information and emotion through the spoken word.

Breathing comes naturally, and it is something you should not be thinking about while performing. From the moment we are born, we are breathing. However, during our formative years, many of us were either taught to breathe incorrectly, or experienced something in our environment that left us with an improper breathing pattern. It may be that we learned to breathe from our chest, using only our lungs. Or perhaps, we adapted to our insecurities and created a mental block that inhibits our ability to breathe properly.

YOUR VOCAL PRESENTATION

Arthur Joseph, a voice specialist and creator of Vocal Awareness, describes vocal presentation as the way in which others hear and respond to you. The way you are perceived by others is directly related to your perception of yourself. If you perceive yourself to be outgoing, strong, forceful, and intelligent, your voice reflects these attitudes and perceptions with a certain loudness and assertiveness. By the same token, if you perceive yourself to be weak, helpless, and always making mistakes, your voice reflects your internal beliefs with qualities of softness and insecurity. How you breathe is an important factor in your individual vocal presentation because breath control is directly related to the loudness, tonality, and power behind your voice.

Your perception is your reality. So, if you want to change how you are perceived by others, you must first change how you perceive yourself — and that requires awareness. In most cases, a problem with vocal presentation is a habit directly related to a lack of vocal awareness — and habits can be changed. Changing a habit requires an extreme technique — discipline, conscious diligence, and constant awareness. A number of vocal presentation problems, and exercises for correcting them, are discussed in Chapter 4, Taking Care of Your Voice.

Many of the exercises in this book will help you discover things about yourself and your voice, of which you might not have been aware. They will also help you improve or change your breathing technique and vocal presentation, and maintain the new qualities you acquire. The lessons you learn about your voice from this and other books will help give you awareness of your voice and will be of tremendous value as you proceed on your voice-acting journey.

Joni Wilson has written an excellent series of books for improving and maintaining the sound of your voice. The first book of the series, *The 3-Dimensional Voice* is the much-needed owner's manual for the human voice and introduces her ideas and techniques. Other books in the series are: *The 3-Dimensional Business Voice, The Young 3-Dimensional Voice, The 3-Dimensional Singer's Voice*, and *The 3-Dimensional Voice for Life*. You can learn more about Joni and her books on-line by visiting her Website at **www.joniwilsonvoice.com**.

BREATH CONTROL FOR THE VOICE ACTOR — (CD track 4)

The first lesson you must learn before you can begin mastering the skills of voice-acting is how to breathe properly. Take a moment to observe yourself breathing. Is your breathing rapid and shallow? Or do you inhale with long, slow, deep breaths? Observe how you breathe when you are under stress or in a hurry, and listen to your voice under these conditions. Does the pitch of your voice rise? When you are comfortable and relaxed, is the pitch of your voice lower and softer? Feel what your body is doing as you breathe. Do your shoulders rise when you take a deep breath? Does your chest expand? Do you feel tension in your shoulders, body, or face? Your observations will give you an idea of how you handle the physical process of breathing that we all take for granted.

Of course, the lungs are the organ we use for breathing, but in and of themselves, they cannot provide adequate support for the column of air that passes across your vocal cords. The diaphragm, a muscle situated below the rib cage and lungs, is the real source of support for proper breathing.

Allowing your diaphragm to expand when inhaling allows your lungs to expand more completely and fill with a larger quantity of air than if a breath is taken by simply expanding your chest. When you relax your mind and body, and allow a slow, deep, cleansing breath, your diaphragm expands automatically. Contracting your diaphragm, by pulling your lower abdominal muscles up and through your voice as you speak, gives a constant means of support for a column of air across your vocal cords. For a performer, correct breathing is breathing from the diaphragm, not from the chest.

Good breath control for a performance begins with a relaxed body. Tense muscles in the neck, tongue, jaw and throat, usually caused by stress, constrict your vocal cords and cause the pitch of your voice to rise. Tension in other parts of your body also has an effect on the quality of your voice and your ability to perform. Relaxation exercises reduce tension throughout your body and have the additional benefit of improving your mental focus and acuity by providing increased oxygen to your brain. Chapter 4, Taking Care of Your Voice, has several exercises for relaxing your body and improving your breathing.

Good breath control and support can make the difference between a voice actor successfully transcending an especially unruly piece of copy or ending up exhausted on the studio floor. A voice actor must be able to deal with complex copy and sentences that seem to never end, and to make it all sound natural and comfortable. The only way to do it is with good breath control and support.

The following piece of copy must be read in a single breath in order to come in at :10, or "on-time." Even though the words will go by quickly, it should not sound rushed. It should sound effortless and comfortable, not strained or forced. Allow a good supporting breath and read the following copy out loud **(CD Track 4)**:

> Come in today for special savings on all patio furniture, lighting fixtures, door bells, and buzzers, including big discounts on hammers, saws, shovels, rakes, and power tools, plus super savings on everything you need to keep your garden green and beautiful.

How did you do? If you made it all the way through without running out of air, congratulations! If you had to take a breath, or ran out of air near the end, you need to increase your lung capacity and breath support. Long lists and wordy copy are commonplace and performing them requires a relaxed body, focus, concentration, and breath support. You need to start with a good breath that fills the lungs with fresh air.

Check your breathing technique by standing in front of a mirror. Place your fingers just below your rib cage, with thumbs toward the back and watch as you take a slow, deep breath. You should see and feel your stomach expand and your shoulders should not move. If your hands don't move and your shoulders rise, you are breathing from your chest.

As the diaphragm expands, it opens the body cavity, allowing the rib cage to open and the lungs to expand downward as they fill with air. If you breathe with your chest, you will only partially fill your lungs. It is not necessary for the shoulders to rise in order to obtain a good breath. In fact, rising shoulders indicates that the breath is getting caught in the chest or throat. Tension, fear, stress, and anxiety can all result in the breath getting caught in the chest or throat, causing the voice to appear weak and shaky and words to sound unnatural.

Breathing from your diaphragm gives you greater power behind your voice and can allow you to read longer before taking another breath. This is important when you have to read a lot of copy in a short period of time, or when the copy is written in long, complicated sentences.

Do the following exercise and then go back and read the copy above again. You should find it easier to get through the entire piece in one breath.

- Begin by inhaling a very slow, deep, cleansing breath. Allow your diaphragm to expand and your lungs to completely fill with air. Now exhale completely, making sure not to let your breath get caught in your chest or throat. Rid your body of any remaining stale air by tightening your abdominal muscles after you have exhaled. You may be surprised at how much air is left in your lungs.

- Place your hands below your rib cage, lower your jaw, and allow two very slow preparatory breaths, exhaling completely after each one. Feel your diaphragm and rib cage expand as you breathe in and contract as you exhale. Your shoulders should not move. If they do, you are breathing from your chest and are getting only a "shallow" breath.

- Allow a third deep breath and hold it for just a second or two before beginning to read. Holding your breath before starting allows you to get a solid start with the first word of your copy and gives stability to your performance.

A slow, deep, cleansing breath is a terrific way to relax and prepare for a voice-acting performance (see Exercise 1 on page 29). It will help center you and give you focus and balance. However, working from a script requires a somewhat different sort of breathing. You will need to find places in the copy where you can take a breath. For some scripts you will need to take a silent catch breath. At other times you might choose to vocalize a breath for dramatic impact, or take a completely silent breath so as not to give away a punch line or in some other way telegraph the moment.

If you breathe primarily from your chest, you will find that breathing from your diaphragm makes a difference in the sound of your voice. Your diaphragm is a muscle and, just as you tone other muscles in your body, you may need to tone your diaphragm.

Here's a quick exercise from Joni Wilson that will help you develop strong diaphragmatic breathing. You'll find other exercises in her book *The 3-Dimensional Voice*[1]:

- Put the fingers of both hands on the abdominal diaphragm and open the mouth in a yawn position. Inhale the air, then say as you exhale the air, "haaaaaaaaaaaaaaa," manually pushing the diaphragm with your fingers in toward the spine for as long as air comes out of the mouth.

- When there is no more air, and what comes out begins to resemble a "death rattle," slowly relax the pushing and allow the diaphragm to drop back down and suck the air back into the lungs. You may experience some dizziness. Stop for a moment, and let it pass before you do the exercise again. You can do this throughout the day to strengthen the diaphragm.

The Elements of a Voice-Acting Performance

There are many aspects to voice-over performing, and as with any skill, a certain level of proficiency is needed before a person is considered to be working at a professional level. Working at a professional level means that a performer has a thorough understanding of the many intricacies of the craft and is a master of many skills and techniques. A voice actor working at this level can make any character believable by unconsciously bringing together the many elements of a performance.

LESS IS MORE

Just because you love what you do does not necessarily mean you are good at what you do. In voice acting, articulate accuracy with pronunciation or an obvious presentation does not necessarily create the highest level of believability. You will find that you can often create a greater level of truth and honesty in a character by simply holding back a little (or a lot). It may be that speaking a bit slower, a bit softer, altering the phrasing, or being somewhat more relaxed might be just the thing to make that emotional connection with the listener. If your character has a specific regional sound or accent to his or her voice, you may find that softening the edge makes your performance more effective. If your character is intended to be an exaggeration, the *less is more* philosophy probably won't apply, and to be effective you may actually have to go overboard on the characterization.

Less is more is a technique often used by filmmakers to create tension and suspense or as a form of misdirection to set the audience up for a surprise. For example, in the Steven Spielberg film *Jurassic Park*, the initial appearance of the T-Rex was not accompanied by a huge roar. Instead, the tension of the moment was created by ripples in a simple cup of water, implying the approach of something huge and menacing.

The same technique of minimalizing in your voice-over performance can create a moment of dramatic tension, or wild laughter. It often has to do with the character's attitude, the twist of a word, the phrasing of a sentence, the pace of the delivery, or simply a carefully placed pause.

Understanding and applying the principle of *less is more* is an acquired skill, much like comedic timing. It requires a mastery of the craft of voice acting to a point where you are not thinking about what you are doing, and your delivery comes from someplace inside you. Although some people seem to have a natural instinct for interpretation and using the *less is more* concept to create a believable performance, most acquire this skill through experience. Use this concept in your daily conversations to add variety and interest, and notice how people change the way they listen to you. In order to use the *less is more* concept effectively as a voice actor, you must have a solid foundation in the basics of proper speech.

KNOW YOUR PVRs

PVRs are the fundamental elements of vocal variety and create the dynamics of a performance. When you understand and apply *pacing*, *volume,* and *range,* you will be able to make any vocal presentation interesting and captivating.

Pacing refers to the speed of your delivery. It is closely related to the rhythm and timing of the copy and to the tempo of your delivery. *Pacing* is how fast or how slow you are speaking at any given moment. I'm sure you've heard commercials or other voice-over that is delivered at the same pace throughout. There is no phrasing, no pausing for impact, absolutely nothing that makes an emotional connection. Only intellectual information being delivered often at a rapid-fire pace. Or you've heard people who . . . seem . . . to . . . take . . . for . . . ever . . . to . . . say . . . what's . . . on . . . their . . . mind. Does either of these styles of delivery get and keep your interest? No! In most cases a steady pace is boring and uninteresting, if not downright hard to listen to. There are some exceptions in projects for which a steady or slow pace may be critical and necessary to the effective delivery of information, as in an educational or training program. However, in most cases, slowing down or speeding up your pacing to emphasize or de-emphasize certain words or phrases will make a big difference in your presentation. Create interesting phrasing by varying your pace within your delivery. Within two or three read-throughs, you should be able to find the pace and phrasing that will allow you to read a script within the allotted time and in an interesting manner. Some directing cues that relate to pace are: "pick it up" (speed up), "stretch" (slow down), "fill" (you have extra time), and "tighten" (take out breaths or pauses between words).

Volume refers the loudness dynamics of your presentation, and is how soft or how loud you speak at any given moment. Just as volume changes in a piece of classical music keep things interesting, dynamic range in voice-over directly relates to the believability of a performance. Performing a script at the same volume throughout is very much like delivering at the same pace throughout. Both result in loss of credibility in the mind of the listener, because real people change how fast and how loud they speak depending on how they feel about what they are saying. The dynamic range of a performance is directly related to attitude and tone —from soft and intimate to loud and aggressive. Dynamic range is expressed as variations in the *volume* (loudness) of your voice as your speak — from a whisper to a shout.

Range refers to the performer's ability to put variety into the performance by adjusting the pitch of the voice to maintain interest. You've undoubtedly experienced a seminar or lecture at which the speaker spoke in a monotone — no vocal range, resulting in the audience tuning out and losing interest. Vocal *range* covers the spectrum from your lowest pitch to your highest pitch. Voice actors for animation have developed a wide range from which to create many characters. You have a normal vocal range for speaking in everyday conversation, and you can speak at a lower or higher pitch when necessary. Practice speaking at a slightly lower or higher pitch and notice how a small change in vocal range can result in a big shift in interpretation.

PVRs refer to the degree of variety in a performance and are achieved by adjusting pacing (rhythm, timing, and phrasing), volume (loudness), and pitch. Listen to the way people talk to each other and you will notice a wide range of speaking styles. Excitement, enthusiasm, awe, sarcasm, pity, wonder, sorrow, cynicism, and sadness are all expressed in different ways by different people. The variations in the way a person expresses herself or himself reflect that individual's vocal range.

Observe how you instinctively adjust your *Pacing, Volume,* and *Range* in your everyday conversations. Practice altering your PVRs as you speak to your friends or at work, and notice how they pay more attention to what you have to say.

Be aware, however, that PVRs can be easily misused, forced, or overdone. The trick to understanding your PVRs is in the interpretation of a script. What is the writer's objective? Who is the intended audience? How should the words be spoken to achieve the maximum emotional and dramatic effect? How should the intellectual content be delivered so the listener can understand and use it? The dynamics of your performance depend on variations in loudness, pacing, pitch, and emotional expression.

Combined, the dynamics of voice acting serve to help create drama, humor, and tension in a performance. When effectively used, they go hand-in-hand to result in a performance that inspires, motivates, and is believable.

ARTICULATION

Complex sentences and awkward word combinations are an everyday occurrence that every voice actor must deal with. Words must be spoken clearly and concepts communicated in a way that can be understood. Voice acting, and effective communication in general, is a blend of intellectual and emotional information delivered in an interesting and understandable manner. Unless a specific speech affectation is called for in a script, it is generally unacceptable to stumble through words or slur through a piece of copy. *Articulation* refers to the clarity with which words are spoken. Most common problems with articulation are the result of *lazy mouth*, or the tendency to not fully use the muscles of the tongue, jaw, and mouth when speaking.

Good articulation, or enunciation, can be especially tricky when copy must be read quickly. Read the copy from page 52 again, this time making sure that your articulation is crisp and clear. Don't worry about getting it in "on-time," just focus on making every word clear and distinct. As an exercise, force yourself to over-articulate — and don't forget to speak the ends of every word. (See "The Cork" exercise on page 32.)

Come in today for special savings on all patio furniture, lighting
fixtures, door bells, and buzzers, including big discounts on
hammers, shovels, and power tools, plus super savings on
everything you need to keep your garden green and beautiful.

When the same letter is back-to-back in adjacent words such as the "s"
in "hammers, shovels" and "plus super," it's easy to slide through the words
sounding the letter only once. It is also easy to drop the letter "d" from
words like "and" and "need," especially when the next word begins with a
"t," "d," "g," or "b." The letter "g" on words, such as "big," can sometimes
be swallowed resulting in the phrase "big discounts" sounding like "bih
discounts." The suffix "ing" can often be modified when in a hurry, causing
words, such as "lighting" and "everything," to sound like "lightin" and
"everythin." With good articulation, the ends of words are clearly heard, but
not overenunciated and suffixes are properly pronounced.

The "s" and "z" sounds should be clearly distinct. The "s" in "door
bells" should have a different sound from the "z" in "buzzers." The
consonant "s" should sound like the end of the word "yes." The "z"
consonant is a bit more complex to form than the "es" sound. To properly
pronounce the "z" sound, the tip of the tongue starts in the "es" position and
is then arched slightly back toward the roof of the mouth. Say the word
"buzz" and hold the "z." You should feel a distinct vibration of your tongue
and teeth.

Plosives are another articulation problem area. *Plosives* are caused by
excessive air rushing out of the mouth when speaking letters such as "P,"
"B," "G," and "K." When this sudden rush of air hits a microphone's
diaphragm, the result is a loud "pop." Plosives can be corrected by turning
slightly off-axis of the microphone or by using a foam windscreen or nylon
"pop filter" in front of the mic. To feel the effect of plosives, place your
hand directly in front of your mouth and say "Puh, Puh, Puh" several times.
Turning your hand to the side will show you how the blast of air is reduced
when turning off-mic.

To achieve a conversational and believable delivery, it is often
necessary to violate some of the basic rules of crisp articulation. However, it
is important to understand and to master the correct way to do something
before you can effectively do that thing incorrectly and make it believable.
In other words, you've got to be good before you can do bad, good. When
delivering in a conversational style, be careful NOT to over-articulate.

Singers have a technique called *linking* in which the end of a word is
dropped and the sound of the dropped letter is spoken as part of the next
word. For example the phrase "he was fast and foolish" might be spoken as
"he was fast an' foolish." With linking, the "d" on "and" would be moved to
the front of the word "foolish." The result would be spoken as "he was fast
an d'foolish." Another trick that works for vocalizing consonants is to
replace "t" and "d," "b," and "p," "f" and "v," "s" and "z," and "c" and "g."
So, for example, "next time" would sound like "nex dime," "a big zebra"

might sound like "a big seebra," and "a grand vacation" could be spoken as "a grand faycation."

DICTION

Diction is defined as the accent, inflection, intonation, and speaking style dependent on the choice of words. Diction is directly related to articulation, the clarity of your delivery, the correct pronunciation of words, and the sound of a character's voice. Diction is important in all voice-over performances — you really do want to say the client's name correctly and clearly. One of the best ways to improve your diction is simply to slow down as you speak and focus on your enunciation and clarity.

If you are creating a character voice, your diction becomes even more important. A character voice may be a dialect or specific speaking style, and it is vital that your words be understood. Listen to yourself closely to make sure you are speaking clearly and at the correct pace for the character. Exercise 9: "The Cork" (or pencil), on page 32, can help with diction.

RHYTHM AND TIMING

All voice-over copy has a built-in rhythm. It is very important for you to find the rhythm in the copy — especially in dialogue copy. *Rhythm* is an aspect of phrasing. It is the flow of the words, the way the words are organized in sentences, and the placement of emphasis on certain words. Poetic copy has an obvious rhythm (or meter). The rhythm of narrative copy is a bit more challenging to find, but it is there.

Dialogue copy has a definite rhythm, which often includes a sort of verbal syncopation, gradually building to a punch line. Dialogue copy also involves timing. *Timing* refers to the interaction between characters or pauses between lines of copy, and is directly related to rhythm. How quickly does one character speak after another finishes a line? Do the characters step on each other's lines? Is there a long silence before a character speaks? These are all aspects of timing.

If you have a natural sense of timing, you are ahead of the game. If not, the producer will direct you into the timing, and you will get a sense of what is needed as the session progresses. As you become comfortable with your character, timing becomes automatic.

Watch TV sitcoms to study timing. Study the interaction between characters and how they deliver their lines. Listen for the jokes, and how a joke is set up and delivered. Watch the physical characteristics of the actors as they work together. What are their gestures? What facial expressions do they use when they deliver a joke? What expressions do they have when they react to something? How do they express emotion? Use what you learn to help develop your rhythm and timing.

Another thing to notice is the difference in rhythm and timing between radio copy and TV copy. The "radio rhythm" is generally a bit slower than the "TV rhythm." Television has a visual aspect, which is almost always the primary focus of a commercial. For this reason, TV copy is written to be paced a little bit quicker than the same copy used for a radio commercial. Because radio uses only one of the senses, the rhythm, timing, and pace are set a bit slower. The slower tempo of radio gives the copywriter an opportunity to quickly establish and develop an interesting story that will grab the listener's attention and hold it while the message is delivered.

PHRASING

Phrasing in voice-over copy is very much like phrasing in music. It refers to the flow of your delivery, the variations in tempo as you speak, and the subtle nuances of your tone of voice. More specifically, phrasing relates to the way you say certain words or sentences. For example, a short statement — "I don't want to go" — can be phrased in several different ways. The first word "I" can be emphasized as the sentence is spoken rapidly to give personal emphasis. By the same token, the word "don't" can receive the emphasis to give an entirely different meaning. Putting a bit of a whine in the voice, and a frown on your face will create a clear image that "going" is something you really do not want to do.

Try this exercise to discover different ways to express this simple phrase. Read each line, emphasizing the word in bold:

> **I** don't want to go!
> I **don't** want to go!
> I don't **want** to go!
> I don't want **to** go!
> I don't want to **go!**

Another way of phrasing this sentence would be to stretch out the word "don't," sustaining the word and those that follow while adding natural vocal sounds and pauses as the phrase is spoken more slowly and deliberately. This technique, called *pulling lines*, adds realism and believability to the character. A pulled version of this line would read like this: "I, uh . . . dooon't . . . mmm . . . waaant tooo goooo."

Phrasing is closely related to pacing, rhythm, and timing in that it refers to how quickly words are spoken within a sentence or paragraph. But, even more than that, phrasing allows you to make the words more real and believable by adding emotional content.

THEE & THUH, AE & UH

Few words in the English language are used improperly more often than the little words "the" and "a." When used correctly, these words can help add power and emotion to your delivery. Used improperly, your message may sound awkward, and might even create an impression of your being "uneducated." Here are a few quick rules to keep in mind when you see these words in a script. Keep in mind these rules are not set in stone, but are only guidelines. Ultimately, whatever sounds best in the context of your performance, or the way you are directed, is the way you should go:

Basic Rules for "the"

1. Pronounce stressed as "thee" (long e):
   - When "the" precedes a vowel: *The English alphabet has 26 letters.* Exception: pronounce as "thuh" if the word starts with a long "U" as in "thuh university" or "thuh United States."
   - When "the" precedes a noun you wish to stress for emphasis (replacing "a" or "an"): *Yes, that is **the** book you gave me.*
   - When "the" precedes a word you wish to indicate as unique or special, or is part of a title: ***the** place to shop, **the** King of France.*
2. Pronounce conversationally and unstressed as "thuh":
   - When "the" precedes a word that begins with a consonant: *The kitchen cabinet is empty. The car ran out of gas. The dog chased the cat.*
   - When "the" modifies an adjective or adverb in the comparative degree: *She's been exercising regularly and looks the better for it.*

Basic Rules for "a" and "an"

1. Use "a" before words that begin with a consonant, "an" before words that begin with a vowel: *a lifetime of choices, an extreme sense of duty.*
   - Words that begin with a vowel but are pronounced with the consonant sound "y" or "w" are preceded with "a": *a European farmer, a united front, a one-room school.*
   - Words that begin with a consonant but are pronounced with a vowel sound are preceded with "an": *an SST, an F in English.*
2. Pronounce stressed as "ae" (as in "hay") (long a):
   - When "a" is intended to emphasize the next word in a singular sense or is referring to the letter "A": *That is **a** singular opportunity. The letter A is the first letter of the alphabet.*
   - The pronunciation of "a" in its stressed form (ae) will be relatively rare for most voice-over copy as it is not generally conversational. However some technical copy may require this pronunciation to properly convey the message or instructions for training purposes.
3. Pronounce unstressed as "uh" when:
   - "a" precedes a consonant: *a horse, a new car, a cat, a personal debt.*
   - Your character is speaking conversationally or casually.
   - This unstressed form of "a" (uh) is used in most situations.

ATTITUDE

What is it that you, as an actor, bring to the performance of voice-over copy? Are you happy? Sad? Angry? What is the mood of the copy? How do you visualize the scene? What is there — in your personal history — that you can tap into to help make the words real and your performance believable? Answer these questions and you will have your personal attitude. Answer these questions in terms of your script, and you will have your character's attitude.

Attitude is the mind-set of the character in the copy. It gives a reason for the words, and motivation for the character's existence. When you read through copy for the first time, find something in the words that you can relate to. Find an emotional hook. Bring something of yourself to the copy as you perform and you will create more effective characters, a strong suspension of disbelief and a believable illusion of reality.

SENSE MEMORY

Every moment of your life is stored in your memory. And every emotional moment you have experienced has a physical tension associated with it. The tension might reside anywhere in your body. There is also a sensory experience associated with the emotional experience that is closely linked to the physical tension.

Your five senses are some of your most valuable tools as a voice actor. Stanislavski, founder of "method acting," developed this tool to help actors create believable characters, and most acting schools now teach some variation of the technique. To truly master the technique of *sense memory* you may need to take some acting classes which involve creative exercises in which you tap into your senses of sight, touch, taste, sound, and smell.

It is said that all creativity originates in the sensory organs. So, to fully utilize your creative voice-acting abilities, you will need to develop skills for recalling and utilizing sensory memories. However, once the basic concept of *sense memory* is understood, anyone can apply this technique to become a better communicator and achieve some amazing results. Here's how you can use this powerful tool:

Close your eyes and think back through your life to a time, event, experience, sensation, or feeling that is similar to what your character is experiencing and hold that memory in your mind. Make the memory as visual as you possibly can. With that memory held in your mind, recall how your senses were affected by what took place. Was there a special smell? A certain sound? Did something taste odd, or especially good? Did you see something unusual? Do you recall touching something in your memory?

As your memory becomes more visual, observe where in your body the physical tension for that memory is being held: neck, shoulders, chest, stomach, legs, arms, etc. Recall the physical tension, body posture, facial expression, etc. and hold onto it. Keep that memory firmly fixed in your imagination. Now, open your eyes and allow your character to speak the words in the script, in a sense filtered through your experience.

Although it may take some time for you to master this technique, even doing just the basics will put you well on your way to becoming a successful voice actor. Many people who do voice-over either don't utilize this technique, or simply are not aware of it.

In Chapter 7, The Character in the Copy, there is an exercise that takes the concept of *sense memory* to a higher level to help create a totally believable character.

SUBTEXT

All commercials have an attitude. In fact, all copy has an attitude. Your job is to find it and exploit it. One way to find the attitude is to uncover the thought or feeling behind the words. This is commonly known in theater as *subtext*. Subtext is what sets your attitude and establishes, or shades, the meaning of what you are saying. It is the inner motivation behind your words. Subtext allows you to breathe life into the words in a script and into the character you create.

Using your sense memory to unlock emotional hooks is a technique for setting attitude. Now take that process a step further and define the attitude in words to arrive at the subtext. For example, let's say you have this line: "What an interesting fragrance." If the thought behind your words is "What is that disgusting odor? You smell like something that's been dead for a week!" the perceived meaning will be quite different than if your thought and/or feeling is "Wow! You smell amazing! That perfume you're wearing makes me want to be close to you." Each of these subtexts results in a completely different mental and physical attitude that comes through in your voice.

What you are thinking and feeling as you deliver your lines makes a tremendous difference in the believability of your character. You have a subtext in your everyday conversations and interactions with others. The idea here is to include a subtext in your performance. Decide how you want the listener to feel or respond to your character — what emotional response do you want to produce? To get the desired response, all you have to do is think the appropriate thoughts and feel the appropriate feelings as you perform.

For some copy, creating a believable character can be challenging, even with a well-understood subtext. The problem may lie in the subtext itself. If you have chosen a subtext that is weak or unclear, try changing the subtext to something completely different, using an entirely different set of emotional hooks. You may find that by shifting your subtext, your entire performance attitude will change.

TONE

Closely related to attitude and subtext, *tone* is the volume of your voice, and the overall delivery of your performance. It is the sum total of *pacing, volume, range, articulation, diction, rhythm, phrasing, attitude,* and *subtext.* It is important to be consistent throughout your performance. Do not change your tone in mid-copy. If you are doing a soft, intimate delivery with a friendly attitude, maintain that tone from beginning to end. If your copy is fast-paced, aggressive, and hard-sell, keep the attitude and tone throughout.

Tone can also refer to the quality of your performance. If you change tone as you read, you will fall out of character and your levels on the audio console will fluctuate, which will drive the engineer and producer crazy. To maintain a consistent tone, do not drift off-mic. Keep your head in the same position relative to the microphone from start to finish. Working close to the mic gives a warm, soft tone, while backing off as little as a few inches gives a cooler tone for straighter, more direct reads.

Occasionally a script is written that calls for a complete change of attitude and tone in mid-copy. If there is a logical motivation for your character to change attitude, then it would be out of character to maintain a consistent tone throughout the copy.

HOLD THAT THOUGHT

Interruptions are a way of life. You experience them every day. You might be in the middle of saying something really interesting . . . and then someone breaks in or cuts you off before you finish what you are saying. This also happens in voice-over, especially in dialogue. The challenge for the voice actor is to make the interruption sound real and believable.

In a voice-over script, an interruption is usually indicated by the familiar ellipsis, or 3 dots (. . .). The ellipsis can also indicate a pause in the delivery, occasionally replacing a comma or other punctuation.

For example:

Boss:	Peterson . . . we seem to be having some problems in your division. What do you have to say about that?
Peterson:	Well, sir, I . . .
Boss:	Now, listen up, Peterson. We need this taken care of right away . . . Understand?

The trick to making an interruption sound real is to continue the thought beyond the last word to be spoken. If the line is simply read as written, the performance can easily sound like the words are being read, or the interaction between characters may sound "off" or artificial. However, if the thought is carried beyond the last word, the interruption becomes real and natural.

To continue the thought, all you need to do is make up something your character might say that is appropriate to the context of the script. Write it on the script, if you like, but at the very least, keep the complete thought in your mind as you deliver the line, and be prepared to speak the words.

For example:

> Boss: Peterson . . . we seem to be having some problems in your division. What do you have to say about that?
> Peterson: Well, sir, *I've taken steps to get things back on track.*
> Boss: Now, listen up, Peterson. We need this taken care of right away . . . Understand?

When the moment of the interruption occurs, simply hold the thought and let the interruption happen. If the other actor is a bit late with the interruption, no one will ever know, because you kept the thought going. If you are the actor who is interrupting, you need to make sure you deliver your line with the appropriate energy and attitude, and that you are cutting off the other person in a way that sounds like a real conversation.

IMITATION

It has been said that imitation is the sincerest form of flattery. This may be true, but as a voice actor, you want to be unique. You can learn a lot from imitating techniques. But do not imitate other voice-over performers. Be yourself, and find the uniqueness of your voice.

Study the work of other performers and actors, and only mimic what they do to learn their techniques. Then adapt what you learn to your personality and style. If you insist on imitating other performers, it could take a long time for you to find your unique voice-acting personality.

Microphone Techniques: Using the Microphone

Microphone technique is a subtle but powerful way of enhancing your character or the emotional impact of your delivery. Mic technique refers to how you use the microphone to your advantage while in the booth.

MICROPHONE BASICS

Before you can use a microphone effectively, it is helpful to first have a basic understanding of how these marvelous instruments work. The basic purpose of a microphone is to convert acoustical energy (sound waves) to electrical energy that can be manipulated and recorded. There are several designs for each of these types of microphones, *dynamic* and *condenser* being the most popular.

- *Dynamic* mics use a moving coil attached to a diaphragm (much like a loudspeaker in reverse) to convert acoustic energy to electrical energy. Dynamic mics are relatively inexpensive and rugged. Sound quality is generally better with the more expensive models. Simply plug it in to the appropriate equipment and start talking.

- *Condenser* mics use two fixed plates very close to each other, but not touching. A constant voltage is placed across the two plates, provided by a power supply (usually from a battery or external power supply). As sound waves strike one plate, a change in the electrical energy is the result. Condenser mics are more expensive, far more sensitive and more fragile than dynamic mics. The sound quality of a condenser mic is generally cleaner and "crisper" than that of a dynamic mic.

Microphones come in two primary pickup patterns: *omnidirectional* and *cardioid* (*unidirectional*). Of these, the most common type of microphone for recording is the cardioid. Omni and cardioid mics can be either dynamic or condenser.

- *Omnidirectional* mics will pick up sound equally from all directions and are not very common for high-quality voice recording. They are, however, usually the least expensive and most rugged.

- *Cardioid* mics (also called unidirectional mics) come in a wide variety of designs, but virtually all of them pick-up sound best from directly in front of the mic. The sound pick-up reduces or fades as you move off-axis of the front center of the mic. The back of the mic is the point of maximum sound rejection.

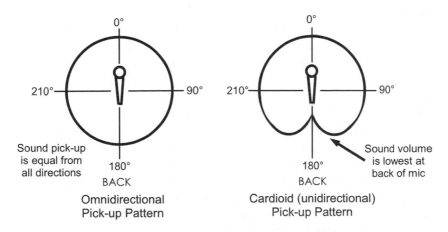

Figure 5-1: Basic microphone pick-up patterns

- A *bidirectional* mic is a single mic that has the pick-up pattern of two cardioid mics placed back to back. With a bidirectional mic, maximum rejection is from the sides at 90° off-axis.

MICROPHONE PLACEMENT

In a recording studio environment you will generally be standing in front of a music stand (copy stand) with a microphone on a boom at about head level. Studio microphones are very sensitive and often have a "pop" screen positioned between the mic and your mouth. The pop screen prevents blasts of air from hitting the microphone's diaphragm. Studio microphones are usually *cardioid* (directional), and most engineers position the mic off to the side or perhaps in front of the performer, above the copy stand at about forehead level about 6-8 inches from the mouth. The acoustics of the voice booth are *dead*, meaning there are no reflected echoes. The result is a very clean sound.

Microphone placement is simple for a single performer, but becomes more critical when there are several performers in the same studio, each with his or her own mic. In this case, the engineer strives to obtain maximum separation from each performer to minimize how much of each actor's voice is picked up by the other microphones.

As a starting point, you should position yourself so your mouth is about 6-8 inches from the mic. You can easily estimate this by extending your thumb and little finger; place your thumb against your chin, and the mic at the tip of your little finger.

WORKING THE MICROPHONE

Microphones really don't care where they are in relation to your mouth. Six inches off to the left will pick up your voice exactly the same as six inches directly in front of you or six inches above your mouth (at about eye level). You should always position yourself so you are talking across the microphone and never directly into it. Speaking directly into the mic can blast the diaphragm. Although this is rarely harmful to the mic, the resulting "popping" sounds can be a serious problem for the recording and are something that cannot be fixed later on.

As you physically move closer to a studio microphone, your voice increases in lower frequencies (bass) and the overall tone of your voice will be more intimate. This phenomenon is called *proximity effect* and is a common characteristic of all directional microphones. As you move away from a studio mic, the mic picks up more of the natural ambience of the room. This results in a more open sound, which is cooler and less intimate. Don't be afraid to experiment, but do let the engineer know what you are doing because he or she will need to adjust recording levels accordingly.

While performing, keep your head in a constant relationship to the microphone. The rest of your body can move as much as you need, provided you aren't making any noise. But your head must remain relatively stationary. If your position drifts on- and off-mic, your voice will appear to fade in and out. This drives engineers crazy because the overall volume of your performance is constantly changing. Even with the best equipment, moving off-mic is extremely difficult to deal with simply because a change of just a few inches can result in a very noticeable change in the *room tone* or ambience picked up by the mic.

NEVER BLOW INTO OR TAP A MICROPHONE

Studio microphones are delicate and *very* expensive. Blowing into a microphone can cause severe damage. When testing a mic or giving a level to the engineer, always speak in the actual volume of your performance. When the engineer asks you to read for levels, consider it an opportunity to rehearse your performance.

Tapping the mic, although not usually harmful, is annoying to most engineers. It's good to keep engineers on your side; they control how you sound and have complete power in the control room. Remember basic studio etiquette — don't touch the equipment!

LET THE ENGINEER POSITION THE MICROPHONE

Always let the engineer adjust the mic to where you will be standing or sitting. Do not move or adjust the mic yourself. The same goes for the pop stopper. After positioning your mic and returning to the control room, the engineer will ask for your level, and may ask you to physically change your position relative to the mic. You may be asked to *move in* on the mic (move closer to the mic), or *back off* a bit (move an inch or so away from the mic). These physical adjustments should be minor, and are intended to help produce the right sound for your voice. If you are popping, you may be asked to change the angle of your face in relation to the mic, or to turn slightly off-mic to prevent your breath from hitting the mic.

HOLDING THE MICROPHONE

You will rarely need to hold the mic during an actual session. However, it may be necessary for some auditions. If it ever happens to you, you need to know how to properly hold the mic for the best sound.

The correct handheld mic technique is to hold it vertically or at a slight angle, with the top of the mic at chin level, about an inch below the lips and slightly away from the chin, not touching the face. In this position, you will be speaking across the top of the mic rather than directly into it. Talking across the mic minimizes breath pops. You can test for proper mic placement by pursing your lips and blowing straight ahead or saying "puh, puh." Slowly raise a finger from below your chin up to your lips and you will know where to position a mic to avoid being hit with your breath.

If you need to hold the mic, do not play with the cord. Just let it hang from the end of the mic. Wriggling the cable can cause noises in the mic that can affect how you are heard. You may not hear anything as you perform, but cable noises can be heard by the producer later on, and may cover up parts of an otherwise good audition.

Acting Classes

You can never take enough classes. You've heard it before, and you will hear it again. Acting classes are where you can learn a wealth of techniques for analyzing copy, developing character, delivering lines, discovering motivation, using body language, interacting with other characters and much, much more.

Acting classes are available at most colleges, as well as from local community theater groups and other sources. Many cities have an actor's studio that offers ongoing workshops. Improvisation workshops are another useful class for the voice actor. Improvisation in voice-over is important because it gets your creative juices flowing and helps with your interaction with other characters in multiple-voice scripts. In an improv class, your creative talents will be expanded and you will discover things about yourself you never knew.

Take classes — you won't be sorry. Then take some more!

---

[1] Wilson, Joni. *The 3-Dimensional Voice.* San Diego: Blue Loon Press, 2000.

6

Voice Acting 101

A voice-over performer is an actor — period. It doesn't matter what the copy or script is for. It doesn't matter if the copy is well written or poorly written. It doesn't matter if you are delivering the copy alone or with others. You are an actor when you stand in front of the microphone.

Acting is an art. Acting skills take time to learn and master. Acting is not difficult; it's just that as we've grown, we've simply forgotten how to play. As a child, you were acting whenever you pretended to be someone you were not. That's really all acting is — pretending!

It's All About Pretending

Voice-over performing — or, more accurately, voice acting — is your chance to bring out the child inside. You may be pretending to be a specific character, an inanimate object that talks, or just pretending to be a spokesperson providing information. Regardless of the copy you are reading, there will always be some sort of character in those words. To be believable, that character must be brought to life. To do that effectively, you must become a master at pretending.

There are many ways to discover a character and bring it to life. The process is very much like telling a bedtime story to a young child. You simply figure out who is speaking and decide what physical attitude and vocal characteristics the character has. Chapter 7, The Character in the Copy, explains in detail how to break down a script for character and story.

Learning how to bring the character to life is the first step of interpreting the copy. Before you can effectively interpret the copy, however, you need to know how to set the physical and mental attitudes of your character.

Use Your Body – Use Your Mind

The two most valuable tools you have as a voice actor (besides your voice) are your body and your mind. This may sound a bit odd, but the fact is that moving your body — using facial expressions, physical exertion, and even the way you stand — can be of immense value in creating and delivering an effective character.

Your imagination is another critical ingredient in creating your character and communicating the message. Your imagination helps you visualize the story and bring your past experiences to the script; that's how you make the copy your own.

These three important tools are fundamental to theatrical acting. If you learn to use them as a voice actor, you will become much more effective with your script interpretation and character performance. However, body movement and imagination are just two of the many skills you need to develop as a voice actor.

Basic Keys to Successful Voice Acting

There are many things you can do to improve the effectiveness of your delivery. As you begin to master these techniques, you will find your delivery becoming increasingly effective. You will also discover that you will become more versatile and better able to handle a wider range of delivery styles. The following sections describe concepts and performing techniques that are basic to theatrical acting, and any or all will be of tremendous value to you as a voice-over performer.

BE IN THE MOMENT

This is basic acting. You need to be focused on your performance. You cannot be thinking about what you are doing later that afternoon and expect to give a good performance. You also cannot be in the moment if you are struggling to get the words right or dealing with interpretation. As long as you are focused on the copy, you will sound as though you are reading. To be in the moment, you must become comfortable with the words to the point where they become yours, and you are not thinking about what you are doing.

Being in the moment means that you understand your character, who your character is speaking to, and the message in the script. It also means that you speak the words in the script with a truth and honesty that comes from the heart of the character. A good way to be and stay in the moment is to practice the following techniques.

LISTEN AND ANSWER

Be aware of what is going on in the copy. Don't just read words on the page — listen to your character, and to the other performers if you are doing dialogue copy. Interact with what is being said. Be real! Respond to the message emotionally and physically. Remember that acting is reacting. Listen to yourself as you deliver the lines. Listen to how you deliver the lines and your internal response to the words you are saying, then react accordingly. This technique can give life to an otherwise dull script.

Your best and most real performance will be achieved when you are truly "in the moment" of the scene taking place — aware of what you are doing, but not consciously thinking about it. As Shirley MacLaine once said in an interview: "It's all about listening, and forgetting who you are."

THE "A-B-C's" OF VOICE ACTING

If you remember nothing else from this book, the following concepts will take you further in voice acting than just about anything else. You can also apply these ideas in any area of your personal or professional life to achieve a high level of communication skill. This technique does not have to be done in sequence. In fact, most of the time one element will help define another, and it may begin with "C."

A = AUDIENCE

Who are you (or your character) talking to? Decide on who will be hearing the message. You would not talk to a ten-year-old with statistics, numbers, and facts. By the same token, you should not talk to adults in the same way you talk to kids. Different styles of delivery are appropriate for different audiences. By knowing your audience, you will be able to figure out the most effective way to reach them.

In most cases, the copy alone will give you a good idea of who the audience is. At other times, it may be helpful to ask the producer who he or she is trying to reach. The more you can learn about the intended audience, the better you will be able to act your part.

The most important thing to remember about your audience, though, is that no matter what the script or project may be, you are *always* talking to ONLY ONE PERSON. Every voice-acting performance is a conversation between the performer and a single listener. It is impossible to effectively communicate a message if you try to reach several people at the same time. Focus your attention on just a single person and talk to that individual as though he or she is your closest friend (or whatever the relationship may be as defined by the script). Attempting to shotgun your performance, by trying to connect with many people at once, will generally result in the listening audience losing their interest and becoming uneasy with you as a performer. There is a very subtle difference between focusing attention on an individual versus a mass of people. You've no doubt experienced seminars where the speaker just doesn't seem to reach the audience, and yet there are others where everyone is hanging on the speaker's every word. In the first instance, the speaker is most likely "shotgunning" the message in an attempt to reach everyone in the audience (or he's just incredibly boring). In the second, the speaker is getting eye contact with individuals in the audience — one at a time. When you focus your attention on one person, and speak with honesty and sincerity, everyone listening will feel drawn in, as though you are speaking only to them. This is an incredibly powerful technique that many people who do conventional "voice-over" simply don't understand or apply.

Describe the person you are speaking to in as much detail as possible and give him or her a name. Use a photograph to get the feeling of having eye contact with a real person. Doing this will make your delivery more conversational and believable. The RISC AmeriScan process outlined in Chapter 7, The Character in the Copy, will give you additional tools you can use to define your one-person audience.

B = BACK STORY

A back story is the specific event that took place immediately before the first word of copy. The back story is the reason why your character is saying the words in the script. If the back story is not clearly defined in the script — make one up! This is a very important aspect of performing from a written script because the back story sets your character's motivation, attitude, and purpose for speaking.

Similar theatrical terms include "the moment before" and "subtext." Both of these can be somewhat vague, so I have my workshop students define a back story in very specific terms that can be described in a single sentence. A back story is not a long, involved story leading up to the first word of the script. It is something very immediate and powerful that has caused your character to speak.

In some scripts, the back story is pretty obvious. In others, you'll have to make up something. Either way, the back story is essential to the development of your character. Without knowing what the specific event is that motivates your character to speak, you cannot know how your character will react to other characters or the situation in the copy as it is written.

A back story can be found for any type of copy. To discover the back story, look for clues in the script that reveal specific details about what is taking place. Use these clues to create your own idea of what took place *before* the story in the script. This is your back story, and this is what brought your character to this moment in time. By understanding what brought your character to this moment, it will be much easier for you to sustain your character and effectively communicate your character's

The A-B-C's of Voice Acting
the   complete   alphabet

A	Audience	Articulate (cork exercise)	Authentic in Attitude
B	Back Story	Benefits	Believe in Yourself
C	Character	Critical Thinking	Commit to Choices
D	Desires	Different Approach	Dynamics for Variety
E	Energy	Effortless (to be real)	Expert
F	Forget Who You Are	Focus	(Have) Fun
G	Grins (use your face)	Gestures	"Go for It!"
H	Hands (use your arms)	How Does Your Character ... ?	Have Alternatives Ready
I	"Into the White"	Inspiration	Imagination
J	Juxtapose (change words to find emotion)	Jargonize (when appropriate)	Journey (explore options)
K	Key Words & Phrases	"Keep It Real"	Kid (let yours come out)
L	Listen Carefully	"Less Is More"	Lose Yourself
M	M.O.V.E.	"Moment Before"	Mark Your Script
N	No Guessing	Never Touch the Mic.	Never Argue
O	"Off the Page"	"Out of the Black"	Observe
P	Play	Practice (for technique)	Pencil
Q	Quality (always do your best)	Question Everything	Quickly Find Your Character
R	Respond	Rehearse (for polish)	Results
S	Sense Memory (use your past experience)	Script Analysis (woodshed your script)	Suspension of Disbelief
T	Teamwork	Think Out of the Box	Truth
U	Understand the Whole Story	Underplay	Use Tools & Techniques
V	Voice Act (not "voice-over")	Visualize the Scene	Vision (the big picture)
W	Warm-up	Water (to stay hydrated)	Woodshed Copy (journalism 5 W's)
X	X-periment	X-plore	X-cite
Y	Yawn to Open Throat	Yell (if appropriate to character)	Yourself (Don't Be)
Z	Zicam (homeopathic cold remedy)	Zeppo (a famous Marx brother)	Z end of Z list

feelings, attitudes, and emotions. Learn how to find the back story and you will learn how to understand the motivation of your character.

C = CHARACTER

Who are you as the speaker of those words on the paper? Define your character in as much detail as you like. How does your character dress? What does the voice sound like? Does the character exhibit any sort of attitude? How does the character move? What is the character's lifestyle? How does the character feel about the product, service, or subject of the script? The more details you can come up with, the more believable your character will be to you and to your audience. Every script has a character, regardless of how poorly the script may be written or what the content of the script may be. Find that character and give it life.

Just as in life, scripted characters have feelings and experience emotions about the stories they tell. Learn how to reveal those emotions and feelings through your voice and you will create believable characters. Chapter 7, The Character in the Copy, will explain many ways for you to do this, and you will find additional tools in Chapter 11, Character Copy.

UNDERSTAND YOUR CHARACTER'S WANTS AND NEEDS

All characters have wants and needs! There is something the character wants from speaking those words. It may be simply to enlighten the listener with a valuable piece of information, it may be to entertain, or it may be to instruct the listener in the fine points of operating a complex piece of machinery. Whatever they may be, your character desires to accomplish something from sharing the message. If that desire is not clearly explained in the script — use the information available to make it up.

MAKE IT THE FIRST TIME EVERY TIME

Be spontaneous, every time! Use your acting and imagination skills to keep the copy, and your performance, fresh. Each performance (or take) should be as though the character is experiencing the moment in the script for the first time. You may be on take 24, but your character in the copy needs to be on take 1 — for every take. Use your imagination to create a clear visualization of a scene, character or situation to help make your performance real and believable take after take.

TELL THE STORY EFFECTIVELY

Don't just read the words on the page. Play the storyteller — no matter what the copy is. Search for an emotional hook in the copy. Find a way to close the gap between the performer and the audience. Find a way to connect with that one person you are talking to, on an emotional level.

Your emotional connection may be in the softness of your voice. Or it may be in the way you say certain words. It may be in the way you carry your body as you speak your lines. Or it may be in the smile on your face. Make that connection, and you will be in demand.

Don LaFontaine, one of the top voice actors in the country, was once asked what he did as he performed. His answer was, "I create visual images with a twist of a word." It is the little shift of inflection or subtlety in the delivery of a word or phrase that makes the difference between an adequate voice-over performance and an exceptional voice acting performance. Effective storytelling is using the subtleties of performance to reach the audience emotionally and create strong, memorable visual images.

BE YOUR OWN DIRECTOR

A part of you needs to be able to look at your performance objectively, as if observing from a distance. This director in your mind will give you the cues to keep your performance on track. Directing yourself is a valuable skill that you can use constantly — even when there is a director on the other side of the glass.

When you are wearing your "director" hat, you need to be listening for all the little things in your delivery that are not working. Look for the important words in the copy that need to be emphasized. Look for the parts that need to be softened. Look for places to pause — a half-second of silence can make all the difference. Listen for the rhythm, the pace, and the flow of the copy. As the director, you are your own critic. Your goal is to constructively critique your performance to increase your effectiveness in communicating the message.

The process of looking at your performance objectively can be quite difficult if you are working by yourself. The difficulty lies in the fact that if you think about what you do as you are performing, you will break character. Your "director's" listening process needs to be developed to the point where it happens at an unconscious level, yet you still have a conscious awareness of what you are doing as your character. You would be wise to work with a voice coach or take some classes to learn what directors look (or listen) for and how they work with performers to get the delivery they want. Watch and learn as others are directed. Observe how the director focuses the performer on the particular part of the copy that needs improvement.

Record your practice sessions and have a skilled director listen to your tapes to give you suggestions on what you can do on your own. As you gain experience, your performance and self-direction become as one, and you will instinctively know how to deliver a piece of copy.

M.O.V.E. (MOVEMENT ORCHESTRATES VOCAL EXPRESSION)

Be physical! Body movement is an expression of emotion, and your expression of emotions or feelings will communicate through your acting and will be heard through the tone of your voice. Move your body in whatever manner works for you to effectively get to the core emotion of the message. Your **M**ovement **O**rchestrates your **V**ocal **E**xpression! M.O.V.E.

Try the following: Find a short paragraph in a book or magazine, preferably with some emotional content. Read the paragraph once or twice to get a basic understanding of its content. Stand straight and stiff, feet together, head up, looking straight ahead with an expressionless face. Hold the book or magazine in front of you at about eye level. Now, read the words out loud — without moving your body or face — and listen to the sound of your voice. Listen to the lack of expression in your voice. Listen to how totally boring you sound.

While keeping the same physical attitude — and still without moving, read the same copy again and try to put some emotion into your reading. You will find it extremely difficult to put any emotion or drama into a reading without moving. When you begin to communicate emotions, your body instinctively wants to move.

Now, relax your body, separate your feet slightly, loosen up, and put a big smile on your face. Read the same copy again — this time moving your arms and body, keeping the smile on your face. Listen to how your physical attitude and facial expression change the sound of your voice. Try this with different physical positions and facial expressions and you may be amazed at the range of voices you will find. A big smile will add brightness and happiness to the sound of your voice. A frown or furrowed brow will give your voice a more serious tone. Tension in your face and body will communicate stress through your voice.

It's a mistake to stand in front of the microphone with your hands hanging limp at your sides or stuffed in your pockets — unless that physical attitude is consistent with your character in the copy. Keep your hands at about chest level and your elbows bent. This allows you the freedom to move your hands as you speak.

The way you stand can also affect your voice performance. Although body stance primarily communicates information visually, it can also be very important when creating a character. Body language, just as facial expression, translates through the voice. For example, to make a character of a self-conscious person more believable, you might roll your shoulders forward and bring your arms in close to the body, perhaps crossing the arms at certain points in the copy.

Physical changes help to create a believable character who is somewhat self-conscious, a bit defensive, perhaps unsure of the situation and who may even be shy and focused on how she or he is perceived by others. Your body posture assists in framing the attitude and personality of the character. The following are some typical body postures that will help you understand how body stance can affect your performance. If used unconsciously, these postures can have an adverse affect on your performance because they will have a direct impact on your speaking voice.   However, if consciously applied to a character or attitude, these and other body postures can be used to enhance any voice performance:

- **Arms behind back ("at-ease" stance)** — This body posture reflects nervousness and implies that the speaker doesn't know what to do with his or her hands or is uncomfortable in the current situation. Clasping the hands in back or in front of the body tends to minimize other body movement and can block the flow of energy through your body. This in turn may result in a "stiffer" sound with a restricted range of inflection and character.

- **Straight, stiff body with hands at the side ("attention" stance)** — Standing straight and tall, with chest out, head held high and shoulders back implies authority, control, and command of a situation. This projection of power and authority can be real or feigned. This stance is sometimes used as a bluff to create an outward image of authority to cover for an inward feeling of insecurity. This body stance can be useful for a character who is to project power, authority, or dominance over a situation.

- **Arms crossed in front of the body ("show me" stance)** — Crossed arms often represent an unconscious feeling of self-consciousness and insecurity, creating an attitude of defiance or being defensive. Crossed arms can also imply a certain level of dishonesty.

- **Hands crossed in front of the body ("Adam and Eve" stance)** — As with the at-ease stance, this posture implies that the speaker doesn't know what to do with his or her hands. This stance, with the hands crossed like a fig leaf, is commonly perceived as an indication that the speaker has something to hide. This stance can be useful in helping create a character who projects suspicion.

- **Hands on the hips ("mannequin" stance)** — This posture makes the speaker appear inexperienced or unqualified. Hands on the hips also blocks the flow of energy through the body and limits the performer's ability to inject emotion and drama into a performance. This stance can be used to create an attitude of arrogance.

FIND THE RHYTHM IN THE COPY

Consider voice-over copy in terms of a musical composition. Music has a range of notes from high to low, being played by a variety of instruments (the voices). The tempo of the music may be generally fast or slow (the pace), and the tempo may fluctuate throughout the composition. The music also has a range of loud-to-soft (dynamics). These elements combine to create interest and attract and hold the listener's attention. Voice-over copy works the same way.

All copy has a rhythm, a tempo, and a flow. Rhythm in voice-over copy is much the same as rhythm in music. There are many pieces of music that run two minutes, but each has a unique rhythm. Many times, the rhythm changes within the composition. Rhythm in voice-over copy is as varied as it is in music. Some copy has a rhythm that is smooth, classy, and mellow. Other copy has a choppiness that is awkward and uncomfortable.

Some of the factors that affect rhythm in voice-over copy are pacing, pauses, breaths, the subtle emphasis of key words, and even diction and intonation. In dialogue copy, rhythm also includes the timing of the interaction between characters. Find the rhythm in the copy and you will win auditions.

Rhythm is something that can only be found by making the copy your own. You cannot get into a rhythm if you are just reading words off a page. Make the words your own by knowing your character, and you will be on your way to finding the rhythm. You might find it interesting to record yourself in a conversation. You may discover that you have a rhythm in the way you speak, which is quite different from the rhythm of others in the conversation.

A conversation has several things going on at once: There is a rhythm to the words, a tempo or pacing and the interaction between the people having the conversation. Listen for pauses, people talking at the same time, the energy of the conversation, and the way in which certain words are emphasized. Observe how they move their bodies, especially when expressing an emotion or feeling. All these elements, and more, go into creating the rhythm of a conversation.

UNDERSTAND THE PLOT OR STORY

Look for the basic dramatic elements of a story in the copy. Ask the basic journalism 5-W's — who, what, when, where, why, and how:

- Who is your character?
- Who are the other characters (protagonist, antagonist) in the story?
- What does your character want or need at this moment in time?
- What is the plot of the story?

- What is the relationship between the characters?
- What is the conflict?
- What complications arise?
- What is the environment?
- When does the story take place?
- When does the peak moment happen?
- Where is the story taking place?
- Why is the character in the situation he or she is in, and what prior events have brought the character to this moment in time?
- How is the conflict resolved, or not resolved?
- How is the message expressed through the resolution or nonresolution of the conflict?

By understanding the story line, you will know your role in the story. A dramatic story structure with a definite plot is most often found in dialogue scripts. However, many single voice scripts have a plot structure that evolves through the course of the story.

Unfortunately, most small-market and lower-end copy is written solely to provide intellectual (or logical) information. Information-based copy, also known as spokesperson copy, rarely has a story or plot, and thus there is little or no conflict. With no conflict to be resolved, it is much more challenging to find an emotional hook. With spokesperson copy, you still need to determine the audience, back story, and character, and you need to find a way to bridge the gap between performer and audience. With spokesperson copy, this can be a much greater challenge than it is with a plot-based story script. However, an emotional connection can still be made with the audience through effective characterization, and a "twist of a word."

MAKE UP A LEAD-IN LINE — (CD track 5)

A lead-in line is simply a short statement of a possible back story. Before delivering your first line, you say something that would be a logical introductory statement, or lead-in. You can say it silently, or out loud. If you say the line out loud, be sure to leave a slight pause before your first line of copy so that the editor can remove the unwanted lead-in line.

For example, if you are reading copy for a spokesperson commercial, you might want to have a lead-in line that sets up who you are talking to. Let's say you have determined that your audience is men and women in their thirties and forties, self-employed, and financially well off. You have set your character as someone who is equal to the audience, so you won't be patronizing; however, you will be conveying some important information.

Here's the copy:

> Health care. It's on everyone's mind. If you're looking for health
> care that really works, get to know FHP, in San Diego. For over
> 33 years, FHP has offered a variety of flexible health plans. FHP,
> an idea whose time has come.

For a lead-in line, you might set up the copy by putting yourself in the
position of talking to your best friend, John. Rather than starting cold, set a
visual image in your mind of a conversation between you and John. Deliver
your lines starting with:

> *(Silently: I learned something really interesting today, and you
> know, John . . .)*
>
> Health care. It's on everyone's mind. . . .

Your lead-in line sets up a conversational delivery that helps you to
close the gap and communicate your message on an emotional level. This
same approach works for all types of copy in any situation. The lead-in line
can be anything from a few short words to an elaborate story leading into
the written copy.

LOOK FOR LOGICAL PLACES TO BREATHE

You need to breathe, and you will sometimes be working a script with
extremely long, complicated sentences. Breath points in most copy usually
occur after a portion of a thought has been stated. Listings provide natural
break points between each item. You probably won't want to breathe or
pause between each item, but there usually is an opportunity if you need it.
To make lists more effective, try to make each item in a list unique by
altering your delivery or inflection.

LOOK FOR KEY WORDS YOU CAN EMPHASIZE FOR EFFECT

Generally, if a client or product name appears in a script, you will want
to do something in your delivery that will help give it some special impact.
There may also be a descriptive phrase or clause that needs some special
emphasis. Giving a word or phrase that extra punch is often referred to as
billboarding.

Emphasis does not necessarily mean speaking the words louder. You
can billboard a word or phrase by hitting it just a bit harder or softer in your
delivery, leaving a slight pause before or after you speak the words, slowing
down slightly, changing your body language or facial expression, changing
the inflection on the word or phrase, or even reducing the volume of your
voice.

If you billboard, or place extra emphasis, on too many words or phrases, your delivery will sound artificial and forced. Experiment with different ways to emphasize names, places, and important phrases in a script and you will soon find one that sounds right. If you have a question about whether or not something needs emphasis, ask the producer.

PERSONAL PRONOUNS — THE CONNECTING WORDS

Personal pronouns — I, we, our, and your — are all words that listeners tune in to. These are *connecting words* that help the voice actor reach the audience on an emotional level. Use these words to your advantage. Take your time with these words and don't rush past them.

In some copy, you will want to give these words a special emphasis for greater impact. At other times, you may want to underplay the personal pronouns and give extra emphasis to words that are the subject of a sentence. For example, the sentence — "It's what you're looking for!" — could have emphasis placed on any of the five words, or a combination of two or more. The contractions — "it's" and "you're" — could even be separated into "it is" and "you are." Each variation gives the sentence a unique meaning. Read the line out loud several different ways to see how the meaning changes. Placing the emphasis on the word "you're" may not be appropriate if the context of the script is all about searching for exactly the right product. In that case, the word "looking" would probably be the best word to receive the emphasis.

THE 2 — 4 SHORTCUT

When you speak conversationally with a fairly relaxed delivery, the result is that certain words are often pronounced in a manner that is not totally accurate. For example, the word "tomorrow" is often pronounced as "tamarrow," "forget" becomes "fergit," "our" becomes "are," and so on.

When you want to correctly pronounce words that have a "to" or "for" in them, simply replace the "to" or "for" with the numeral "2" or "4." Your brain is trained to say the numbers as "two" and "four," so as you are reading a script, your brain sees the number and you automatically speak the word more precisely. For a word like "our," change the spelling to another word that has the sound you want, like "hour." One student of mine had difficulty speaking the word "cellular" when used in the context of a script discussing cellular telephones. By simply changing the spelling of the word on his script from "cellular" to "sell-ya-ler," he was almost immediately able to deliver the lines perfectly. This little trick fools the brain and works with most sound-alike words.

LOOK FOR TRANSITIONS IN THE COPY

A copy transition can take many forms. It may be a transition of a character's mood or attitude. Or it may be a transition in the rhythm or pace of delivery. It might be a transition from a question asked to an answer given. It could even be a transition between concepts or products within a list. Transitions help "hook" the audience and keep their attention. Look for transitional phrases in the script and decide how you can make the transition interesting. Avoid keeping your delivery the same through all the transitions as you read a script. Give each transition a unique twist. Change your physical attitude, movement, mental picture, or use some other device to let your audience know that something special has happened, or that you have moved on to a new idea. Sometimes all that is needed is a slight change in your facial expression or body posture. And sometimes, a simple pause in your delivery will do the trick. Experiment with different techniques to find out what will work best for the copy you are performing.

"Woodshed" Your Copy

SCRIPT ANALYSIS

The process of studying a script for information about the message, the intended audience, your character, and your overall interpretation is called *woodshedding,* or *script analysis.* As you begin working with voice-over copy, you may find that it will take you a few minutes to make the choices about your character and other aspects of the copy. However, as you gain experience, you will be able to do a thorough "woodshedding" in the time it takes you to read the copy a few times.

The Script Analysis Worksheet on pages 83 and 84 can be used when working with any piece of copy. Once you've done this process a few times, the process will become automatic and you won't need the worksheet any longer. By answering the questions on the worksheet, you can quickly learn everything you need to know about a script and your character. If an answer is not clear from the copy, then make it up. You won't be graded on your answers, I promise. The answers you come up with are a tool for you to use in developing effective characters and delivery. For you to maintain a consistent performance, it is important that you stick with the choices you make in your script analysis. If something isn't working for you, of course, you can change your mind. But any new choices or changes should only be made to make your performance and your character more real and believable.

Script Analysis Worksheet

Answering the following questions, based on the copy, will help you discover the audience you are speaking to, your character, and any special attitude you need to incorporate into your performance.

Who is the advertiser or client? _____

_____

What is the product or service? _____

_____

What is the delivery style?
- ☐ Hard-Sell (fast and punchy)   ☐ Single Voice   ☐ Corporate/Narrative
- ☐ Medium-Sell (mellow)   ☐ Dialog, multiple
- ☐ Soft-Sell (relaxed)   ☐ Character/Animation

Who is the advertiser/client trying to reach (target AUDIENCE)? Determine the age range, income, sex, buying habits, and any other specific details that become apparent from the way the script is written. Who is the "other person" you are talking to? Visualize this individual as you perform the copy.

_____

_____

_____

Find important words or phrases in the copy that you can emphasize using dynamics of loudness or emotion. These include the advertiser's name, product, descriptive adjectives, and an address or phone number. These elements of the copy need special attention in your performance. Underline or highlight the words or phrases you want to emphasize.

What is the message the advertiser/client wants to communicate to the target audience? What is the story you are telling through your performance? What is the USP (Unique Selling Proposition)?

_____

_____

How does the story (plot) develop? For dialog copy, find the setup, the conflict, and how the conflict is resolved or not resolved. Discover how the plot flows. Are there any attitude changes with your character or others? Plot development is critical to effective dialog copy. Determine your role in the plot and how your character develops.

_____

_____

Use arrows ↗ ↘ to indicate copy points for changes in inflection or attitude.

What is role (your CHARACTER in the story) in terms of how the story is being told? Do a basic character analysis to define your character's age, life-style, clothing, speaking style, attitude toward the product or situation in the script, etc. What are your character's motivations? What are your character's WANTS and NEEDS at *this moment in time* (DESIRES)? What happened to your character in the moment immediately before the copy (BACK STORY)? Be as detailed as necessary in order to discover your character.

_____

_____

How does your character relate to any other characters in the script, or to the audience in general? Is your character an active player in telling the story (as in a dialog commercial), or is your character that of a narrator imparting information to a captive audience (as in a single-voice "spokesperson" commercial)? What can you do to create a bond between your character, other characters in the script, and the audience?

_____

_____

What can you do to make your character believable? Any special vocal treatments or physical attitudes?

_____

_____

Does your character have any unique or interesting attitudes, body postures, or speaking characteristics? (Speaks slowly, fast, with an accent, squeaky voice, etc.) If so, identify these.

_____

_____

Study the copy for pauses that might be used to provide emphasis, and for places to breathe. This is especially important in industrial copy which frequently contains long, run-on sentences with technical terminology. Mark breaths and pauses with a slash mark (/).

Find the rhythm of the copy. All copy has a rhythm, a beat, and timing. Discover the proper timing for the copy you are reading. Dialog copy has a separate rhythm for each character as well as an interactive rhythm.

Look for transitions in the script (similar to attitude changes). These may be transitions from asking a question to providing an answer (common in commercial copy), or a transition between attitudes of your character.

Look for words you can emphasize and that will connect you with the audience. Personal pronouns, such as "you," "our," "my," and "I," may be written into the script or simply implied. If connecting words are implied, find a way to make that implied connection through your performance (without actually saying the words).

SUBSTITUTE AND JUXTAPOSE TO FIND THE EMOTIONS

Sometimes it can be challenging to find just the right emotional spin, attitude, or verbal inflection for delivering a script or sharing a message. Woodshedding is the perfect time to experiment with interpretive ideas.

One very good way to work with troublesome copy is to literally change the words or context of the copy. These changes are only temporary and are intended to help you discover what you need to know to deliver the real words effectively. The idea is to put the subtext of the script into a form that you can personally relate to (remember "sense memory"?).

For example, the script you are performing is extolling the virtues of a particular brand of exotic fruit, but you may have never experienced that particular fruit, so you have absolutely no idea of how to create a believable delivery.

You can start by first *substituting* words that describe one of your favorite foods every time you see the name of the fruit. Use *sense memory* to tap into the sensation and physical tension associated with your favorite food. Hold onto those feelings and *juxtapose* your recalled feelings as you deliver the real words.

You won't need to use this tool very often, but it will come in handy when you are having a hard time getting to a believable emotion.

Physical Attitudes to Help Delivery

Don't be afraid to be physical in the studio. Remember, Movement Orchestrates Vocal Expression! I have seen voice-over performers do some of the strangest things to get into character. The basic rule is "whatever works — do it." I once worked with a voice actor who arrived at the studio wearing a tennis outfit and carrying a tennis racket. Throughout the session, he used that tennis racket as a prop to help with his character and delivery. I've seen other voice actors go through a series of contortions and exercises to set the physical attitude for the character they are playing. A friend of mine was working a dialogue script and her male dialogue partner was having trouble getting into the right delivery. To get into the proper attitude, the two of them actually lay down on the studio floor as they delivered their lines. Your analysis of the copy can give you a starting point for your physical attitude. When you've decided on your physical attitude, commit to it and use your body to express yourself.

Many people are self-conscious when just starting in this business, and that's normal. However, when you are in the "booth," you really need to leave any judgments you may have about your performance outside. If you are concerned about what the people in the control room think about *you* as you are performing (rather than what they think about *your performance*), you will not be able to do your best work. It comes down to taking on an attitude of "I don't care" when walking into the booth or studio. It's not that you don't care about doing your best, or making the character in the copy real and believable. You must care about these things. But you cannot afford to care about what others think of you and what you are doing as you perform to the best of your abilities. And besides, it's not you delivering those words anyway — it's really your character who's speaking!

If getting to your best performance means that moving your entire body and waving your arms wildly are appropriate for your character, that's what you need to do. You can't afford to worry that the people in the control room might think you are crazy. The engineer and producer certainly don't care! They are only interested in recording your best performance as quickly as possible, and they have seen it all anyway.

Usually you can perform better if you are standing, but in some cases, being seated may help with your character. If you sit, remember that a straight back will help your breathing and delivery. If possible, use a stool rather than a chair. Sitting in a chair tends to compress the diaphragm, while a stool allows you to sit straight and breathe properly. If a chair is all that's available, sit forward on the seat rather than all the way back. This helps you keep a straight back and control your breath. Most studios are set up for the performers to stand in front of the microphone. Standing allows for more body movement and gives you a wider range of motion without being restricted.

Your physical attitude is expressed through the relaxation and tension of your face and other muscles. All human emotions and feelings can be communicated vocally by simply changing physical attitudes. Often, the copy expresses a specific emotion or attitude. Find a place in your body where you can feel the tension of that emotion or attitude — and hold it there. Holding tension in your body contributes to the realism and believability of your character. Focus on centering your voice at the location of the tension in your body and speak from that center. This helps give your voice a sense of realism and believability.

A tense face and body will communicate as anger, frustration, or hostility. A relaxed face and body result in a softer delivery. Try reading some light copy with a tense body; you will find it very difficult to make the copy believable. You can make your delivery friendlier and more personable simply by delivering your lines with a smile on your face. Turning your head to the side and wrinkling your forehead will help convey an attitude of puzzlement. Wide-open eyes will help create an attitude of surprise. Practice reading with different physical attitudes and you will be amazed at the changes you hear. Your physical attitude comes through in your voice. Remember to M.O.V.E.

Your Clothes Make a Difference

Wear comfortable clothes. Tight or uncomfortable clothing can be restricting or distracting. You do not want to be concerned with shoes that are too tight when you are working in a high-priced recording studio. Stay comfortable. The voice-over business is a casual affair. Remember that voice actor who came into the studio in his tennis outfit?

Another note about clothing: The microphone in the studio is very sensitive and will pick up every little noise you make. Be careful not to wear clothing that rustles or "squeaks." Nylon jackets, leather coats, and many other fabrics can be noisy when worn in a recording studio. Other things to be aware of are: noisy jewelry, loose change in pockets, cell phones, and pagers. If you insist on wearing noisy clothing, it may be necessary for you to restrict your movement while in the studio, which can seriously affect your performance.

Commit to Your Choices

As you work with a piece of copy, you will be making decisions and choices about who your audience is, who your character is, what the back story is, and many other aspects of your performance. It is important to commit to these choices in order to be consistent throughout the recording session.

Of course, as new choices are made to enhance your character, you must commit to these also. In some cases, you may find that the choices you have committed to are not working as well as you or the producer might like. You may find it necessary to change or revise some of your choices. As new choices are made, commit to them to maintain a consistent character. As you commit to choices that develop the character and strengthen the delivery or emotional impact of the performance, you will be creating realism and believability in your performance.

The Magic of Your Mind:
If You Believe It, They Will!

Believability is one of the secrets of success in voice acting. One of the objectives of voice acting is to lead the audience to action. The most effective way to do that is to create a suspension of disbelief during the time you are delivering your message. You suspend disbelief whenever you go to a movie or to the theater and allow yourself to be drawn into the story. In reality, you are fully aware that the people on the stage or screen are just actors, and that life really isn't that way. However, during the time you are experiencing the performance, you suspend your disbelief and momentarily accept the appearance of the reality of what is happening in the story.

Suspension of disbelief in voice-over is essential for creating a sense of believability in the message. The audience must believe you, and for that to happen, *you* must momentarily believe in what you are saying.

Use your imagination to create a believable visual image in your mind for the message you are delivering. The more visual you can make it, the more believable it will be for you and for your audience. On a subconscious level, your mind does not know the difference between illusion and reality. Just as your physical attitude affects the sound of your voice, if you create a strong enough visual illusion in your mind, your words will be believable.

Creating a visual illusion is a technique used by most great actors and virtually all magicians. For a magician to make the audience believe that a person is really floating in the air, he must momentarily believe it himself. The performer's belief in what is taking place contributes to establishing the suspension of disbelief in the audience. If the magician is focused on the mechanics of his illusion, he will not give a convincing performance.

Any performer focused on the technical aspects of the performance cannot possibly be believable. This is every bit as true for a voice-over performer as it is for a theatrical performer. The technical aspects and techniques of your work must become completely automatic to the point where you are not even aware of them. The words on that script in front of you must come from within you — from the character you create. Only then will you be able to successfully suspend disbelief. This is what's meant by the phrases "making the words your own" and "getting off the page."

Creating visual images is a good technique to use when you are delivering dialogue copy and single-voice or industrial copy that is technical or difficult. If you create the visual mental illusion of being an expert in the area you are talking about, that attitude of authority will communicate through your voice.

Read your script a few times to get an understanding of what you are saying. Then, set your visual image and let your character come in and be the storyteller, the expert, the spokesperson, the salesperson, the eccentric neighbor, the inquisitive customer, and so on. By allowing your character to take over, you automatically shift your focus from the technical aspects of reading the copy to the creative aspects of performing and telling the story.

Creating a visual image helps give life to your character, reason for its existence, an environment for it to live in, and motivation for its words. Visualization helps make the character in the copy believable to you. If the character is believable to you, its words become true, and the message becomes believable to the audience. To put it another way: If you believe it, your audience will.

Trends

A considerable amount of voice-over work is in the form of advertising as radio and television commercials. The advertising industry is generally in a constant state of flux simply because its job is to reach today's customers in a way that will motivate them to buy the current "hot item." In order to do that, advertisers must connect on an emotional level with their audience. And, in order to do that, the delivery of a commercial must be in alignment with the attitude and behavior of the target audience. Each new generation seems to have its own unique lifestyle, physical attitude, slang, and style of dress. These constantly shifting *trends* are reflected in the advertising you see and hear on television and radio. You will notice different trends for different market groups, but the most obvious will be for products intended for the younger generation. In other words, what is "in style" today may be "out of style" tomorrow.

As a voice actor, it is important that you keep up with the current trends and develop flexibility in your performing style. You may develop a performing style that is perfect for a certain attitude or market niche, but if you don't pay attention to the changes going on around you, you may find that you are getting fewer bookings, simply because your style is no longer in demand.

Probably the best way to keep pace with current trends is to simply study radio and television advertising that is on the air today. Listen to what the major national advertising producers are doing in terms of delivery attitude, pace, and rhythm. Observe the energy of the music and how the visuals are edited in commercials and notice how the voice-over works with or against that energy. Look for commonalities among the commercials you study, and you will begin to notice the current trends. One thing you will notice is that most locally produced advertising does not follow the trends presented in national advertising.

You don't really need to do anything about these trends, other than to be aware of what they are and how you might adapt your performance. That awareness will prove to be another valuable tool for you to use when you audition or are booked for a session. Use it to your advantage.

7

The Character
in the Copy

When you read copy as a voice actor you are performing a character. The character may be well defined by the manner in which the words are written, or you may need to discover it. Scripts written for specific or stereotyped characters occasionally have some directions written on the script. The directions may be something like: "read with an English accent," or "cowboy attitude." Many times, producers or writers will be able to give you additional insight into their vision of the character. It will then be up to you to create an appropriate voice for that character.

The character you create may be defined as simply an "announcer" or spokesperson doing a hard-sell sales pitch or, perhaps, a "friendly neighbor" telling the story about a great new product he has discovered. In other cases, the character you need to define may have a complex personality with a range of emotions.

Woodshedding a script by reading through it once or twice usually gives you an idea of what you need to do to bring your character to life. However, there will be times when the attitude or personality of your character is not clear, and you might need some help in figuring out the best way to perform the copy.

In theater, this process of defining the attitude and personality of a character is called a *character analysis*, which can be as detailed as you like. The more details you include in your character analysis, and the more you understand your character, the better you will be able to take an attitude and personality to "become" that character for your performance. Or, to put it another way, the more you understand the character in your copy, the easier it will be for you to find those emotions, attitudes, and personality traits within you that you can use to create your character and bring life to the words in the script.

Let's review some of the key elements of copy that can help determine your character. For a more complete explanation, please refer to Chapter 6, Voice Acting 101.

- **The structure of the copy** (the way it is written) — Is the copy written in a dialect style? Is the wording "flowery" or expressive in one way or another? Is the copy a straight pitch? What is the pace of the copy? What is the mood of the copy? What is the attitude of the character?

- **Know the audience** — Knowing the target audience is a good way to discover your character. Experienced copywriters know that most people fit into one of several clearly defined categories. The words and style they choose for their copy will be carefully chosen to target the specific category of buying public they want to reach. Specific words and phrases will be used to elicit an emotional response from the target audience. Your character may be defined in part by the words spoken to convey a thought, or his or her attitude may be clearly expressed within the context of the copy.

- **What is the back story** (the moment before) — What happened before the first word of copy? The back story is the specific event that brought your character to this moment in time. This may or may not be obvious in the script. All dialogue copy has a back story. There can also be a back story for single-voice copy. If a back-story is not defined within the context of the script, make one up.

- **Who are the characters** (in a dialogue script) — Who is your character and how do other characters interrelate with your character and each other? This interaction can give solid clues about your character.

- **What is the conflict** — What happens in the copy to draw the listener into the story? Where is the drama in the story? How is conflict resolved or left unresolved? Is the conflict humorous or serious? How is the product or message presented through the resolution or nonresolution of conflict?

There are many other clues in the copy that will lead you to discovering the character. As the performer, you may have one idea for portraying the character, and the producer may have another. If there is any question about your character, discuss it with the producer.

Your Best Tool Is Your Own Personality

The best tool you have to define a character is your own personality. When you know yourself, you can tap into parts of your personality to give life to the character in the copy.

Personality analysis is a subject that has been studied for thousands of years. Hippocrates developed a system of defining personality traits, which placed individuals into four separate personality types with dominant and recessive traits. The extrovert types were called Sanguine and Choleric, and the introvert types were Melancholy and Phlegmatic. The Hippocrates system of personality analysis was very restrictive in its definitions of personality types but it did provide a basic structure within which people could be placed.

More recently the psychologists of our world have developed highly refined methods of determining specific personality types. Some of their studies have shown that personality is largely a result of the chemical makeup of the brain. Cultural upbringing and conditioning further contribute to personality development.

There are several excellent books available that will help you discover some fascinating aspects of your personality. Many of these books are written as aids to improving relationships. Three excellent personality books are: *Please Understand Me — Character and Temperament Types* by David Keirsey and Marilyn Bates (1984), *Are You My Type, Am I Your Type* by Renee Baron and Elizabeth Wagele (1995), and *Dealing with People You Can't Stand* by Dr. Rick Brinkman and Dr. Rick Kirschner (1994). These books look at personality types from different points of view and offer some fascinating reading.

An advertiser's understanding of who buys the company's products is crucial when it comes to a marketing campaign. Your understanding of yourself is equally necessary when it comes to creating a character that will effectively communicate the message in the advertiser's copy. The best way for you to learn more about yourself is to ask questions and find the most appropriate answers. Based on your answers, you will be able to determine some of your dominant and recessive personality traits.

Most studies of personality type start with several basic categories, then divide those into subcategories. Every person has characteristics in several categories, but certain areas are dominant, and others are in the minority.

The books referred to earlier can help give you an in-depth analysis. In addition, the following simple questions will give you an idea of some basic personality differences.

- Do you respond to problems emotionally, or do you think about them before responding?

- Do you have a strong need to express yourself creatively, or do you prefer quiet activities?

- Do you avoid unpleasant emotions (including fear), or are you inclined to take risks?

- Do you rely on your instincts for information, or do you rely on what you see and hear?

- Do you seek approval from authority figures, or do you rebel?

- Do you play the role of a nurturer, or do you treat others in a detached manner?

- Do you express anger readily, are you accommodating and out of touch with your anger, or do you see anger as a character flaw?

- Do you prefer literal writing or a more figurative writing style?

- Are you more realistic or speculative?

- Do emotions impress you more, or do principles?

- Are you attracted to creative, imaginative people, or to more sensible, structured people?

- Do you tend to arrive at events early, or are you generally late?

- Do you do things in the usual way, or do you do things in your own way?

- Do you feel better having made a purchase or having the option to purchase?

- Do you operate more from facts or from principles?

- Do you find it easy to speak to strangers, or is this difficult?

- Are you fair-minded or sympathetic?

- Do you prefer planned activities or unplanned activities?

Your answers to these and other questions will only scratch the surface of your personality. When you gain an in-depth understanding of who you are, you will be ahead of the game when it comes to creating a believable character. With an understanding of yourself, you will be able to tap into some of the core elements of your own personality as you create a unique character.

Sociocultural Awareness

You should also know that the corporate business world uses highly refined methods of personality and social analysis to define the demographics (statistical data) of the marketplace for selling products and services. These studies define the buying attitudes and purchasing habits of consumers and aid advertisers in reaching their desired market.

There are several companies whose entire business is based on analyzing the buying trends of different types of people. By understanding what motivates a person to buy, an advertiser can write in specific words and phrases, or a particular style. For TV commercials and print advertising, editing techniques and use of color, type style, and other visual elements are used — all of which are "hot" buttons designed to trigger a buying impulse in the listener, viewer, or reader. In radio commercials, similar hot buttons are triggered through the careful choice of words and phrases, the use of appropriate music and various production techniques. In any case, the desired result is to reach the audience on an emotional level and to motivate the audience to take action.

Today, advertisers are faced with a marketplace of "occasional" consumers who are no longer characterized by predictable buying habits and who no longer exhibit strong brand loyalty. The key objective of marketing sociocultural research is to identify the links between personal motivations and buying behavior in order to understand the consumer and why he or she is attracted by certain propositions and not by others. Simply studying consumer behavior is not adequate, nor is analyzing buying habits in terms of age or class. To understand modern society, it is necessary to look much deeper at the sociocultural diversity of society and find the trends and characteristics that can make the difference between commercial success or failure.[1]

Marshall Marketing & Communications, Inc. (MM&C) is one of the leaders in sociocultural analysis for the purpose of marketing on a local and regional basis. MM&C, in association with the International Research Institute on Social Change (RISC), which has operated nationally in the United States since 1987 and internationally since 1978, uses a program called RISC AmeriScan[2] to help advertisers understand and adjust to purchasing behaviors of present and future consumers. The RISC AmeriScan program is quite extensive and could be the subject of a book of its own, so only those aspects that relate to voice acting are included here.

Through a series of studies, both on national and local levels, a probability sample of people is surveyed with a carefully developed questionnaire. The questions don't ask for opinions, but rather register relevant preferences and facts about the individual. The results of the survey capture the person's sociocultural characteristics.

To more easily view the results, a chart is created that takes on the basic appearance of a compass. The first axis (pointing north and south) is linked to attitudes of change. At the north are people who see change as a positive force in their lives (Exploration). To the south are people who prefer stability, structure, and consistency (Stability). The other axis of the compass (east-to-west) relates to the balance between the individual and society. To the east are those who are more independent and seek immediate pleasure (Individual); to the west are people with strong ethics and more community oriented (Social).

Respondents are scored on each of approximately 40 sociocultural characteristics. Their scores result in a specific placement on the compass, and can be represented as a "cloud of dots" in multidimensional diagrams (Figures 7-1 and 7-2).[3] The diagram is then divided into ten territories to result in the RISC AmeriScan map (Figures 7-3 and 7-4). Individuals positioned close to each other tend to have shared values and similar preferences, while those at opposite extremes have little in common.[4]

A basic understanding of how advertisers target their message will be beneficial to you as a voice actor. Knowing what the cultural and social norms are for any specific demographic group will give you some much-needed information to aid in the development of a believable character. For example, let's say that, based on the copy you are given, you can determine that your audience is outgoing, youthful, interested in experiencing new things, and likes to live on the edge. You make this determination based on your analysis and interpretation of the words and phrases in the copy. With this information you can now make reliable choices and adapt your character and performance energy to something your audience can relate to, thus creating a sense of believability.

For the audience described here, you would most likely need to perform with considerable energy and excitement in your voice. A slow, relaxed delivery probably would not be an effective way to reach the audience, unless the script was specifically written for that attitude.

THE TEN CULTURAL TERRITORIES

Each of the ten segments on the RISC AmeriScan map (Figure 7-4) represents a cultural territory with specific attitudes, beliefs, preferences, motivations, and buying habits. Advertisers use these cultural territories to aid in targeting their advertising and marketing plans. All aspects of a campaign, including words, visuals, colors, music, and sound effects, are carefully chosen to match the characteristics of the territory being targeted. The closer the match, the more likely it is that the message will reach the target audience.

These ten RISC AmeriScan cultural territories can also be useful in developing a believable character. Understanding the motivations, attitudes, and belief system of your audience will enable you to tap into those parts of your own personality and bring them into the character you are creating. When you create a believable character, an emotional connection can be made with the audience, giving the message a stronger impact.

The following pages separate the ten cultural territories into their sociocultural profiles, key attributes as defined by RISC, and other useful information to help you understand your audience and create a believable character. As an exercise to develop your acting skills, use these territory charts as a guide to create a variety of characters with different attitudes. Find a paragraph in a book or newspaper and read the same copy from the attitude of a character in each of the ten territories. Allow your mind and body to take on the characteristics, body posture, belief system, and attitudes in each territory and observe how each character can be unique.

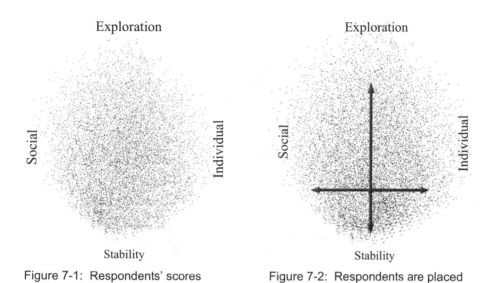

Figure 7-1: Respondents' scores create a "cloud of dots."

Figure 7-2: Respondents are placed on the compass based on sociocultural characteristics.

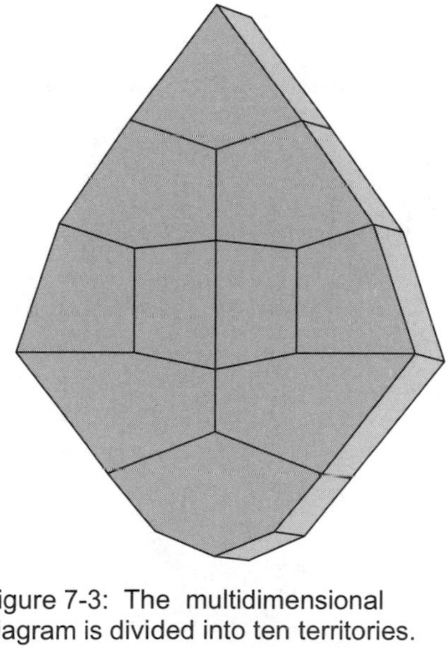

Figure 7-3: The multidimensional diagram is divided into ten territories.

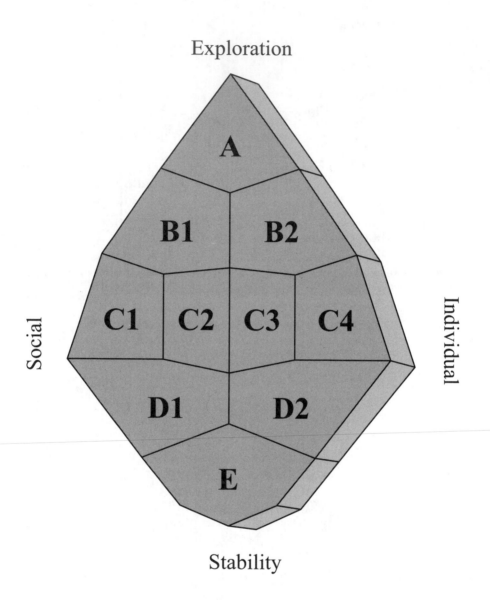

Figure 7-4: RISC AmeriScan ten cultural territories map.

TERRITORY A — Personal Growth, Socially Involved, Connected

TONE OF VOICE CONSUMER WILL BEST RESPOND TO: Persuade

Key Attributes	Sociocultural Profile	Motivations
• Exploring human potential • Community ties • Networking • Empathy • Personal growth • Social commitment • Coping with uncertainty • Social flexibility • Well-being	• Integrate society and the self • Combine traditional and modern ideas • Active involvement in the growth and change of society • Social and personal development important	• Belongings, culture, novelty • Rely on own sense of style and instinct • Interest in newness, curiosity, and the unusual • Acceptance of ambiguity and paradox • Interaction, experience, and diversity are important

© RISC, 1997

TERRITORY B1 — Community, Spirituality, Social Responsibility

TONE OF VOICE CONSUMER WILL BEST RESPOND TO: Legitimize

Key Attributes	Sociocultural Profile	Motivations
• Exploring human potential • Community ties • Spirituality • Social commitment • Order and vigilance • Integrity • Global world • Empathy • Well-being	• Comfort and well-being of others is most important • Caregivers and nurturers • Family values • Concern for others • Religious tolerance • Uphold tradition while also creating new rituals for special occasions • Focus daily life on family and social gatherings	• Belongings, culture, novelty • Rely on their own sense of style and instinct • Interest in newness, curiosity, and the unusual • Acceptance of ambiguity and paradox • Interaction, experience, and diversity are important

© RISC, 1997

TERRITORY B2 — Independent, Experimental, Interest in New

TONE OF VOICE CONSUMER WILL BEST RESPOND TO: Seduce and Enliven

Key Attributes	Sociocultural Profile	Motivations
• Exploring human potential • Coping with uncertainty • Personal growth • Networking • Pleasure • Risk-taking • Strategic opportunism • Emotions	• Intense and eager to explore • Open and optimistic • Invigorated by diverse, multiple connections • Active and involved • Always push their limits • Strongly individualistic yet open to a broad view of community • Uncertainty equals a challenge	• Culture, novelty, understanding, independence • Fascinated by the avant-garde and unexpected • Will pay more for what they want • Intrigued by the one-of-a-kind and impossible, and the experiences that come with it

© RISC, 1997

TERRITORY C1 — Rituals, Loyalty, Duty, Conventional

TONE OF VOICE CONSUMER WILL BEST RESPOND TO: Build on Trust

Key Attributes	Sociocultural Profile	Motivations
• Order and vigilance • Spirituality • Community ties • Organized life • Well-being • Clear-cut principles	• Defined by duty, morality, family, and community • Lead principled and routine lives • Seek reassurance and stability • Adhere to a firm moral code and a strong sense of values • Observe traditional rituals	• Belongings, understanding, nurturance, stability • Good deeds equal goodwill • React to community involvement • Primary concern is family • Always defined in relation to others • Comforted by the familiar

© RISC, 1997

Source: RISC AmeriScan Sociocultural Territories, copyright RISC, 1997.
Reprinted by permission of Marshall Marketing & Communications, Inc.

TERRITORY C2 — Rules, Principles, Need for Recognition

TONE OF VOICE CONSUMER WILL BEST RESPOND TO: Inform and Position

Key Attributes	Sociocultural Profile	Motivations
• Clear-cut principles • Organized life • Social fairness • Environment • Competitive drive • Integrity • Roots	• Tentative and unsure • Mediate the needs of the family and the individual • Less willing to sacrifice for the common good • Not certain among those outside of family circle • Unbalanced in desire to explore their individuality • Simple and collective enjoyment for well-being	• Recognition, understanding, nurturance, stability • Need positive reassurance from others • Driven by commitment to provide comfort for family • Simple, straightforward messages and symbols are important keys

© RISC, 1997

TERRITORY C3 — Achievement, Exhibition, Trend Setters, Self-Indulgent

TONE OF VOICE CONSUMER WILL BEST RESPOND TO: Inform and Position

Key Attributes	Sociocultural Profile	Motivations
• Strategic opportunism • Risk-taking • Emotions • Pleasure	• Rely on others to promote their own achievement • Focus on short-term gains and personal risk-taking • Indulge in the pleasures of immediate gratification • Lack a strict moral code • Materialism important • Unconcern for community • In constant pursuit of being "number one"	• Thrills, accomplishment • Identity is reflected in the display of awards, status symbols, and possessions • Need to succeed and to have success recognized • Live life to the fullest • Seek immediate advantages from products and services

© RISC, 1997

TERRITORY C4 — Materialism, Seek Pleasure, Need for Recognition

TONE OF VOICE CONSUMER WILL BEST RESPOND TO: Stimulate and Flatter

Key Attributes	Sociocultural Profile	Motivations
• Strategic opportunism • Risk-taking • Emotions • Pleasure • Social flexibility • Blurring of the sexes	• Point of view is pleasure • Put themselves first • Willing to take social and personal risks • Tend to be the fashion leaders • Driven by impulse and immediate gratification • Intense and self-centered • Live life in the present, moment by moment	• Thrills, diversion, exhibition, sexuality • Highly attracted to "new" • Want to be entertained • Seek ways to express their uniqueness • Sexual innuendo and overt eroticism hook their interest in being cutting edge

© RISC, 1997

TERRITORY D1 — Need for Structure, Control, Respect for Authority

TONE OF VOICE CONSUMER WILL BEST RESPOND TO: Demonstrate

Key Attributes	Sociocultural Profile	Motivations
• Organized life • Roots • Security • Clear-cut principles	• Strong beliefs in duty and clearly defined rules • Unquestioning respect given to authority figures • Routine balances the uncertainty of life • Brand loyalty is more habit than conviction • Basic pleasures and familiarity shape their structured lifestyles	• Control, stability, dependence • Abundance is a sign of prosperity • Not particularly selective about purchases • Promotions, gimmicks, price incentives are key • Basic benefits more important than image and style

© RISC, 1997

Source: RISC AmeriScan Sociocultural Territories, copyright RISC, 1997.
Reprinted by permission of Marshall Marketing & Communications, Inc.

TERRITORY D2 — Personal Style, Spontaneous, Concern About Future

TONE OF VOICE CONSUMER WILL BEST RESPOND TO: Gratify

Key Attributes	Sociocultural Profile	Motivations
• Security • Status • Pleasure • Aimlessness • Blurring of the sexes • Risk-taking • Fear of violence	• Pleasure is a feeling of power • Aspire to set themselves apart from the masses • The "wannabe's" of the Rich and Famous • They are both whimsical and spontaneous • Fashionably antiestablishment • Resist tradition	• Nonconformity, sexuality, exhibition • Need options that allow them to be different • Resist the persuasions of mass culture • Developed sense of style • Appreciate parodies of conventional values, norms, and status

© RISC, 1997

TERRITORY E — Need for Security, Worriers, Suspicious of Change

TONE OF VOICE CONSUMER WILL BEST RESPOND TO: Reassure

Key Attributes	Sociocultural Profile	Motivations
• Aimlessness • Fear of violence • Security	• Security is the prevailing tendency • Yearning for stability makes them suspicious of change and reluctant to be a part of it • Resist pleasure • Fearful outlook on world • Strong preoccupation with health problems • Possessions equals security	• Security, dependence • Need to feel free of the threat of harm • Want the comfort of knowing that they and loved ones are protected • Expect immediate results from products and services • Long-term or preventive benefits seen as misleading

© RISC, 1997

Source: RISC AmeriScan Sociocultural Territories, copyright RISC, 1997.
Reprinted by permission of Marshall Marketing & Communications, Inc.

Theater of the Mind

Voice acting is theater of the mind. You do not have the advantage of props, flashy lighting, or scenery. All you have are the words on a piece of paper — and your individual creativity. From the words alone, you must create an illusion of reality in the mind of your audience. In order for you to create a believable illusion, you need to know what is going on in the mind of the character you are playing. You also need to know the relationships of the characters in the script to the *unique selling proposition* (USP) — the advertiser's message or unique product benefit. To learn what is going on in the character's mind, and to understand the USP, you need to analyze the script.

Analyzing a voice-over script is very much like reducing a play to its essential parts. The more information you can discover in the copy, the easier it will be to create a believable performance. Single-voice spokesperson copy is frequently information-based and may not require much analysis. However, dialogue copy and plot scripts are short theatrical pieces and must be understood to be effectively performed.

Although analyzing a script is helpful in understanding its component parts, it is important to realize that *overanalyzing* a script can kill spontaneity and cause the voice actor to place too much focus on technique and thinking about what he or she is doing. Remember, to be effective, technique must become automatic and occur without any conscious effort. Study a script just long enough to discover what you need to know, then put the script down and let your instincts do the rest.

To create effective theater of the mind, your performance must reflect real life, exhibit some sort of tension, contain something the listener can relate to, and have a sense of honesty and a ring of truth. These are all elements of good theater and should be incorporated into any voice-acting performance, regardless of the type of copy or the length of the project.

When creating a character for your performance, keep in mind the following basic elements of good theater:

- Interesting characters with wants and needs "at this moment in time"

- A story or sequence of events that leads to a climax

- Conflict in one or more forms

- Resolution or nonresolution of the conflict, usually in an interesting or unexpected manner

- Closure in which any loose ends are satisfactorily resolved

Uncover these elements in a voice-over script and you will better understand your character.

Creating a Performance Road Map: Analyzing and Marking a Script

One of the first things you should do as you begin working with a script is to quickly analyze it; *woodshed* it, searching for clues to help you create a believable character and effective delivery. Look for words and phrases that describe the attitude and emotion. Notice the context of the copy and how the message is presented. Look for places where you can add variety by using the dynamics of pacing, energy, attitude, tone of voice, and emotion. Look for natural breaks, shifts of attitude, and transitions in the copy.

By the time you read a script once or twice, you should be able to make some solid choices on how you intend to perform it. You should know who the one person is you are speaking to (the audience), who you are as the speaker (your character) and why you are speaking the words in the script at this moment in time (your back story).

Mark the copy and make notes to create a map of how you will deliver it. These markings are your personal cues to guide you through an effective performance of the copy.

Practice marking magazine or newspaper articles or short stories and you will quickly find a system that works for you. In a short time, you will refine your system to a few key markings which you can use regularly to guide you through almost any script.

Here are a few suggested markings and possible uses. Adapt, modify and add to them as you like:

- Underline (———) — emphasize a word, phrase, or descriptive adjectives
- Circle (O) — key elements of conflict in the script
- Box (□) — the peak moment in the copy — put a box around the words or phrase at that point in the copy
- Highlight (▒▒▒▒) or different color underline — resolution or nonresolution of conflict
- Arrow pointing UP (↗) — take inflection on a word up
- Arrow pointing DOWN (↘) — take inflection on a word down
- Wavy line (~~~) — modulate your voice or inflection
- Slash or double slash (//) — indicate a pause

The degree to which you mark your script may vary from project to project, but it will certainly help to have a system in place when you need it. Practice your system on newspaper articles or any printed ad copy.

Discovering Your Character

Just as you have a personality, so does the character written into every script. The character for a single-voice script is often simply that of an announcer or spokesperson delivering a sales pitch of some sort, or communicating basic information. But, even this announcer has a personality that is appropriate to the copy. Scripts written for dialogue or comedy have multiple characters that are often more easily defined. For all types of copy, finding the personality of the character allows you to give the character life and helps make your performance believable. Remember, making your performance believable is what voice acting is all about.

CHARACTER ANALYSIS

As you have seen, there are many clues in copy that will help you discover the character and his or her personality. The target audience, the mood or attitude of the copy, the writing style, and any descriptive notes all give you valuable information. The sociocultural data in the RISC AmeriScan map can be another useful tool in helping to uncover a character's personality.

The process of analyzing, or discovering, your character is something that will become automatic in time. Once you know what to look for, you will soon be able to define your character after reading through the copy once or twice.

Voice-over performing does not require the same sort of in-depth, detailed character analysis that might be necessary for a theatrical performer. However, to be believable, you do need to have a good idea of the character you are portraying. Refer to the RISC AmeriScan territories earlier in this chapter to get a clear picture of the attitudes and motivations of the character you are creating.

Here are some things to look for and consider as you read through your copy to discover and define your character:

- Who is this character talking to? (target audience)

- What is the environment for the copy? (mood)

- What is the character's age? (young, old, middle-age)

- How does the character stand? (straight and tall, hunched over, arms crossed, hands on hips, etc.)

- Where is the character from? (geographic region, country)

- Does the character speak with an accent or in a dialect? (If so, what would be the country of origin? A poorly done dialect or accent can have negative results unless done as a parody or characterization.)

- How would the character dress? (well dressed, high-end business suit, or casual)

- What would you guess to be the character's economic status? (financially well off, struggling, etc.)

- What is the overall mood or attitude of the copy? (fast-paced, slow and relaxed, romantic feel, emotional, aggressive, etc.)

- What is the pace of the copy? (Slow-paced copy often calls for a relaxed type of character while fast-paced copy demands a character with more energy.)

- What is the product or service for which the copy is written? (The subject of the copy often dictates a specific type of character.)

- What is the character's purpose, or role, in the script? (protagonist, antagonist, delivering the message, part of a story script, comedic role, or that of straight-man)

- What life events or actions brought the character to this moment in time?

- What does the character want from telling the story?

Finding answers to questions like these will help you develop a visual image of your character. With a well-formed visual image, you will instinctively know what is needed to deliver the copy effectively and believably. You will know, for example, if the character needs to speak quickly or slowly, with an accent, or with an attitude.

Creating a visual image of your character and the environment he finds himself in will help to develop the necessary tension for drama. The tension here is not between characters, but rather a physical tension located somewhere in your body. It is this tension that will allow you to give life to the character in the copy.

Discovering the character in the copy may appear to be a lengthy process, but, in fact, it happens quickly once you know what to look for.

FIND THE BACK STORY

All copy has a back story, also known as "the moment before." A *back story* is simply the specific event that occurred immediately before the first word of the copy. The back story is the result of the wants and needs of the character that has brought him or her to this moment in time. It is the story that provides the motivation for the words, actions, and reactions to what happens in the environment of the story.

In theater, the back story is frequently unveiled during the course of the performance. With voice-over copy, there is rarely enough time to reveal the back story or provide much character development. A 60-second radio commercial must be a self-contained snippet of time — the telling of a story with a beginning, middle, and an end — and with fully developed characters from the outset.

In a dialogue script, you will often be able to figure out the back story with ease. A dialogue script back story consists of the life experiences of all the characters in the script and the specific event that brought each to the moment of their story, and more important, the relationship between those characters. The interaction between characters often reveals clues to the back story.

It can be more of a challenge with a single-voice script. A single-voice script back story consists of the life experience of only the speaking character. There may be few, if any, clues that reveal what brought him or her to the point of speaking the words in the copy.

If a back story is not clear from the copy, make one up. After all, you are an actor and you do have permission to pretend. The idea is to create a believable motivation for your character that brings him or her to the particular moment in time that is taking place in the script. The back story will reveal your character's wants and needs at this moment, and that information will help guide you in your delivery.

Define the back story and what the character wants in just a few words. Keep it concise, believable, and real.

UNVEIL THE CONFLICT

Conflict is an essential part of dialogue copy, and can also be present in a single-voice script that tells a story. Conflict rarely occurs in information-based copy in which the message is more of a sales pitch or instructional in nature than a story. Conflict creates drama, and drama holds interest.

A dialogue script without conflict will be boring and uninteresting. On the other hand, a dialogue script with a well-defined conflict can be funny, emotional, heartwarming, and informative — all at the same time. Look for the primary conflict in the script. Usually, this will be some difference of opinion, a crisis, an impasse, or some other obstacle. Define this primary conflict in a few concise words.

Once you have defined the primary conflict, look for any complications that support or exaggerate it. These are often secondary or minor conflicts that serve to add meaning and importance to the primary conflict.

Follow the development of the conflict to reveal its peak moment, which is the climax — the key moment in a commercial. It will usually be found immediately prior to the resolution or nonresolution of the conflict.

During the course of developing the conflict, the advertising benefit (*unique selling proposition*) should be revealed. The peak moment often is the point in the copy where the advertiser's name is mentioned or the purpose of the commercial is revealed.

DISCOVER THE RESOLUTION OR NONRESOLUTION OF THE CONFLICT

In commercial copy, it is through the resolution or nonresolution of the conflict that the message is expressed. Sometimes ending a commercial with an unresolved conflict can actually create a memorable impression in the mind of the listener. An unresolved conflict leaves the end of the story up to the listener's imagination, and that can be a very effective motivation for action. For example, a radio commercial we produced for the high-end toy store, Toy Smart, presented a conflict between a mother and her "child." As the story developed, the mother tried to coax her "child" to eat his green beans with less than satisfactory results. This conflict appeared to resolve when the "child" turned out to be the husband who said "I'll be happy to eat all the green beans you want, as long as you put them with a T-bone steak!" However, at the very end of the commercial, the husband had one more line, which left the conflict in a state of nonresolution: "What do I get if I eat all my brussels sprouts?" This left the resolution of the conflict to the imagination of the listener and created a memorable impact moment in the commercial.

Look for details in the copy that give clues as to how the message is actually communicated. Are there a series of gags, jokes, or a play on words that lead to expression of the message? Do characters in the copy shift roles (reversals)? Is there a list of information that ends with an unusual twist? Does the story take place in an unusual location? Is there something in the story that appears to be out of context with what is taking place? Is there a personality problem or physical limitation with one or more of the characters? How are these resolved — or not?

MAKE THE COPY YOUR OWN

As you analyze a script, remember that there are no right or wrong answers to the questions you ask. Use your imagination and bring something of yourself into the copy. The idea is to create a believable character and situation for the copy you are reading. Bringing your personal experience into the character you create will aid in making him or her real to the listener.

Use what you learn from the copy and the tools at your disposal to make the copy your own. If you have a naturally dry and sarcastic style of speaking, you may be able to apply that trait to your character to make it unique. If you have a bubbly speaking style, that trait might give a unique twist to a character. Don't be afraid to experiment and play with different approaches to performing a character.

To Be More Believable

The best way to effectively communicate a scripted message is to create a believable character telling a believable story. To be believable, your performance must include variety, tension, and sincerity. It must also be easy to listen to and in a style that the audience can relate to. To be believable, you must develop a performing style that is conversational and real. The best way to be more believable is to eliminate punctuation marks.

TAKE OUT THE PUNCTUATION MARKS

Periods, exclamation points, commas, and question marks are all necessary ingredients in printed copy. Punctuation marks give us visual clues as to how we should interpret a sentence as we read, where the emphasis should be, and the attitude of a written concept.

Punctuation marks in a voice-over script also give us clues as to how we should interpret the copy. They guide us as to how we should pace our timing and delivery, the attitude of the message, and even give us information about our character and the interaction between characters. However, if the punctuation marks are taken literally and performed as written, an otherwise well-written script can sound flat and lifeless.

Taking the punctuation marks out of the copy doesn't mean literally going through the script with white-out (although I do know of some voice-actors who actually do that, and it is a technique I teach in my workshops!). What it does mean is performing the copy in a real, believable, and conversational manner. A real-life conversation is punctuated with pauses, changes of inflection, dynamics (soft, loud), emotional attitude (excitement, sadness, and so on), vocalized sounds (uh-huh, hmmm, etc.), and many other subtleties. Voice-over copy should be delivered the same way. Let your delivery dictate the punctuation.

The only way to achieve this is to allow the scripted punctuation marks to guide you, but not to take them too literally. Sometimes, changing a comma to a hyphen, or a period to an exclamation point can make a big difference in the interpretation, improving the performance. Allow the lines of a script to flow into one another as they would if you were telling the story to another person, not reading it. Take the punctuation marks out of your performance and your performance will be on its way to being more believable.

CREATING TENSION

When making copy your own, it is important to be specific when defining a scene or character and to commit to the choices you make. Using specific terms creates a tension in your body that you can use in your voice. Without tension you will be unable to create drama, which is essential for capturing and holding the attention of the listener, and communicating the message.

To create tension in your body, begin by observing your feelings and emotions as you read the copy. Allow your senses to be open to experience whatever sensations might appear and make a mental note of where that sensation occurred in your body. As you begin to add life to your character, recall the memory of the sensation you just experienced (*sense memory*). Focus on placing your voice at that place in your body. This technique may be somewhat difficult to master at first, but keep working at it — the result is truly amazing once you get the knack of doing it.

AN EXERCISE FOR CREATING "REAL" CHARACTERS — (CD/6)

The first time I used this exercise in my workshop, the result was absolutely amazing. We witnessed a total transformation and the student, who was having difficulty finding the proper voice and attitude, was able to create a completely believable character that she did not know existed within her. Visualization is a powerful technique that can help bring your characters to life, and this exercise will do just that! As I've mentioned before, for a character in a script to be "real" to a listener, everything about the character must flow through you just as if you were the character.

Once understood, the following visualization process can take as little as only a few seconds to a minute or so. However, as you learn this technique you may want to spend some additional time relaxing your body and mind prior to doing this exercise. Of course, in an actual session you won't have much time for a lengthy visualization, but by then the process should be second nature.

Begin by thoroughly woodshedding your script and making choices for your audience, back story, and character. Define your character in as much detail as you possibly can, including physical appearance, clothing, hair, posture, mannerisms, and other features. Visualize this character in your imagination. This character description and image will become important later on, so don't skimp on the details.

You may find it helpful to do this as a guided visualization by listening to track 6 on the CD or recording the script yourself. Take your time with this, and don't rush it. The more clearly the visualization, the better the results, and the more believable your character will be.

Script for "Creating a Character" Visualization

- With your character in mind, close your eyes and take a slow deep breath through your nose. Fill your lungs completely. Exhale slowly through your mouth to relax. Repeat with another long deep breath . . . and slowly exhale. Don't forget to keep breathing.

- Imagine yourself standing in front of the microphone, or in the voice-over booth. See yourself in your imagination — it's as though you are observing yourself from across the room. Create the image of yourself as clearly as you possibly can, in whatever manner works for you. When you have a sense of seeing yourself standing in the room, take another long deep breath . . . and slowly exhale.

- Now, imagine the character you will be playing coming into the scene in your imagination. See the character walking in. Notice how the character is walking. Observe the posture and physical movement. Notice what the character is wearing — what do the clothes look like? What kind of shoes is your character wearing? Is your character wearing glasses or jewelry?

- As you observe this scene, see yourself look at your character's face. Notice any facial details, color of the eyes, appearance of the skin. Does your character appear to present any sort of attitude or have interesting facial expressions? When you have a clear image of the character in your imagination, take a long deep breath . . . and slowly exhale.

- Now, as you are observing the two of you in the room, imagine seeing the real you step out of your body and come to the place where you are observing. As the real you steps out of your body, imagine the character stepping into your body. Everything about the character is now reflected in your body. The character's posture, the way the character stands and moves, the character's physical appearance, facial expressions, and mental attitude — everything about the character is now expressed through your body, mind, and voice.

- Allow yourself to fully experience this transformation. Notice any tension in your body. Be aware of how you feel as this character, physically, mentally, and emotionally. When you have a sense of the transformation, take a slow deep breath, exhale, maintain the physical, emotional, and mental state, open your eyes, and begin speaking the words in your script.

At first glance, this visualization may seem a bit unusual. However, if you give it a try, you'll probably be surprised at what you are able to come up with, not only with physical changes, but also with the sound of your voice that results from creating a believable character.

TIPS FOR MAKING YOUR CHARACTER BELIEVABLE

Many of the following tips apply to dialogue copy, and you will see some of them again in Chapter 10. However, they can also be applied to single-voice copy, whether it is for a commercial, an animated character, a corporate sales presentation, or some other narrative.

- Take the punctuation marks out of your delivery. Keep your performance conversational. Add your personal spin to make the copy your own.

- Be careful not to overanalyze your copy. It's easy to fall into the trap of analyzing a script to death. Overanalyzing can cause you to lose spontaneity and cause your delivery to become flat and uninteresting.

- Don't become so focused on your character that you lose sight of the whole story, the drama and the relationships between characters and conflict.

- Be careful not to exaggerate your character's attitude, speech patterns, or other characteristics, unless the script specifically calls for an extreme characterization.

- Try to internalize the wants and needs of your character, both physically and emotionally. Find the place in your body where a tension develops. Hold it there and read your lines. In theater, this is called *setting the character*. Don't set your character too soon. Only after running through a script several times will you be able to find the true voice for your character. Stay in the moment, listen and answer, and react authentically to the other characters.

- Speak your lines to another person, real or imagined, expecting that they will respond. Pretend you are speaking to your best friend. Keep in mind the wants and needs of your character and express those to someone, with tension in your body, expecting a response.

- Underplay, rather than overplay. Louder is not better. If in doubt, pull back, speak more softly, and be more natural. Remember, "less is more."

- Keep your body posture (physical attitude) in a stance consistent with the character you have decided on. Maintain this attitude throughout your performance.

- Don't read! Be conversational. Talk *to* the audience, not *at* them. Be careful not to overenunciate. Less is usually more.

- Find the rhythm in the copy. All copy has a rhythm. Find the rhythm and phrasing and be consistent throughout the copy.

- Keep it real. Speak as quickly as you would if you were talking to someone and speak as quietly as you would if you were in a real conversation. If "uhhh's," "hmmm's," or "ahhh's" seem appropriate for your character, ad-lib them into your delivery even though they might not be written into the copy. This is a technique for making a scripted character more human.

- Get into the moment by ad-libbing situations or lines. Give yourself a realistic lead-in to the copy and ad-lib that lead-in before you start. Make your lead-in specific and concrete.

- Stay in the moment. Pick up cues. Interact with other performers. Don't let your lines be separated from those of the other performers. Listen to yourself, the director, and the other performers and respond appropriately (*listen and answer*).

- Don't allow any air between your line and the other character's line. The only exception is when a pause for timing is logical or makes sense in the context of the story.

- Create a powerful visual image of your character in your imagination and let the character "live" through your body, mind, and voice.

All voice-over performances are a form of theater, and you are the actor. When you become the character in the copy, you will be believable to the audience, creating a suspension of disbelief. When the audience suspends their disbelief in what they hear, they become more open to the message being communicated. Remember, it all starts when you discover the character in the copy.

---

[1] "Understanding Consumers and Markets," *Why People Buy*, RISC, 1997 (1-2).
[2] RISC AmeriScan compass, map, and other materials copyright RISC, 1997. Used by permission of Marshall Marketing & Communications, Inc.
[3] "Understanding Consumers and Markets," *Why People Buy*, RISC, 1997 (3).
[4] *MM&C RISC AmeriScan Guidebook*, copyright RISC, 1997 (5).

8

Words That Sell

This chapter reviews many of the techniques discussed in Chapters 5, 6, and 7. Chapters 9, 10, 11, and 12 include a variety of scripts that have been aired as radio and television commercials, used for corporate presentations, or for other real-world applications. These scripts will give you a good idea of the types of copy you may be asked to perform as you begin to do auditions and work sessions. Each script is reproduced as accurately as possible, including typos, awkward phrasing, grammatical mistakes, and other things that might seem odd, yet are commonplace in voice-over copy.

The Director in the Front Row of Your Mind

As a performer, over time, you will develop instincts as to how to develop your character, deliver your lines, and create drama in your performance. These instincts are good and necessary for a professional performer. However, if they are simply left at the level of instincts, they will limit your abilities to find the nuances and subtlety of the performance — those seemingly insignificant things that make the drama powerful, or the dialogue interesting, or a comedic script hysterical rather than just humorous.

All voice-over copy is written for the purpose of selling something — a product or service, information, education, or an emotion or feeling. However, it is not the words in and of themselves that sell, it is the *way* in which *the words are spoken* that sells. It is the details of the performance behind the words — the nuance — that allow a performer to bring a script and a character to life. And behind every performer, there is a director. Somewhere in your mind is a director. You may not have realized it, but that director is there. Allow your director to sit front row, center in your mind so he or she can objectively watch your performance to keep you on track and performing at your best.

115

Voice-over copy is theatrical truth — not real-life truth — and your internal director is the part of you that gives you silent cues to keep you on track when you forget this. As you work with copy, you will find a little voice in your head that tells you, "Yeah, that was good" or "That line needs to be done differently." Your mental director is the result of critical thinking. He or she is the part of you that keeps you on track, helps you stay in the moment, and gives you focus and guidance with your performance. Think of this director as a separate person (or part of you) who is watching your performance from a distance, yet close enough to give you cues.

Over time, your internal director and your performance will become as one — a seamless blending of director and performer resulting in a truly professional dramatic artist, without any conscious effort. This is the level to strive for. This is what theater is all about. This is what you, as a voice actor, can achieve with any type of copy you are asked to read.

The Process of Pretending

Acting is the process of pretending. An actor momentarily pretends to be someone or something other than his or her true self. Effective acting is making the process of pretending believable to the audience. To make a performance believable, the actor must understand the character in the script and must temporarily take on the appropriate personality traits and other attitudes of that character.

Effective actors will search within themselves to find something from their personal experience that can be applied to their character's situation or to the performance in general (*sense memory*). If there is nothing in the actor's past to draw on, then the actor simply makes something up! The idea is to create an emotional, mental, and physical connection between the performer and the character in the script. This connection, which exists purely in the mind of the actor, helps give life to the character in the script, making the character more real and believable to the audience.

Bring a part of you to the words on the page and your performance will become more believable. Decide on what your thoughts and feelings will be as you perform your lines (*subtext*) in order to make the copy your own. Let's review some of the keys to successful voice acting that have already been discussed elsewhere in this book.

LET GO OF JUDGMENTS AND INHIBITIONS

One of the major keys to success with voice acting is to let go of any judgments, inhibitions, and concerns. It is important to leave your self-critic outside. The director in the front row of your mind is not a critic, but, rather a coach and an advocate whose sole purpose is to make your performance better. There is an important difference between being critically analytical about your performance and judgmental.

Judgmental thinking would be:

- "The way I delivered that last copy was just horrible! I'll never be able to do these lines right."
- "I just can't get into this character!"
- "I can't do this kind of copy!"
- "I shouldn't feel embarrassed when I do copy like this."

Analytical, or critical, thinking would be:

- "I didn't like the way I delivered the copy — it just didn't seem real."
- "I know I can be more effective than that last read."
- "What can I do to make my character more believable?"

Judgmental thinking usually approaches the subject from a negative point of view, stops you in your tracks, and prevents you from discovering the solutions you need. Critical (analytical) thinking is constructive and helps move you toward solutions that will make your performance more believable.

UNDERSTAND THE COPY

As you study a script, do a quick character analysis to figure out who your character is. Also determine to whom you are speaking (your one-person listener or *audience*), why your character is speaking (your *back story*) as well as any special requirements of the scene, including emotional or attitude changes, dynamics, interactions with other characters, etc. What is the subject of your copy? Do a mental script analysis as you run through the copy once or twice. Commit to your decisions. Use a pencil to mark your script as needed and allow the words to become your own.

To effectively orchestrate your performance you need to have a solid understanding of the following:

- Who is the audience?
- Who are you as the character?
- Why is the character speaking these words? (What is the character's motivation or purpose in speaking and what gives your character the authority to be speaking the words in the script?)
- What are the performance dynamics? (pacing, volume, timing, etc.)

- What are the key words and phrases that may need special emphasis?

- What is the overall attitude of the script?

- What are the emotional hooks in the copy?

- What is the producer or copywriter's vision for the "sound" of the performance?

WORK BACKWARDS

To quickly get an idea of the copywriter's intent, the target audience, the client's message, and some solid clues about your character and the story in the copy, try looking at the last line of the script first. The end of a script is where the resolution or nonresolution of conflict occurs and is usually the point where a character's attitude or true motivation is revealed. It is also where the most important part of the client's message usually resides. By working from the bottom of the script to the top, you will be able to learn important information that you can use to quickly create a basic character and attitude. Then use other clues in the copy to more fully develop your character.

M.O.V.E.

Remember — "**M**ovement **O**rchestrates **V**ocal **E**xpression." Don't just stand in front of the microphone stiff and rigid! Relax! Let your character move. Keep doing exercises to develop the habit of being relaxed and condition your body and mind to the experience of relaxation. A relaxed mind and body will make it easier to release your inhibitions and be nonjudgmental. Use your face, arms, and upper body to "act out" the scene in the copy. Use gestures when the script has you talking to someone. Make a fist when emphasizing a strong point in the copy. Use a smile, a frown, and other facial expressions to help convey the feeling or emotion in the copy. Feelings must be expressed in your body and your face in order to become real through your voice. Keep moving!

FIND THE RHYTHM TO ADD VARIETY

Find the rhythm in the copy! Don't deliver every line with the same inflection and intonation — unless that is specifically requested of you. Add some variety to the way you deliver your lines, staying in character, of course. Broaden you vocal range (changes in pitch and intonation) and your dynamic range (soft to loud). Use a soft, gentle voice to emphasize something tender or romantic or to create a feeling of warmth, intimacy, or friendliness. Use a louder voice to project anger, aggression, or hostility. A soft voice with tension can be an effective way to project a character's pent-up emotions. Be real!

Use your face and body to add variety and feel the rhythm of the copy. Put a smile on your face to create a feeling of fun or happiness; frown to create a mood of frustration or anger. Use breath control to support your voice as your character expresses the emotions present in the copy.

Ad lib natural human sounds like "uh," "hmm," and so on, in appropriate places as you deliver the copy. You might also leave a short pause for timing between words or sustain certain word sounds to add variety and create realism.

ADJUST YOUR PHRASING

Look at voice-over copy as if it were classical music. Classical music constantly shifts from loud, fast sections to slower, softer sections. Each of these sections has its own unique tempo (*pace*) and rhythm according to the feeling or emotion being communicated. A voice-over performance can do exactly the same thing. Don't be afraid to slow down, speed up, or even leave a second of complete silence, if you feel it is necessary to create realism and believability in the copy you are reading.

STUDY OTHER PERFORMERS

Study film and television actors. Watch how they deliver their lines and interact with other characters. Listen to the dynamics of their voices. Notice that most actors use a lot of variety and inflection — they don't speak in monotone or with limited range (unless those attributes are part of the character). They also move and express emotion physically as well as verbally, just as they would in real life. Mimic and imitate what you see other actors do and how they speak so you can get the experience of what they are doing. Study the techniques they use and apply them to your style of performance. You will soon find the boundary of your comfort zone — the point where your stretch becomes uncomfortable. To grow as a performer, you need to find a way to work past that boundary.

TAKE THE "VOICE" OUT OF "VOICE-OVER"

Don't just read your copy. Have a conversation with the listener. Talk *to* your audience, not *at* them, always striving to motivate, persuade, or move the listener to action. Remember that even if you are the only person in the booth, the *other* person is always there. Visualize your best friend, wife, or husband on the other side of the microphone, and talk *to* them.

Do whatever you can to draw the listener into your story and expect a response. You are a storyteller! Remember:

- Use drama (*emotional hooks*) to attract and hold the listener's attention.
- Talk in phrases, not word by word.
- Don't read.
- Let the content and subtext of the copy determine your dynamics.
- Have a conversation with the listener.
- Talk out loud to yourself to find hidden treasures in your delivery.
- Experiment with different attitudes, inflections, and emotions.
- Take out the punctuation marks in the script to make the copy flow more naturally and conversationally.
- Have a mental attitude that allows you to create a feeling of reality and believability. If you believe your character is real, your listener will.

LOOK FOR QUESTION MARKS IN THE COPY

Question marks are opportunities for dramatic punctuation. I'm not referring to the punctuation mark — ?. I'm referring to words or phrases in the copy that give you the opportunity to ask a question. If the copy specifically asks a question, you should make that clear with your performance. Question marks that do not ask questions are usually found in sentences that describe or explain something. Someplace in the sentence there will be an opportunity to answer the unasked question.

Find those spots and figure out your own answers to the questions. Your answers will be valuable to your character because they are part of the character's knowledge or history, which helps make the character real. Here's a :30 TV script with places where question marks present opportunities for discovering information noted in parentheses:

She's just a few days old (HOW MANY DAYS?) and you're already worried (WORRIED ABOUT WHAT?).
What kind of world will she grow up in? (COPY ASKS A SPECIFIC QUESTION – COME UP WITH AN ANSWER.)
How will she get the education she needs? (ANSWER THIS QUESTION.)
And learn the values (WHAT VALUES?) to sustain her in trying times?
She's counting on your knowledge (WHAT DO YOU KNOW?) and concern (WHAT ARE YOUR CONCERNS?).
Shouldn't you have a newscast you can count on for that same thing? (WHAT THINGS CAN YOU COUNT ON?)
KNSD News. Coverage (WHAT KIND OF COVERAGE?) you can count on.

You can take this process as far as you like, even to the point of asking questions about every word in the script. As you decide on your answers to the unasked questions, you will be creating the foundation of your character's attitude and personality. Commit to the answers you come up with and use them as tools for giving your character life. However, be prepared to modify your answers as your character develops and as you receive direction from the producer.

FIND EMOTIONAL HOOKS

These are the words or phrases that carry an emotional impact. Call on your past experience to recall a memory of a similar emotion (*sense memory*). Notice that the memory of the emotion creates a certain tension someplace in your body. Observe the tension's position in your body and what it feels like. Hold this tension or sensation as you deliver the copy, reexperiencing the emotion or feeling. Now speak from that place in your body, fully expressing the tension. This technique helps to make your performance more believable and your character more real.

STAY IN THE MOMENT

Don't let your mind wander — stay focused. Don't be thinking about what you are having for lunch or dinner, or about how bad the traffic was when coming to the studio. Stay focused on the performance at hand. Allow yourself to experience the moment taking place in the script. Concentrate on staying in character and maintaining that role throughout the session. Then let it go so you don't have to think about it.

MAKE EVERY TIME THE FIRST TIME

Make each and every performance seem as if it is the first time. It is very easy to get sloppy by take 27. Take 28 should sound as fresh and real as take one — only better. Unless the producer or director tells you otherwise, you should maintain the same energy and attitude for each take. Use the director's guidance as a tool to help you focus in on your best performance. Add a little spin to a word, or shift your emphasis here or there with each take, but keep your energy and attitude consistent. This becomes very important to the editor who needs to put the final project together long after you have gone. Many times, bits and pieces from several takes are assembled to arrive at the finished product. Variations in your performance energy can stand out very clearly if you are not consistent, and make the editor's job a nightmare.

LISTEN AND ANSWER

Most people have a hard time listening. Allow the director in the front row of your mind to listen carefully as you perform the copy. Then, listen to what your internal director has to say. Listen to the producer or director for instruction on how to modify your delivery. If you are doing dialogue, listen to the other performers. Listen for opportunities to inject small human sounds: uh-huh, ummm, clearing your throat, breath sounds, and so on, all to make dialogue more real and believable. An inexperienced actor will just do his or her lines. An experienced actor will give the same lines life by adding the little details that make the conversation real.

ADD DRAMA

Even dry, boring copy can be made interesting if it is performed with drama. A dramatic performance is much more than just reading the words on the page. It involves body movement, a wide range of vocal pitch and dynamics, body tension, a thorough understanding of the character, and a mastery of story telling techniques. When done properly, even reading the phone book can be a dramatic experience.

The key to effective drama is the element of surprise. Lead the audience in one direction, and suddenly end up someplace else. This is also the key to effective comedy. In both types of performances, the actor must never tip his or her hand and let the audience in on what's happening too soon. Variations in vocal tone, dynamics, and physical energy are what make a voice-over performance interesting and captivating.

PRACTICE DIFFERENT ATTITUDES

Practice developing your basic acting skills by pretending different moods or attitudes at times when you are by yourself. Read from a book striving for intensity, clarity, and meaning in every word. Perform the same copy or section of a book as different characters with different attitudes. Record these practice sessions and listen for the believability in your performances. To achieve drama, try changing your energy or attitude for different sections of the copy. Use your emotions to express the mood of the copy and don't hold back. To express anger, be loud and aggressive. To express tenderness or romance, be soft and gentle. Practicing in private helps you overcome your self-consciousness and gradually opens you up to being able to express powerful emotions and feelings when in a working environment.

STRETCH YOUR BOUNDARIES

Don't worry about how you will appear or sound to anybody! As a voice actor, your job is to perform the copy and your character in the best manner possible. If you need to make strange faces, or wave your arms wildly to get into the character, then that is what you need to do. Leave your inhibitions and self-conscious attitudes outside the studio door.

Stretch beyond what feels comfortable to you, even in a recording session. It is better to stretch too far rather than not far enough. It is easier for a director to pull you back after setting a character that is too far out there than it is to stretch you further. Remember, there is no absolutely right or wrong way to perform. Each performer is unique and different techniques work better for different performers. Do whatever works best for you to make your performance real and believable.

As you stretch your abilities, you will probably feel uncomfortable at first. Remember to be nonjudgmental and to not worry about how well you are doing. Each of us has an individual concept of some point at which we feel we would be going too far, or over the edge. This is usually the line between what we would call *normalcy* (sanity) and *craziness* (insanity).

Practice taking yourself just a little bit over that line until you begin to feel uncomfortable. Then take yourself a little bit further. The more you take yourself beyond the point where you think sanity ends, the faster you will develop the ability to take on any character — and momentarily become that character.

BE WILLING TO TAKE RISKS

You must be willing to risk total failure. Intend to perform to the best of your abilities. Become the character and do whatever it takes for you to get *into* character. Remember that you are uniquely you, and that you are interesting just as you are. Also remember that the people you are working with have insecurities of their own and may actually know less about the business than you do. Know that you know what you are doing. If you never risk, you can never learn. Use each audition or session as a learning experience. Keep an attitude of always being in training.

ACT PROFESSIONAL

Play the part! Act professional and you will be treated with respect. Enter a studio with the attitude of a professional there to do a job. Be friendly, cooperative, and ready to work. Making money does not make you a professional. Acting professionally makes you money. When you act like a pro, the people hiring you will believe you are a pro and will respect you.

Remember that this business is all about creating believability in the mind of the audience. When you enter a studio, your first audience will be the people who hired you. Make them believe you are good at what you do and prove it with your performance.

> Become the child you once were!
> Pretend!
> Play!
> Have fun!

Tips for Performing All Types of Copy

Remember, voice acting is theater of the mind, and you are the actor. When you become the character in the copy, you will be believable to the audience, and a suspension of disbelief will be created. When the audience suspends their disbelief in what they hear, they become more open to the message. This all starts when you discover the character in the copy.

- Don't overanalyze your copy. Overanalyzing can cause you to lose spontaneity and cause your delivery to become flat and uninteresting. You can also become so focused on your character that you lose sight of the whole story, the drama and the relationship between the characters and the conflict.

- You need to be able to get just enough information from the copy to understand your character and know what is taking place. Understand the drama, then add your personal spin to make the copy your own. Find the USP in the copy and let everything you do lead to that goal.

- Rely on your instincts, and the director in your mind will guide your delivery to keep it on track.

- Tell the story. All scripts tell a story, even dry, technical scripts. Storytelling is always about relationships. As a voice actor, it is your job to understand the relationships, discover the story, and communicate it to the audience. To be believable, make the relationships seem real.

- Play, have fun, be natural, and feel free to experiment. If you go too far, the producer or director will pull you back.

- Keep a strong mental image of your character and the story in your mind. Pretend that what you are saying or that the situation your character is in is real. Make your character believable by adding something of yourself. Let your imagination run wild. If you believe in the reality of your performance, the tension of your belief will come through in your words and the audience will believe.

9

Single~Voice Copy

Single-voice copy is written for a solo performer who will deliver the entire message, with the possible exception of a separate tag line. There is no interaction between characters, since there is only one, although there may be some implied interaction between the performer and the listener. Most radio and television commercials, public service announcements, corporate narratives, telephone messages, books-on-tape, and some CD-ROM projects fall into this category.

All single-voice copy is communicating information, often attempting to reach the listener on an emotional level. To communicate effectively, it is essential to grab the listener's attention, and hold it. Reading or announcing copy will not achieve either of these goals. Both reading and announcing direct the performance inward and imply that the performer is speaking to himself or herself. The target audience of a single-voice script can usually be determined pretty easily; however, sometimes it can be a challenge to define the character speaking. Well-written copy that clearly tells a story makes the character easy to define. Poorly written copy that contains only information in the form of facts and figures can make this difficult.

Consider single-voice copy as a story you are telling. Find your storyteller and commit to the attitude and style choices you make. Deliver the copy from a set point of view by finding the subtext (how you think and feel) behind the words you speak and express it through your voice. Study your script closely to determine if it was written to match a current trend.

One key to effective single-voice copy is to use the basic dramatic principle of having a conversation with another person — talking to the listener who is not really there. Another key is to find the appropriate attitude for your delivery. Make your conversation natural, believable, consistent, and keep it candid — and remember to speak to only one person at a time. *Shotgunning*, trying to speak to several people at once, tends to make your delivery sound more like a speech than a conversation.

Make the other person someone you know — anyone who might be a good candidate for the message. Do not have the conversation with a pet or stuffed animal but rather give the subject of your conversation a base in reality. Make the person real in your imagination. A strong visual image will help lead to feelings and emotions in your conversation. When you have feelings and emotions, your experiences communicate through your voice.

In single-voice scripts, as in others, there can be many different written references to the performer, such as VO:, MAN:, WOMAN:, TALENT:, ANNCR: (announcer), VOICE 1:, AVO: (announce voice-over), and so on. These all refer to the performer and are often used interchangeably. Scripts also include references to music and SFX (sound effects), which are not to be read by the performer. A TV script may or may not include a separate column for video instructions. If the column is there, use the video description to your advantage to glean valuable information about the audience, your character, overall energy, and how you can best perform the copy.

Tips for Performing Single-Voice Copy

Remember, single-voice copy always tells a story and stories are always about relationships. The relationships can be between people, between people and other things, or even between things. Stories and relationships are present even in dry narrative copy that contains only intellectual information. If the story is not clearly written in the script, use your imagination to make it up. If a relationship is not clear, it might be simply a relationship between the character speaking and the audience. The following suggestions will help you create effective performances for single-voice copy.

- Analyze the copy for character, mood, attitude, conflict, rhythm, etc. (See Chapter 7, The Character in the Copy).

- Find the unique selling proposition (USP) in the copy. What is the ultimate message, image, feeling or unique quality about the product or service that the advertiser wants to communicate to the listener? What makes this product or service unique from its competitors?

- Find the subtext for the words you are speaking. What are you thinking, and how do you feel?

- Determine who your primary audience is and why they should be listening to what you have to say. Use a photo to help make the conversation real.

- Determine what places your character in a position of being an authority on the subject of the script.

- Determine the creative strategy that will enable you to build dramatic tension and allow for expression of the message. Use sense-memory techniques to recall your past feelings in a similar situation. Locate where the tension is in your body and speak from that place.

- Keep your delivery conversational and in the appropriate attitude. Remember that the other person is always there, just not visible. Make the other person real in your imagination. Keep the attitude of moving or persuading them with your words, and have the expectation of a response. Talk *to* the other person, *not at* him or her.

- Be believable by staying in the moment, keeping spontaneity, and making the copy your own.

- Be careful not to telegraph the message or send a message of "here comes another commercial."

- Talk to a single person. A photograph can be used to give you focus.

Single-Voice Scripts

As you work with the following scripts, you might find it interesting to read through the script before reading the Copy Notes provided for each one. Come up with your own interpretation for attitude, pacing, character, and performance, and then read through the notes to see how close you came to what the producers of these projects intended. After working with the script for a while to come up with your interpretation and delivery, play the corresponding audio track on the CD that came with this book to hear the actual commercial. You may find it useful to use the CD track as a tool for understanding the various elements of the performance.

BC HYDROPONICS — (CD track 7)

Title: "Science" Local Radio :60
Agency: One Stop Voice Shop — **www.onestopvoiceshop.com**
USP: "Start Growing Today"
Target Audience: All ages, people interested in growing their own plants and food
Style: Calm, yet friendly
Character: Storyteller
VO Talent: Ross Huguet — **www.greatpipes.com**
Copy Notes: The slow pace and classical music used to underscore this commercial create a sound that contrasts most radio programming. The result is that the spot quickly gets the listener's attention. The unusual subject holds the attention of those interested.

(Comfortable, calm delivery. Classical music fills pauses)

Hydroponics . . . the science of growing plants without soil. Imagine a calming, peacefully rewarding pastime that gives you hours of stress relief and satisfaction. Experience the world of hydroponic gardening. Heighten your awareness of the environment while keeping it under control. Your plants will grow faster, be more productive, and love you. No need to spray on harmful pesticides . . . everything is cleaner, looks better, and lasts longer. Hydroponics allows you to work with less space and maintenance. BC Hydroponics is here to help you with everything you need to get started. Call 1-888-346-GROW. That's 1-888-346-GROW. Or visit us on-line at BCHydroponics.com and start growing . . . today.

BIDBAY.COM — (CD track 8)

Title: "BidBay Bucks" Regional TV :30
Agency: The Commercial Clinic — **www.commercialclinic.com**
USP: "Get 100 BidBay Bucks when you register for free"
Target Audience: Women 30-50
Style: Friendly, with a moderate touch of sarcasm
Character: Spokesperson
VO/On-camera Talent: Mary Pinizzotto — **www.shamonfreitas.com**
Copy Notes: This is a :30 television commercial. The VISUAL side of the script describes the picture, while the AUDIO side of the script contains the copy. You can often get a good idea of how to deliver your copy if you know what the producer is planning to do visually. Sometimes a storyboard will be attached to the script. A storyboard is much like a cartoon strip with drawings that show the intended visual flow of the commercial.

This spot was written specifically to attract new visitors to the website **www.BidBay.com**. Although this script is for a television commercial, the entire audio was pre-recorded for the client so he could approve the voice and delivery attitude. The pre-record was then used as a guide track during the videotaping to achieve proper timing and pacing.

When was the last time someone handed you a hundred bucks to play with? That's what I thought! Well, when you register at BidBay.com, that's exactly what you get . . . a hundred BidBay bucks you can use right away to buy just about anything from toys to cars to other really cool stuff. This offer won't last forever. So why are you still sitting on that couch? Get up! Turn on your computer and register at BidBay.com. You're still there . . . Go!

LAKE ARROWHEAD HILTON LODGE — (CD track 9)

Title: "Come Up for Air!" Local Radio :60
Agency: The Ganyon Idea Factory, San Diego (for Western Media Corp.)
USP: "Come Up for Air" Enjoy a relaxing get-away at a rustic resort
Target Audience: Adult men and women
Style: Friendly attitude projecting a sense of beauty and quality
Character: Spokesperson
VO Talent: Phil Ganyon
Copy Notes: When this radio commercial aired in 1986, the Arrowhead Hilton Lodge was overwhelmed with a response that resulted in the largest number of calls in a single day in their history, and sold-out weekends. The overall style of the delivery is very casual and friendly, conveying the experience of a world-class resort while emphasizing the extensive amenities and very reasonable price. Note that the phone number is repeated three times. Phone numbers in radio scripts are rarely of any value unless the listener is in a position to write it down or unless the number is repeated several times in a manner the listener can easily remember.

The beautiful <u>Lake</u> <u>Arrowhead</u> <u>Hilton</u> <u>Lodge</u> invites you to come up for air! . . . clean . . . clear . . . fresh mountain air!

In the time it takes to watch a movie on TV, you can <u>drive</u> up to gorgeous, mile-high Lake Arrowhead . . . It's <u>that</u> <u>close</u>! And, the <u>Arrowhead</u> <u>Hilton</u> <u>Lodge</u> makes this invitation irresistible with prices as low as <u>eighty-nine</u> dollars for <u>three</u> days and <u>two</u> nites!

Rustic, luxury lakefront accommodations; <u>five</u> restaurants; <u>three</u> entertainment lounges; complete exercise club, with indoor running track; organized activities for children . . . The <u>quality</u> service and ambiance of a world-class Alpine resort/ spa . . . In the famous <u>Hilton</u> tradition—<u>all</u> for as low as $89 for 3 days & 2 nites!

And, you're just minutes away from great skiing at <u>eight</u> resorts: Gold Mine . . . Green Valley . . . Mountain High . . . Mount Baldy . . . Ski Sunrise . . . Snow Forest . . . Snow Summit . . . and Snow Valley!

So, come up for air! . . . At the beautiful, affordable Lake Arrowhead Hilton Lodge!

For more information & reservations, call this toll-free number, now:
1-800-223-3307 . . . . 223-3307 . . . . 1-800-223-3307.

NATIONAL LITERACY HOTLINE — (CD track 10)

Title: "You're not alone" TV :30
Agency: LAK Advertising, San Diego
USP: "Reading is power"
Target Audience: Adults who cannot read
Style: Relaxed, friendly, compassionate
Character: Helpful friend
VO Talent: MJ Lallo — **www.creatingvoices.com**
Copy Notes: This script almost has the appearance of a public service announcement (PSA), but it is, in fact, a commercial. The product/service being advertised is training for people who cannot read. Notice that there is not a lot of copy for the :30 spot. Knowing that this is a :30 commercial, and judging by the tone of the script, who the audience is, and how short it is, you can get a good idea of a delivery style and pacing. Deliver with a friendly, compassionate attitude at a fairly slow pace. This script actually has only about 25 seconds of copy. The rest of the commercial audio is filled with a peaceful, yet uplifting musical background. Notice that the telephone number is only given once. Television commercials have the advantage of being able to provide the contact information visually, so a single mention of a phone number is not a problem, as it would be in a radio commercial.

If you need help reading, you're not alone. One in five adults is functionally illiterate. Learn how to fill out a job application, read traffic signs, and vote.

Reading is power. Call us at the National Literacy Hotline — 1 800-228-8813 for a program near you.

Copyright MJ Productions, Los Angeles, CA, used by permission

ENERGY CONSERVATION — (CD tracks 11, 12, 13)

Title: "Feels good," TV :30
Agency: Commercial Clinic — **www.commercialclinic.com**
USP: "Do your part!" Educational; conserve energy
Target Audience: Environmentally concerned adults; general adult audience
Style: Storyteller
Character: Concerned friend
VO Talent: James R. Alburger — **www.voiceacting.com**
Copy Notes: This commercial is a good example of what can happen when a client delegates the creative and production responsibilities of their project but when the product is delivered they have either changed their mind — or don't like what they get. The goal of this project was to encourage energy

conservation at a time when utility rates were at an all-time high, and energy producers could not generate enough electricity to meet the demand.

The CD contains two different versions of this spot that clearly show how a subtle change in delivery can totally affect how the message is perceived by the listener. The first version is delivered in a serious tone with a relatively low energy level, creating an overall serious tone. The second version is more upbeat, with a positive spin and more "smile" in the voice. Notice the differences in pacing, energy, and attitude between the two versions.

A music-only version is also included on the CD so you can work with this script on your own. Experiment with different attitudes, pacing, and energy levels as you work with this copy. Change your character, audience, and back story to see how that affects your interpretation and delivery.

> We take lots of things for granted — like flipping a light switch, turning on the TV, or the air conditioning — or using a computer. We'll always be able to do that, right?
>
> Well, right now we're in a serious energy crisis and we have to do our part to reduce the burden on an already overworked power grid.
>
> Do **your** part. Leave your laundry 'til after 7pm. Power down your computer when you're not using it, and leave the lights off when you're not in the room.
>
> If we **don't** all do our part . . . we may soon have far **LESS** to take for granted.

FRANK POMERLEAU, INC. — (CD track 14)

Title: "College Mom" Local Radio :60 (:50 body/:10 tag)
Agency: Kern Media, Inc.
USP: "On Sale at Pomerleau's"
Target Audience: Persons 25-54, parents of college students and students
Style: Storyteller
Character: A "mom" of a first-year college student
VO Talent: DB Cooper — **www.voxvobiscum.com**; Chuck Morgan
Copy Notes: This :50/:10 radio spot was written for a fall "back-to-school" campaign in combination with print. The format of this commercial is typical of retail store ads that promote a single seasonal product or service for a limited time. The first portion of the spot is an interesting story, which integrates the store's name several times. The last :10 of the spot is a tag, usually performed by a different voice actor. The tag is sometimes called the "sell" because it is here where the details of the sale and store locations

are given. Proper delivery of the tag is every bit as important as delivery of the body of the script. A poorly performed tag (often "read" by the station DJ) can absolutely destroy the mood and motivation built through a wonderfully performed story, resulting in a much lower response than if the tag is professionally voiced and attached to the produced spot. This commercial includes a built-in tag.

Although this spot has two separate voices, there is no dialogue. So even though this is technically a multi-voice spot, it is more accurately a commercial with two single-voice sections. Both performers may have been at the studio at the same time, but they were recorded separately and the tracks edited together during post-production.

MOM: My kid's an honor student! You wouldn't believe how smart he is . . . he's off to school next week . . . he gave me the list for his dorm room. First is a desk and a rug . . . that makes sense to me, he needs a comfortable place to study. Next on his list is a TV/VCR combo . . . to watch the PBS science shows, he says. Well that's a good reason, and besides they're on sale now at Pomerleau's. But why does he need a mini-fridge and a microwave? I'll just think of the money he'll save eating in! So smart . . . plus they're on sale at Pomerleau's. Big item he's gotta have is a DVD . . . he calls it a "degree value device" or something like that . . . anyway, guess who's got 'em on sale? Yep, and Pomerleau's is where I'll get his "loafa-sofa" too, for extra dorm comfort. Ya know, I gotta draw the line at a satellite dish! For watching foreign films, he says! He's smart, but mom's got a thing or two to teach him.

TAG ANNC: Essentials for the dorm room! And non-essentials too. All on sale at Pomerleau's — corner of Bridge and State streets in Augusta.

10

Dialogue Copy: Doubles and Multiples

Your understanding of the whole story and your character's part in it will directly affect how your performance is received during an audition. The casting person, producer, or director is looking for performers who can make their character and the situation appear real. If you perform your lines the same way twice at an audition, chances are you will not be considered for the role. Casting people are generally looking for much more than just a voice. They are looking for performers who can take direction well, deliver lines with variety and realism, and bring a character to life.

Types of Dialogue Copy

THE CONVERSATION

As with single-voice copy, dialogue copy involves a conversation between two or more characters. The primary difference with dialogue copy is that your one-person audience is in the studio with you and is participating in the performance.

Unlike most single-voice copy, dialogue copy usually involves a story with a specific plotline and interaction between two or more characters. It is important for you to understand the whole story, not just your part in it. If you limit your understanding to just your role, you may miss subtle details that are vital to effectively interacting with the other characters. You may have difficulty creating the dramatic tension that is so necessary for giving the characters life and making them real to the listener.

Another form of dialogue script is one in which the characters are not talking to each other, but are both speaking directly to the audience. In this

133

case, a conversation is still taking place, but it may be a bit more one-sided and informational in nature.

COMEDY

Comedy is a very popular form of dialogue copy. It is not the words on the page that make a script funny; it is the intent behind the words. In part, comedy is based on the unexpected — leading the audience in one direction and then suddenly changing directions and ending up someplace else. Comedy is often based on overstating the obvious or placing a totally serious character in a ludicrous situation. Comedy can also be achieved by creating a sense of discomfort in the mind of the audience.

Don't play a comedy script for laughs, think of it as life — with a twist. If you play your lines for laughs, you won't get them. The laughs will only come when the audience is surprised.

Rhythm and timing are essential with comedy dialogue copy. The interaction between characters can make or break a comedy script. Overlapping lines, or stepping on lines, usually gives a more natural, real feeling and helps set the rhythm and pace of the copy. A feeling of realism can also be achieved by adding pauses (where appropriate), and adding natural vocal sounds.

Jokes are good examples of comedy that lead in one direction and end up someplace unexpected; for example:

VOICE 1:   Class, it is an interesting linguistic fact that in the English language a double negative makes a positive. However, in other languages, like Russian, a double negative still makes a negative. There is no language in which a double positive makes a negative.

VOICE 2: (*sarcastically*) Yeah, right!

It is a good idea to ask the producer or director before you take too many liberties with any copy; this is especially true with comedy copy. If the producer understands comedy, he or she will usually let you experiment with your character and how you deliver your lines. It might be a good idea to do the lines as written for at least a few takes before experimenting with ad-libs or taking your character too far out.

The most important thing about comedy is to not telegraph the punch line. Don't let your character's attitude tip off the ending. Say your lines in a natural, conversational way, appropriate to the situation, and the comedy will happen.

Tips for Performing Comedy Dialogue Copy

To be effective, comedy dialogue must have a sense of reality, even if the situation is ludicrous and the characters are exaggerated. The following tips and suggestions will help you perform comedy copy effectively.

- Be real. Keep your character spontaneous and natural. To help you get "in the moment" of the dialogue, you can create a believable back story or lead-in line.

- Find the comedy rhythm. This might include appropriate "beats" or pauses, which can provide the punch necessary for the peak comedic moment. Remember, dialogue copy has a rhythm for each character and a rhythm for the overall dialogue.

- Speak your lines to another person, real or imagined, expecting him or her to respond. Pretend you are speaking to your best friend. Keep in mind the wants and needs of your character and express those to someone, with tension in your body, expecting a response.

- Where appropriate, add natural sounds and reactions, such as "uhh," "yeah," "uh-huh," "mmm," or a groan or clear your throat. All of these sounds help give the feeling of a real, natural conversation. Ask the producer before making changes to the copy.

- *Subtext* — how you think and feel as you perform — is especially important with comedy. If your character is that of a normal person in a ludicrous situation, you need to have a subtext of normalcy. If your thoughts anticipate the punch line, it will be communicated through your performance.

- Do not telegraph the punch line. Be careful that your character's attitude doesn't give the audience more information than they need to know.

Tips for Performing Dialogue Copy in General

The following tips and suggestions will help you perform more effectively in all types of dialogue sessions.

- Internalize the wants and needs of your character, both physically and emotionally. Find the place in your body where a tension develops. Hold the tension there and read your lines. In theater, this is called *setting the character*. Don't set your character too soon. Only after running through a script several times will you be able to find the true voice for your character. Stay in the moment, listen and answer, and react authentically to the other characters.

- Underplay, rather than overplay. Louder is not better. If in doubt, pull back, speak more softly and be more natural.

- Don't read! Be conversational. Be real. Talk *to* the audience or other performer(s), not *at* them. Be careful not to overenunciate. Less is usually more.

- Find the rhythm in the copy. All copy has a rhythm. The rhythm for a comedic script will be different from that of a more serious script. Find the rhythm and be consistent throughout the copy.

- Keep it real. Speak as quickly as you would if you were actually talking to someone and as quietly as you would if you were in a real conversation. If "uhhh's," "hmmm's," or "ahhh's," hesitations, and other reactions seem appropriate for your character, ad-lib them into your performance, even though they might not be written into the copy. This is called *pulling lines* — a technique for making your character more human by altering the pacing of your delivery.

- Get into "the moment" by ad-libbing a situation. Give yourself a realistic lead-in to the copy and ad-lib that lead-in before you start. Make your lead-in specific and concrete.

- Stay in "the moment." Pick up cues. Interact with other performers. Listen to yourself and the other performers and respond appropriately (*listen and answer*). Don't allow any air between your line and the other character's line. The only exception is when a pause is logical and makes sense in the context of the story.

Dialogue and Multiple-Voice Scripts

As you work with the following scripts, you might find it interesting to read through the script before reading the Copy Notes provided for each one. Come up with your own interpretation for attitude, pacing, character, and performance. Then read through the notes to see how close you came to what the producers of these projects intended. As you listen to the CD tracks for these commercials, notice the interaction between characters and how these characters sound real, even though the voice or attitude may be somewhat exaggerated.

UNITED FURNITURE WAREHOUSE — (CD track 15)

Title: "5 minutes" Radio :30
Agency: The One Stop Voice Shop — **www.onestopvoiceshop.com**
Production: The Commercial Clinic — **www.commercialclinic.com**
USP: "Brand name furniture at half the price"
Target Audience: Adults in the market for new furniture
Style: Very conversational
Characters: Lonely Man: very low key, dry, droll, almost depressed delivery; Mom: overbearing, controlling
VO Talent: Lonely Man: Ross Huguet; Mom: Penny Abshire
Copy Notes: This is one of a series of radio commercials designed to "brand" United Furniture Warehouse as a source for high quality furniture at great prices. The story line for these commercials follows the love life of Lonely Man, who is constantly losing girlfriends because of his bad taste in furniture. Of course, Mom comes to the rescue by taking her son to UFW to get his new furniture. As much as Lonely Man wants to be independent, his life is completely at the whim of his Mom.

Even though Lonely Man has relatively few lines, his personality and boring life style need to be clearly communicated. This is done by defining the character, setting the desired attitude, and allowing the character to come through. The same process can be used to create the personality and attitude for the voice of Mom.

SFX – Telephone Ring

LM: Hello

Mom: So, how's my precious boy today?

LM: Fine, Mom.

Mom: How's the new couch? Did we get a deal, or what?

LM: It looks good mom, but I . . .

Mom: I told you United Furniture Warehouse was a wonderful place!

LM: Yes, Mom, but I . . .

Mom: But nothing! We paid half price for name brand furniture? You told me you liked it!

LM: I do Mom, but I still have to sit on it all by myself.

Mom: Oh, sweetheart, mother can be there in 5 minutes.

LM: Yes, Mom.

JINGLE: *United Furniture Warehouse!*

GEORGE TANNOUS & AFFILIATES — (CD track 16)

Title: "Teddy" Radio :60
Agency: The Commercial Clinic — **www.commercialclinic.com**
USP: "Now They're on Our Side!"
Target Audience: Adult men and women who need tax preparation
Style: Serious tone, conversational
Characters: Wife (seductive); Husband (very focused); Tag annc.
VO Talent: Wife: Penny Abshire; Husband: James Alburger; Tag: John Turner
Copy Notes: This award-winning commercial is one of a series of seven spots designed as a radio campaign for George Tannous & Affiliates tax preparation firm (1-800-taxtax5). At the time, GTA had 5 offices in the Los Angeles area, and was in the process of expanding to new locations. The company's primary competition was viewed to be H&R Block, the nation's largest tax preparation firm. The purpose of the campaign was to create top-of-mind awareness for GTA through the use of radio commercials that people would remember. On a subtle note, there is a reference to the competition made in a rather off-handed manner. Of the seven multi-voice commercials produced, six were set as interactive dialogue scenes and one was written as a rhyming story told by several voices.

H: Honey, do you have the hotel receipts for that trip to Mazatlan – I think I can write that off as a business expense . . .

W: Hotel?

H: . . . we did see your boss down there – and I'm sure we talked about work, didn't we?

W: You've been working on these taxes for hours and you're only on line 12 – how about a little R & R?

H: I gotta to get this done!

W: Oh, that can wait 'til later – why don't you come with me – the kids are asleep, and I've got something to show you . . .

H: Where did you put the calculator?

W: I bought a new teddy today, wanna see?

H: I told you we can't afford to buy any new toys for the kids right now!

W: It isn't for the kids, you Blockhead! It was for you!

(SFX DOOR SLAM)

H: Oh . . . Ohhh . . . Honey . . .

(SFX GIGGLES UNDER)

TAG: If there are more enjoyable things in your life you'd rather be doing than taxes – and we know there are – then call 1 800 Tax Tax 5 and have George Tannous & Affiliates prepare your taxes. Every office is run by a former IRS agent. These are the people who used to handle audits and they know the tax laws inside out. Call today – George Tannous & Affiliates – 1 800 Tax Tax 5. Now they're on our side.

TOYSMART — (CD track 17)

Title: "Green Beans" Radio :60
Agency: The Commercial Clinic — **www.commercialclinic.com**
USP: "Your Birthday Headquarters"
Target Audience: Adults with children
Style: Playful
Characters: Mom: frustrated, trying to get her "child" to eat; Child/Dad; Tag annc.
VO Talent: Mom: Penny Abshire; Child/Dad: James Alburger; Tag: James Alburger
Copy Notes: The owner of ToySmart was frustrated with the commercials being produced by his ad agency and wanted to try something different. The concept for this commercial was to create an interesting story that would get attention and draw customers to the stores. While brainstorming for this project, it was determined that there needed to be a way of tracking the success of the commercial. A number of ideas were suggested which led to the "green beans" idea. The spot evolved into a message that ultimately promoted a 10% discount for customers who brought in a can of green beans. Of course, even a mention of the green beans would get the discount. When asked about how the commercial was working for him, the client put it this way: ". . . everybody else in town is down. We're up!" The ToySmart stores collected a considerable number of cans of green beans, which were then donated to their local food bank.

The characters in this spot need to be real people in an identifiable situation. We have all known the frustration of trying to get a child to eat something they don't want to. Use your knowledge of that sort of experience to find the attitudes for both characters.

When you listen to the CD, notice the voice placement for the "child" voice and how it transitions to the adult Dad voice. Also notice how the Mom voice moves through a series of emotional levels and ends up with an attitude of amusement at the situation and her "child's" behavior.

ToySmart
Radio :60
"Green Beans"

Jingle music BG:

Mom: Come on honey – We'll go to Toy Smart this afternoon if
      you'll just eat your green beans.

Baby noises – protesting! (they're icky)

Mom: But you know how much you like seeing and playing with
      the best toys from all over the world – Remember how nice
      the store is and the friendly and helpful clerks? You liked
      them, didn't you?

Baby noises – excited!

Mom: I know you don't like green beans, sweetie, but finish 'em
      we can go to Toy Smart. Come on – open big – here
      comes the choo choo . . .

Baby noises protesting (uh,uh!)

Mom: Now be a big boy! We can buy a present for Jimmy's party
      and they'll gift wrap for free! I might even buy you a
      present too! Won't that make you happy? *(exasperated)*
      Come on - **<u>Please finish your green beans</u>!**

Dad: I'll eat all the green beans you want. Just put 'em with a
      T-bone steak!

Mom: Oh honey, you are such a child!

TAG: Come into Toy Smart today! Bring in a can of **green beans
      for the homeless** and get 10% off your total purchase.

Jingle sing: Toy Smart, gotta get a gift!

Tag: Toy Smart – Savannah's birthday headquarters – 309
      Eisenhower Dr. next to Kid's Space and River Street at
      Lincoln Ramp

Jingle Sing: Toy Smart, Toy Smart!

Dad: What do I get if I eat all my brussels sprouts?

IKEA BACK TO SCHOOL EVENT — (CD track 18)

Title: "Back To School Event" IK01R7-1 Radio :60
Agency: AM Advertising, San Diego — **www.amadvertising.com**
Copywriter/Producer: Elliot Rose
USP: "Be Yourself!"
Target Audience: Parents of first-time college students
Style: Playful with a touch of sarcasm
Characters: Announcer: tongue-in-cheek making "fun" of the girl's attitude; Girl: stereotyped high school ditzy blonde
VO Talent: Annc: Elliot rose; Girl: Erin Ashe (**www.shamonfreitas.com**)
Copy Notes: The San Diego Radio Broadcasters Radio In Achievement Awards honored this commercial as "Best Radio Commercial Written and Produced in San Diego."

Announcer: "The following message furnished by IKEA:"

Music in: Pomp and circumstance

Girl: . . .as we, the graduating seniors go out into life . . . we'll all face like, many really, really big challenges: Like staying true to ourselves in a world that demands, like, total conformity . . . all the time. Right?

Announcer: She should "like" go to Ikea's "Be Yourself: Back To School Event." With dozens of unique furnishing and accessories at Ikea's everyday low prices it'll be easy for her to express her true personality, . . . if she has one.

Girl: . . . and like so many of us are going off to college y'know . . . leaving home for the first time . . . to like, spread our wings and stuff?

Announcer: With Ikea's unique colors and matching patterns it'll be lots of fun for her to put together a dorm room or apartment that lets her be herself. And with Ikea's no hassle return policy she can bring it all back if she decides to be someone else.

Girl: . . . so as we go forth seniors, let's not forget all of the friends who helped us get here . . . for they are "The wind beneath our wings." Thank You! Oh . . . and Go HAWKS! Richie I love you

<applause>

Announcer: Go forth to the "BE YOURSELF" Back to School Event happening now at Ikea ½ Mile West of Qualcomm Stadium on Friars Road. Ya know?

GEORGE TANNOUS & AFFILIATES — (CD track 19)

Title: "Now, Spit!" Radio :60
Agency: The Commercial Clinic — **www.commercialclinic.com**
USP: "Now, They're on Our Side!"
Target Audience: Adults who need tax preparation assistance
Style: Conversational with a developing attitude
Characters: Patient: an unsuspecting foil for the dentist's aggression; Dentist: friendly at first, but gradually becomes more incensed as he seeks revenge; Tag Annc: storyteller who provides the necessary contact information
VO Talent: Dentist: Marc Biagi; Patient: Dave Rivas; Tag: John Turner
Copy Notes: The overall pace and interaction between the two characters must be fast, yet natural. The dentist starts out friendly enough, but as he realizes who he is working on, his frustration with the IRS is revealed. The patient becomes reactive to the situation, almost to the point of panic.

SFX:	(Dentist's office with typical overhead music)
Dentist:	Open wide, please - First time with us Mr. Green? Who referred you? What do you do for a living?
Patient:	I'm an IRS Examiner . . . OW!!!!
Dentist:	Oh, sorry. Open . . . You say you're an IRS examiner? The one who does the audits?
Patient:	Uh huh . . .
Dentist:	I was audited last year - cost me a lot of money.
SFX:	(Painful drilling sounds)
Patient:	It wasn't my fault!
Dentist:	Hmmm, this looks like a possible root canal - You say you've been flossing, but did you keep a log to prove it to me? And I see you claim to use a fluoride toothpaste and have regular checkups. Do you have your receipts and cancelled checks? I can't just take your word for it, you know. This may cost you big, Mr Green!
Patient:	(undecipherable protesting mutterings)
Dentist:	Now, stop complaining, or I'll dig even deeper . . . just like that IRS auditor did to me . . .
Patient:	(moaning)
TAG:	Time to turn the tables on the IRS? Call George Tannous & Affiliates at 1 800 Tax Tax 5 where former IRS agents will assist you with all your tax preparation needs. Now, they're on our side.

BOSTON MARKET — (CD track 20)

Title: "Blue House" Radio :30 (:18/:12)
Agency: Suissa Miller (Feb. 13, 2001)
Client: Boston Market/Low Fat
Production: Dick & Chris @ The Radio Ranch — **www.radio-ranch.com**
USP: "Boston Market. Slow Down"
Target Audience: Families who eat out together
Style: Conversational, rapid-fire
Characters: Guy: friendly but forgetful; Wife: helpful and forgiving
VO Talent: Guy: Dick Orkin; Wife: Christine Coyle;
ANNCR: Brian Cummings
Copy Notes: Dick Orkin and Christine Coyle @ The Radio Ranch have a reputation for producing some of the best and most effective commercials to come out of Hollywood. The Radio Ranch is consistently one of the top award-winning creative houses in LA. If you listen to the radio you've probably heard Dick and Christine no matter where you are in the country. And if you're old enough to remember the famous "Chicken Man" radio vignettes — yep . . . that was Dick Orkin in the chicken suit. Brian Cummings is an extremely busy voice actor who does commercials, animation, and film trailers. You've probably heard his voice on numerous Disney movie trailers.

This commercial is part of an on-going national campaign for Boston Market. In each of the spots, the theme line "Boston Market. Slow Down" is dramatized by creating stories about people who haven't connected in a while. There is usually an offer that tags out the spot. This commercial presents a husband who is so busy he has forgotten what his house looks like. His wife is one of those people who can get along with everyone and nothing seems to affect her. The dialogue is a very fast-paced repartee. There are no pauses during this interaction. The challenge here is to create believable characters in conversation, telling a story that everyone can relate to — and do it in :15! The ANNCR tag is another :03 taking the produced body of this commercial to :18. The remaining :12 is for the offer, which could be either produced as part of the commercial or read by the local station DJ.

Practice delivering the script on the next page with someone to get a feeling of just how fast :15 really is. Then listen to Dick and Chris on the CD. Notice that even with very little time available, you can immediately get a sense of the characters.

BOSTON MARKET:

Blue House—Radio :15/:03/:12

GUY: (ON PHONE) Hi, Honey . . .

WIFE: Hi.

GUY: I've been driving around the neighborhood and I'll be darned if I can remember what color our house is.

WIFE: Blue.

GUY: Blue? That's right. I've been so busy lately, I feel like I've hardly been home.

WIFE: Want me to stand in the driveway and wave so you don't miss it again?

GUY: Okay, now are you a blonde or a brunette?

WIFE: Redhead.

GUY: That's right . . . A tall—

WIFE: Short.

GUY: Short, blue-eyed—

WIFE: Brown-eyed.

GUY: Redhead. Right?

WIFE: Right.

GUY: Right.

ANNCR: Remember? It's about dinner as a family. Boston Market. Slow down.

ANNCR: (:12) OFFER (local station VO)

11

Character Copy

Vocalizing Characters

Most character and animation voices are an exaggeration of specific vocal characteristics or attitudes, which enable the performer to create an appropriate vocal sound for the character. In some cases, a character voice can be difficult to sustain for long periods of time. Be careful not to overexert or injure yourself when doing character voices, especially when it is for a talking inanimate object or some other unusual character.

It can be tempting to force a vocal sound or attitude in an attempt to create a voice. A forced voice is rarely the most effective, is difficult to sustain, and can actually cause physical damage to your vocal cords. The most effective character voices are those that emphasize or exaggerate the attitudes and emotions of the character you are portraying, or that take a small quirk or idiosyncrasy and blow it out of proportion.

ANIMATION AND CHARACTER VOICES

Character and story analysis are most important with this type of copy. Many factors will affect the voice of the character, so the more information you can uncover about your character, the easier it will be to find its true voice. Since animation and character work can be in the form of single-voice or dialogue copy — and the voice may have many special attributes — all the principles of good voice acting apply even more here.

Consistency is extremely important in character voice work. When you find the character's voice, lock it into your memory and keep the proper attitude and quality of sound throughout your performance, adapting your character's voice when the mood of the script changes. The important thing here is to avoid allowing the sound of your character to *drift*. To make your character believable and real to the audience, the quality of the voice must not change from the beginning of the script to the end. Consistency is especially important in animation work because sessions can be lengthy and a script can be recorded out of sequence over a period of several days.

Most animation voice actors have a repertoire of several voices. A typical session may begin with one voice, followed by lines for a different voice later on. After lunch, they may do lines for yet another voice and then go back to record more lines for a character they did earlier in the day. This sort of schedule means character voice actors must be extremely versatile and must be able to accurately repeat and sustain voice characterizations. These demands make animation work a challenging niche to break into, and one of the most creative in voice-over.

In addition to voices and sounds for animation, character voice work can also include dialects, foreign and regional accents, and even celebrity impersonations. Special accents and dialects require an ability to mimic a sound or attitude that is familiar to a portion of the listening audience. Usually, this mimicking is a *stylized* interpretation and doesn't necessarily have to be 100 percent accurate unless the character is represented as being authentic to a region or culture. Many times, the best accent is one that reflects what a community "thinks" the accent should sound like, which is often not the real thing. However, when authenticity is required, in order to give the character believability, vocal accuracy is important. Most of the time, however, a slight exaggeration of certain regional vocal traits tends to give the character attitude and personality. Personal familiarization with the culture, region, or dialect is also helpful.

Celebrity voice impersonations are often the most challenging because the celebrities are usually well known. The voice actor's job is to create a voice that offers recognition of the celebrity, yet hints at being just a bit different. Celebrity impersonations are usually done in the context of a humorous commercial in which some aspect of the celebrity's personality or vocal styling is exaggerated or used as a device for communicating the message. Any commercial using a voice that represents a known person must have a disclaimer stating that the celebrity's voice is impersonated. If the voice is recognizable, this is a legal requirement whether or not the person's name is included in the copy.

In most cases, if a producer wants an extremely accurate celebrity voice, he or she will hire the celebrity. It may cost more to hire the actual person behind the voice, but the increased credibility is often worth it. Also, a disclaimer is not required if the real person is performing.

VOICE PLACEMENT — FINDING YOUR VOICE BY BODY

Begin creating a character's voice by doing a thorough character analysis to discover as much as you can about him or her (or it) and the story. Based on the copy, make the decisions and commit to who you are talking to and if your character has any special accent or attitude. Finally, decide where in your body the character's voice will come from.

Visualize the voice coming from a specific location in your body and work with the copy until the voice *feels* right. Use your choices about the character's physical size and shape to help you localize the voice in your body. Use the "sweep" (Exercise #10, page 33) to locate a suitable pitch for your character voice. Once you have found a pitch, you can position the voice in that area of the body to create a unique sound. A voice coming from the top of your head might sound small and tiny; a voice from deep in the chest may sound big and boomy. The following list includes some physical locations and their associated vocal sounds:

top of head (tiny)	under tongue (sloppy)	nose (nasal)
behind eyes (nasal)	diaphragm (strong)	chest (boomy)
top of cheeks (bright)	loose cheeks (mushy)	throat (raspy)
front of mouth (crisp)	back of throat (breathy)	stomach (low)

Practice different voices with different attitudes. Use computer clip art, comic strips and other drawings to get ideas for character voices. Record yourself doing a variety of voices and listen to your tapes. If all of your voices sound the same, you need to work on range and characterization.

VOICE PLACEMENT BY COLOR

As you experiment with voices that originate in different parts of your body, notice how each voice makes you feel. Close your eyes as you speak in a character voice and observe any images that pop into your imagination. You may find that a particular physical characteristic or facial expression feels right, or is needed in order for you to get the proper sound and attitude. Remember: *Physicalize the moment and the voice will follow.*

As you work with voices from different parts of your body, you may be able to sense a color for each region: Lower pitch voices are often represented by dark colors while higher pitch voices are represented by brighter colors. The energy level and attitude of a voice are frequently sensed through the intensity of the color.

You can use these colors to help you recall the voice at a later time. Make copies of the "Voice Placement by Body & Color" worksheet and make note for each character voice you create. Keep a notebook of these worksheets for future reference. Eventually, you will be able to switch between voices quickly. But as you are developing your voices, it is important that you have a way to document their characteristics.

CHARACTER VOICE WORKSHEET

If you are doing voice-over for animation, it is essential that you be able to recall a voice on demand. If you cannot recall the sound and placement of a voice, your voices will vary widely and your marketability as a voice actor may be affected.

Voice Placement by Body & Color

CHARACTER NAME: _____

Find a place in your body that is appropriate for the sound of your character's voice. Use the "sweep" to find a suitable pitch, and adapt the vocal sound at that pitch to develop texture and nuance for the sound of the voice. You can have several different sounds at any level of pitch, and you can combine body areas to create unique voices. As you are developing voices at different locations, you may be able to associate a color with those parts of your body. This associated color will help you recall the voice at a later time.

BODY PLACEMENT   ASSOCIATED COLOR

_____   ABDOMEN   _____

_____   CHEST   _____

_____   THROAT   _____

_____   ADENOID   _____

_____   NASAL   _____

_____   FACE   _____

_____   EYES   _____

_____   HEAD   _____

ADDITIONAL COMMENTS:

Character Voice Worksheet

Use this worksheet to document your character voices.

CHARACTER SOURCE: _____
(Where did the idea for this voice come from?)

CHARACTER NAME: _____

AGE: _____   SEX: _____   ATTITUDE: _____

KEY PHRASE: _____
(A short phrase to trigger voice placement, physicalization, and attitude.)

APPEARANCE (HAIR, CLOTHING, ETC.):

_____

STANCE: _____
what is the character's physical posture and attitude?

QUIRKS: _____
anything odd in appearance or movement?

PITCH: _____
where is the voice placement?

TEMPO: _____
at what pace does the character speak?

MOUTH WORK: _____
anything unique about the character's speaking manner?

WALK: _____
how does the character walk and move?

LAUGH: _____
how does the character laugh?

PLACEMENT: _____
where in your body are you placing the voice?

TONE: _____
what is the character's attitude and vocal tone?

DIALECT: _____
what accent or dialect is appropriate, if any?

If _____ (name) was a character, what and who might it be like?

Other notes about your character:

There are many ways to document and recall the voices you create. The "Character Voice Worksheet" covers most of these, and is a good way to document the characteristics of each voice you create.

Character Source: Make a note about where you got the idea for the voice. A great way to get voice ideas is to simply sit at a shopping mall and listen to people as they walk by.

Character Name: Give a name to the character portrayed by the voice you create. Just because a script gives a character a certain name does not mean that is the name you need to use for your voice characterization.

Age, Sex, Attitude: Make initial choices as to your character's age, sex, and overall temperament. Be willing to adapt your choices as your characterization develops.

Key Phrase: This is perhaps the key to recalling a character voice. Find a short phrase that perfectly reflects the character you are creating. You will know the phrase is correct when you speak it using your character voice, and it simply sounds like something your character would say.

Appearance: Be as detailed as you possibly can about the look of your character. Include interesting items of clothing and props the character might use.

Stance: How does your character stand? Does he/she stand stiff and rigid, constantly shift weight, slump, etc.?

Quirks: What sort of physical, facial, or speaking quirks does your character exhibit?

Pitch: What is the overall pitch of the character's normal speaking voice? (refer to the Body & Color worksheet)

Tempo: Does your character speak fast, slow, constantly shift tempo, never finish a sentence, etc.?

Mouth Work: How does your character articulate? Are words spoken crisply or is there a lot of wet and sloppy tongue?

Walk: How does your character move? Slow, fast, with a limp, with high energy, in pain, etc.?

Laugh: How does your character laugh? Visit a shopping mall or some other place where you can find people having a good time and listen to the incredible variety of laughs.

Placement: Where is your character's voice placed in your body?

Tone: What are your character's overall attitude and speaking dynamics?

Tips for Character and Animation Copy

Character voice work can be challenging, but lots of fun. Use the following tips and suggestions to help find your character's voice.

- Understand your character and the situation. Remember that acting is reacting. In animation, you often must make up what you are reacting to.

- Discover who the audience is and understand how the audience will relate to the character.

- Maintain a consistent voice throughout the copy and be careful not to injure your voice by stretching too far to create a character. It is better to pull back a little and create a voice that can be maintained rather than push too hard for a voice you can only sustain for one or two pages.

- If a drawing, photo, or picture of the character is available, use it as a tool to discover the personality of the character.

- Use your *physical-ness* to take on the physical characteristics of the character. *Physicalize the moment and the voice will follow.*

- Find the place in your body from which the voice will come.

Character and Animation Scripts

As you work with the following scripts, you might find it interesting to read through the script before reading the Copy Notes provided for each one. Come up with your own interpretation for attitude, pacing, character, and performance. Then read through the notes to see how close you came to what the producers of these projects intended. Listen to the corresponding track on the CD that came with this book to hear how the actual projects were performed. These scripts are reproduced as closely as possible to the original copy, including grammatical errors and awkward phrasing.

USING THE CHARACTER VOICE WORKSHEETS

To help you understand exactly how the Character Voice Worksheets can be used to discover and document your voices, MJ Lallo will take you step-by-step through the process of creating a voice for an animated character. For this character you will be provided with a sketch drawing of the character and a few brief lines of copy. As a voice actor, it is your job to give life to this character.

"BUMPY" — ANIMATED CHARACTER — (CD track 21)

Title: "Bumpy"
Agency: MJ Productions
Style: TBA
Character: Very young, somewhat of a prankster
VO Talent: MJ Lallo — **www.creatingvoices.com**
Character Sketch Artist: Aliki Theofilopoulos
Copy Notes: MJ Lallo is one of the busiest animation voice coaches in Los Angeles. She has an extensive background in commercial jingles as a composer and singer, and as an award-winning voice actor in film looping, television, and animation. MJ offers a variety of workshops in commercial and character voice-over and is in constant demand as a character voice actor.

The following script is typical of what you might encounter at an audition for an animation voice-over. The sketch gives you a certain amount of information about the character. The copy lines give you some additional clues. Don't simply read the lines. Instead, use the drawing of the character and the phrasing of the copy to help you find an interesting and creative way to speak the lines.

Use the Character Voice Worksheets to help you find a voice for this character, and listen to the CD as MJ guides you through the process of finding and documenting your character voice.

That little girl's lunch pail looks like it's full of cookies.

I bet she won't even miss a few.

HMMMM, my mouth is watering just thinking about chocolate chips.

TGIF PHONE MESSAGES — (CD track 22)

Title: "Outgoing Answering Machine Messages"
Agency: TGIF, The Ganyon Idea Factory
Style: Various
Character: Various recognizable and "oddball" characters
VO Talent: Phil Ganyon
Copy Notes: The Ganyon Idea Factory began as a one-man shop in 1977. During those early days, Phil would often be out of the office meeting with

clients or in recording sessions. His telephone answering machine was his "front line," and since his business was creative advertising, it didn't seem right to simply have a "generic" outgoing message on the machine. But there was another problem: The PhoneMate model of answering machine he had would not allow for a message shorter than 20 seconds. That meant either a long delay until the "beep," or fill the time. The challenge was to record something that would hold callers and motivate them to leave a message. Humor seemed to be the way to go. So Phil created a cast of characters who would "just happen" to be in the office to answer the phone while Phil was out. It didn't take long for the local media reps to catch on, and TGIF began getting calls just to find out who would answer the phone next.

Use the descriptions below and the Character Worksheet to come up with your own voices for these characters. Use variety in pacing, attitude, and voice placement, and physicalize each character. Then listen to the CD to hear the original phone messages.

Tom Twist: proud of his work, however odd it may be.

"My name is Tom Twist, a professional nut and bolt tightener."

Sleepy: formerly a dwarf, now a mattress tester.

"(sigh) My name is Sleepy. I used to be a dwarf, but now I'm a mattress tester."

Ingmar Instep: a foreign athlete, from . . . we're not quite sure where — but he could be Swedish.

"I am Ingmar Instep, a professional soccer player."

Trigger Burke:

"Hello, my name is Trigger Burke. I applied for the job firing the cannon after Charger touchdowns."

Wilfred Dodds: a feisty janitor who would pick up the phone while he was "just cleanin' up 'round the desk," then complain about how messy the office was, or something Phil had done, or was doing.

"Well, it's secretary's week, and Mr. Ganyon decided to take Debbie out to lunch. Yeah . . . secretary's week . . . they oughta be back from McDonald's in about 20 minutes. Leave a message and he'll call you back."

Oliver Paisley: An English butler type who would make dry comments about Phil's behavior and whereabouts.

"Rumor has it that Mr. Ganyon has absconded with the coffee filter again."

Sir Roger Billingsley: a gruff old English gentleman who loved to tell stories.

> "Sir Roger Billingsley here. I was right in the middle of a story, when Mr. Ganyon was rudely called away."

Sidney Tannucci: an Italian Jew, who used to be a mobster.

> "Hey, this is Sidney Tannucci, eh. (unintelligible mumbles) . . . my buddy Ganyon, he says . . . (unintelligible mumbles) . . . Hey, make me look good, uh? Leave a message and he'll call you back. Thanks a lot."

Marty Copazzano: a loud-mouthed Brooklyn type who loved to complain.

> "Marty Copazzano . . . just the name tells you somethin'."

Rashid Fazool: a wealthy middle-eastern businessman who'd use Phil's office whenever he was in town trying to sell one big thing or another.

> "I was in town, visiting my friends, when suddenly, from nowhere, I saw myself . . . it was a scary moment."

The Godfather: would warn the caller that the call had already been traced, and "strongly suggest" that a message be left "if ya know what's good for ya."

> "This is a very close personal friend of Mr. Ganyon's. Since this call has already been traced, I strongly suggest that you leave a message for my friend . . . I strongly suggest! If ya know what's good for ya."

Sylvester Peeps: a sensitive, budding author whom Phil let use his typewriter on weekends to work on his novel.

> "Hello, this is Sylvester. Mr. Ganyon is letting me use his computer, 'cause I'm writing a novel. It's about two people who are so similar. They have the same kinds of haircuts . . . wear the same brand of underwear . . . and, uh . . . well, that's as far as I've gotten."

Former Secretary of State, Henry Kissinger: would ask the caller to leave a message, then turn and say, "You know, Phil . . . I vouldn't do dis for anybody else."

> "That's right . . . well, I will look into it as soon as possible . . . No . . . I'm sorry, but I can't talk now . . . I'm very busy . . . yes. Well, could you call me back again, please. Alright . . . Goodbye."

EESOO — AUDIO BOOK DRAMATIZATION — (CD track 23)
www.eesoo.com

Title: "Eesoo: The Epic Begins . . ." Full-cast audio drama
Executive Producers: Eesoo Productions in association with Celeen Publishing, written by Kathleen Boettcher — **www.celeen.com**
Production: The Commercial Clinic — **www.commercialclinic.com**
Music: David Helpling — **www.dhmmusicdesign.com**
Target Audience: Men and women who listen to audio books & Sci-Fi
Style: Dramatic, Science Fiction
Characters/VO Talent: The produced audio drama has a cast of 12 characters. The scene included here is one with only three characters.

Narrator (Nancy Cota): You're telling a story to a group of people you love. It's a story that's personal. You're Angela as an older woman telling what happened. The narrator's voice should not be an older woman's voice, but rather a normal voice. Angela's age has no relevance to the part of the narrator. It's just to give you a mood.

The narrator is used to set up scenes and provide transitions between dialogues, and is, therefore, as much a part of the scenes as the characters. The narrator sets the overall mood for each scene.

Angela Evans K'Sada (Penny Abshire): Kind, compassionate, loving doctor. Patients adore her. She's easy going and likeable. She's genuine. Assertive, but not aggressive. Never confrontational or rude. Quietly stubborn. Brave. Intelligent. Likes dealing with people. Has backbone.

Angela falls in love with T'hur the moment she lays eyes on him and strikes out at him because she can't understand the flood of emotion that washes through her. She thinks it's hatred, but it's not.

Angela isn't a fearful person, but this situation unnerves her at first. That's what Shantar meant it to do. He wanted her to be afraid of T'hur and lash out at him. But it didn't work. After she meets T'hur, the fear goes away. From then on, it's a battle of wits between them. Angela always firmly stands her ground.

Consul General Tanar Cala (James R. Alburger): He's the kind of man who steps over other people to get ahead. Cold, hard, calculating, thinks he's better and smarter than anyone he deals with. Has a sinister, nasty side. Intimidation is his most used quality. Always talks down to people and lets them see he thinks they're stupid and incompetent. He's the sort of person who once they get a bit of power, wields it like an axe.

That is, unless he's dealing with Leader/Shantar. Cala knows Shantar wouldn't hesitate to kill him if he fails the Leader in any way. Sometimes he trips over himself trying to please Shantar. He worries his life could be in danger if he fails. He's right.

Synopsis: (from the website **www.celeen.com**) — The N'daran solar system is unique. Circling its sun are five planets sustaining life. The N'darans, having evolved in the same way as humans of Earth, are considered a handsome race with black hair and eyes, tan skin, and athletic bodies. Similarities end there, however, as they are a more aggressive race whose society differs in many ways from those on Earth. Terrans and N'darans meet for the first time when both try to mine the same asteroid belt. Conflict arises over mining rights and war ensues. Diplomats end the conflict and Space Station Harmony is built through an act of cooperation between N'dar and Earth.

Blue-eyed, red-haired Dr. Angela Evans joins Harmony's staff and meets Ambassador Shantar Ineetu K'sada. Shantar and Angela fall in love, marry, have a child, and move to Iowa where Shantar oversees the building of Earth's first interstellar alien embassy. Shantar is killed in an accident and, when settling his estate, Angela is informed of a N'daran law which requires his unmarried twin brother, T'hur Ineetu K'sada, to take responsibility for her and Shylar, their three-year-old daughter. Angela angrily refuses the order to marry T'hur, but she and T'hur are forced to comply by T'hur's father who is the N'daran Domain's ruler. Angela's father Edward, mother Elaine, and aunt Lucille are outraged when it is decreed T'hur will move into their home in Iowa where Shantar and Angela lived. Refusing to soften his warrior demeanor gets T'hur into humorous situations.

Navarch T'hur Ineetu K'sada is heir to the N'daran throne. He and an elite squad run the formidable N'daran Warriors. Sirdar officers Ganar, Kia, Tela, Mikal, Zenda, Lana, Neela, and Mela enforce his edicts. The women are required to service the Navarch in all ways and willingly do so. T'hur's demanding, arrogant manner complicates his personal life. At odds with his father, Supreme Regent Tava Ineetu K'sada, T'hur seems to have little regard for anyone outside the military. Furious at being ordered to comply with a rarely used antiquated law, T'hur does so with a chip on his shoulder and a defiant attitude.

Intertwined with the relationship development is a plot to usurp T'hur, overthrow Tava, and undermine all interstellar diplomatic relations.

The saga moves from Warrior space stations circling N'dar to Des Moines, Iowa, to Space Station Harmony, to the planet Minda, and ends on T'hur's home of N'dar.

Copy Notes: This project was originally produced as a demo for the purpose of testing the concept of the full-cast audio drama and to pitch the project to audio book publishers. The original goal was to produce the original novel (all 654 pages!) in the full-cast dramatization format. Although this demo project tested successfully, it was determined that the novel in its original format was a "difficult read." The author decided to rework the novel by splitting it into several shorter books. The new goal is to simultaneously release several of the new, shorter novels, along with a traditional single-voice narrative audio book. This will be followed by a series of full-cast adaptations that will be released over a period of time.

The full-length 33-minute audio drama demo can be heard on-line at **www.eesoo.com**. The scene included here is one in which Angela first meets Consul General Tanar Cala and takes place near the beginning of the story. The emotion in the scene can be clearly seen in the script. As you listen to the excerpt on the CD, notice the voice placement for Tanar Cala — very throaty and "gravelly" with a definite edge and an "I'm better than you" attitude. Also note that Angela speaks in two distinctly different ways: introspectively, as she speaks (or thinks) to herself, and outwardly in conversation. To differentiate between the two thought processes, Angela's voice was given a special effect for those times when she was speaking introspectively. Also notice that there are certain additions to the dialogue that were ad-libbed, and are not written into the script. These ad-libs make the scene more believable and real to the listener.

MUSIC: NEW DAY. BRIGHT, HAPPY, BIRDS SINGING

NARR: It was autumn in Iowa. Gentle breezes caressed trees ablaze in red and gold. Dr. Angela K'sada stepped into the N'daran Embassy.

ANGELA: (thinking, sadly) I haven't been here since Shantar died. I wish it looked as desolate and empty as I feel. I suppose this meeting with the Consul General is to settle Shantar's estate. Is hope it doesn't take long. I want to get out of here!

ANGELA: (shouting) I will not marry his brother! It's not going to happen!

CALA: Is this your signature on our standard mating contract?

ANGELA: Yes.

CALA: Then you obviously know what I'm talking about.

ANGELA: I don't have a clue what you're . . .

CALA: (interrupting) The contract reads . . . Female agrees if mate dies before children reach 21, to mate with closest unmated blood kinsman. This provision is added so our government isn't burdened with supporting the fatherless.

ANGELA: Shantar and I discussed the contract and that clause wasn't in it! Why's there a problem? Shantar was wealthy. Shylar and Is won't need help from anyone.

CALA: Shantar's wealth goes to the House of K'sada. The
           Clause is your only inheritance.

ANGELA: Still no problem! I have a successful career and we
           live with my family! We'll manage just fine!

CALA: This isn't about finances. It's about honoring a
           commitment.

ANGELA: I won't do it! You can't make me do it! I'll get legal
           help!

CALA: Your defiance will jeopardize negotiations between
           our governments. Terran officials won't intercede on
           your behalf. They won't risk offending us.

ANGELA: You're not going to bully me! I don't care if you're
           offended or not!

CALA: Let's move along and discuss the penalty for failing to
           comply with the contract. If you don't mate with
           Shantar's older, unmarried twin brother, the child will
           be given a fatal injection and responsibility for her
           simply . . . goes away. Oh? Did I fail to mention she's
           in our custody here in the embassy?

ANGELA: You give me my daughter right now! Where is she?

CALA: Ridiculous demands are pointless. The bottom line is
           you mate with Shantar's brother, warrior commander
           T'hur K'sada, or the child dies. This Embassy is
           N'daran territory. Any attempt to remove her from our
           custody will be considered an act of war. Shylar stays
           here until you're pregnant with T'hur's child. He's
           N'dar's next ruler and needs heirs. T'hur will assume
           his brother's duties as head negotiator, take Shantar's
           place at the embassy and in your home. You have
           two days to make a decision.

ANGELA: (thinking) Maybe he's lying! I've got to get home and
           check on Shylar.

12

Corporate and Long-Form Narrative Copy

Sales presentations, marketing videos, in-house training tapes, point-of-purchase videos, film documentaries, telephone messages, and many other projects all fall into the category of corporate and narrative. Frequently, these scripts are written to be read and not spoken.

Writers of corporate and narrative copy are often not experienced writers, or usually write copy for print. There are exceptions to this, but overall you can expect copy in this category to be pretty dry. Corporate and narrative copy is often full of statistics, complex names or phrases and terminology specific to a business or industry. These can be a challenge for even an experienced voice-over performer.

As you perform a corporate or narrative script, you are still performing a character telling a story, just as for any other type of copy. You should know who your character is, who you are talking to, and what you are talking about. You also need to find a way to create an image of knowledge and authority for your character. What is it about your character that gives him the authority to be speaking the words? Is your character the owner of the company, a satisfied customer, the company's top salesperson, or a driver for one of the delivery trucks? To create an image of credibility, figure out an appropriate role for your character and commit to your choice.

A corporate or narrative script for a video project might have several on-camera performers. These are often professional actors, but may include employees of the business. There also may be several voice-over performers for different sections of the script. Many scripts in this category are written for a single voice-over performer, but there may be two or more performers alternating lines or doing different sections. There may also be some dialogue sections of the script. The complexity of a corporate script will vary greatly depending on the intended purpose and the company's budget.

It is sometimes more challenging to deliver a script of this nature in a conversational manner, but it is possible. Facts, numbers, unusual terms, and complex names all contribute to a presentation more like a lecture than a conversation. However, the information is important, and the audience must be able to relate to the presentation as well as clearly understand what they hear. If the presentation of the information (your performance) is interesting and entertaining, the effectiveness of the communication will be much better.

Tips for Performing Corporate and Narrative Copy

The following tips and suggestions will help you with corporate and narrative copy in general.

- Talk *to* the audience on their level, not *at* them, even though the script might be full of facts, statistics, and unusual names or phrases.

- Take your time delivering the copy. Unlike radio or TV copy, which must be done within a specific time, there is rarely any time limitation for corporate and narrative copy.

- Be clear on the facts and pronunciation of complex words. These are important to the client and need to be correct and accurate.

- Slow your delivery or pace in sections where there is important information; speak more quickly in other parts of the script.

- If you are alternating lines with another performer, and the script is not written for dialogue, be careful to not overlap or step on the other performer's lines. Keep your delivery more open for this type of script, unless the producer specifically requests that you tighten your delivery.

Tips & Tricks for Audio Book Narration

William Dufris is an audio book narrator and producer with more than 200 projects to his credit. He also teaches audio book narration workshops.

Here are some tips from William for doing audio book sessions, which will frequently run into several days of work. These tips are good advice for any type of voice-over work, and reinforce everything you've already read in this book.

Listen to audio books to study techniques.
- "Wannabe" actors study films and go to plays
- "Wannabe" writers study other writers
- So . . .

Develop stamina:
- Audio book sessions can be very long, often lasting several days (or weeks).
- Books can be hundreds of pages—some of which can be very boring and dry.

Take frequent breaks, step out of the studio, stay hydrated

Audio book performers fall into two categories:
- Actors—excellent cold readers who add interpretation and "spark"
- Narrators—read only what is written

Read the book AT LEAST twice (preferably 3 times):
- 1st time—to get the "feel" of the story
- 2nd time—to mark the book
  - color code characters in dialogue sequences
  - note mood and/or signpost with adverbs
  - write in the remainder of incomplete sentences, or at least to a natural break to eliminate potential noise from page turns.
- 3rd time—not critical, but a third read just prior to the session will always stand you in good stead with the producer.

3RD PERSON NARRATION:

Picture the story (visualize) — if you don't see it, your listeners won't.
- Be involved in the story
- Savor words
- Attend to the punctuation
- Separate the narrative from the dialogue

CHARACTERS:

Characters must be well defined
- The listener must never ask "Who?"
- Build a vocal library to accommodate several voices with a range of styles

THE MICROPHONE:

The microphone "HEARS" everything
- Work the mic 6" - 8" from your nose, with the mic at eye level
- Use your eyes when reading down the page—moving your head will cause a shift in the sound of your voice
- To achieve a "clean" recording:
  - Soften plosives—p's, b's, f's
  - Stay hydrated to minimize mouth noises
  - Herbal tea with honey and lemon will help open the throat (regular tea contains tannin and caffeine)
- Avoid thick liquids, coffee, soda and dairy products
  - Thick liquids create a "clammy" sound

- Coffee, tea, and cola drinks contain caffeine and tannin which constrict the throat
- Caffeine is a diuretic and will dry your mouth
- Movement should be silent
  - Avoid noisy clothing and jewelry

BREATHING:

Breathing should be natural or imperceptible
- Take shallow, quieter breaths
- Keep breathing unobtrusive and soft
- Only accentuate breathing when needed as a "character breath"

PAGE TURNS:

Page turns should be as silent as possible.
- For sentences that are incomplete on a page—finish the sentence at the bottom or top of a page.
- Narration — SILENCE — page turn — SILENCE — Narration

MISTAKES (BLOOPERS):

Monitor your performance
- Return to the nearest clause, or beginning of line
- Choose pick-ups that will make the editor's job easier
- Leave a beat of silence—then start the pick up.
- Picking up a line before where the mistake occurred can often work well to help keep your delivery consistent.
- Remember—nobody's perfect—mistakes will happen.

RE-TAKES, INSERTS, AND REPLACEMENT LINES:

When replacing lines days (or weeks) after the original session:
- If at all possible, listen to your delivery from the original recording
- Match your original attitude, pacing, pitch, and tone of voice
- Make an effort to maintain a consistent performance—noticeable edits and obvious changes in the sound of your voice become a distraction for the listener

Corporate and Narrative Scripts

As you work with the following scripts, you might find it interesting to read through the script before reading the Copy Notes provided for each one. Come up with your own interpretation for attitude, pacing, character, and performance. Then read through the notes to see how close you came to what the producers of these projects intended. The following scripts are reproduced as accurately as possible, including typos, grammatical errors, and awkward phrasing.

COULTER MEDICAL — (CD track 24)

Title: "Introducing AcT," Multimedia Presentation
Agency: Hansell 'Maginations
USP: "The first family of hematology analyzers — imagine the possibilities."
Target Audience: Medical industry sales representatives and buyers
Style: Authoritative spokesperson
Characters: Expert on the Coulter AcT equipment and its history
VO Talent: Don Ranson
Copy Notes: This multi-screen multi-media presentation was presented at a trade show many times during the a single day. A preproduced portion had interaction with live actors who had done some of the introductory voice-over (not included here). At the end of the produced video, the program moved back to live action for the final two minutes. The entire production was underscored with music and sound effects where appropriate.

The message is designed for a very specific audience in the medical industry and contains a few long sentences with a few technical terms. The first sentence is a good test of your breath control and enunciation. Try reading the line out loud at a constant volume and energy level. If you run out of air, you probably need to work on breath control and increasing your breathing capacity.

Only a portion of the program is included here, but it will give you the idea of a typical corporate marketing script. Notice how the performer's attitude shifts from an "announcery" or "billboarded" introduction to a conversational message. It is important to maintain an attitude of knowledge and authority in order to establish credibility with the audience. The music and sound effects were added after the voice track was recorded.

> **SHOW BEGINS** — *MUSIC is bold and dynamic, loud and attention-getting.*
>
> ANNCR: And now, Coulter (*pronounced Coal-ter*), the same company that brought you the ONYX high volume analyzer and MD series of medium volume analyzers, introduces the first inexpensive, low volume hematology analyzer.
>
> For the fourth time in the last 5 years, Coulter, the world leader in hematology analysis, introduces its newest analyzer, designed for the alternate care market . . .
>
> The AcT (*ACK tee*)
>
> SFX—*MUSIC is exciting and dynamic, building to climax.*
>
> Coulter brings you a complete family of hematology analyzers with a product to fit every customer's needs.

TIMBERLAND SAVINGS M-O-H — (CD Track 25)

Title: "Timberland Bank MOH" — Telephone outgoing message
Agency: Williams & Company
USP: "Your neighborhood bank"
Target Audience: Adults 18 and older
Style: Friendly, helpful
Characters: Friendly, neighborhood spokesperson
VO Talent: DB Cooper — **www.voxvobiscum.com**
Copy Notes: You've undoubtedly called a business only to be put on Hold, which can seem more like "ignore" if you are left for very long with nothing to listen to. To fill the void of telephone silence, some businesses will simply play some music for you. However, the savvy business owner will use the time you spend on Hold as an opportunity to deliver a sales message.

Message-On-Hold (M-O-H) production is rapidly becoming a big part of the voice-over business. M-O-H is similar to single-voice work in that there is generally only one voice presenting the message. However, unlike radio commercials, M-O-H rarely has any time limits. Knowing this, some business owners will make the mistake of producing a single, long narrative that includes everything about their business including terminology that may not be familiar to the caller. The result is sensory overload with too much information for the caller to remember or absorb.

The most effective M-O-H projects consist of several short messages, each of which focuses on a single product or service provided by the business. Because the message will be heard over the telephone, it is very important that the pacing is not too fast, and that enunciation is clear. Use of technical words should be kept to a minimum, unless it is known that callers already have an understanding of the business terminology. Most callers really don't care about the model number of a specific piece of equipment that is used by the business.

Most M-O-H projects should be delivered with a friendly, positive attitude, and perhaps with a smile on your face. When you listen to the CD track for this M-O-H, notice that the entire script is underscored with music. Most projects of this type will have about :10 of music between scripts. This track has been condensed a bit for time. Music serves two purposes: first, it confirms to the caller that they are still connected, and second, the music should help to support the mood and image of the business. The purpose of a message-on-hold is twofold: 1) to keep callers on the line until a company representative can assist them, and 2) to inform callers about products and services they may not be aware of.

Come home to a no-fee checking account when your mortgage is at Timberland Savings. You can also have automatic mortgage payments withdrawn for your convenience. You'll never have to pay to see a teller at Timberland Savings and when you open a new checking account, you'll receive a neighbor-to-neighbor gift certificate to use at local participating neighbor-to-neighbor businesses. Thanks for holding. Your call is important to us.

With Timberland Savings telephone banking services, you can access information about account activity and make transfers between your accounts 24 hours a day from anywhere. Using your Timberland Savings Master Money Debit card saves you time at the checkout. Our debit cards can be used anywhere a MasterCard is accepted, so you'll never be caught without cash again. Thanks for your patience! Someone will be with you as soon as possible.

Refinancing your home could be the right decision for you. Talk to our lenders in our 6 local offices for timely information and decisions. Our newest mortgage option is a ten-year mortgage that helps you build equity quickly and save on the overall cost of the loan. Timberland Savings trust company offers a variety of financial services for proven money management. Our sound investment advice could help you meet your financial goals. Appointments can be made in Springfield or at any of our local offices. Thanks for holding. Your call is important to us.

Sneakers in the bank is one way Timberland Savings help teach your children how to save money. Your children will have their very own savings book and a colorful sneakers zippered bag to keep it in. What better way to learn about money than at Timberland Savings? Your call is important to us. Thanks for holding.

COVIGO — (CD Track 26)

Title: "CTIA Short Script — 3 minutes" — Rich Media e-mail
Agency: Flashpoint Studios, San Diego — **www.flashpointstudios.com**
USP: "Your neighborhood bank"
Target Audience: Customer Prospects
Style: Corporate, professional
Characters: Spokesperson
Producer: Marc Lyman — **www.flashpointstudios.com**
VO Talent: Stephanie Donovan
Original Music: David Helpling — **www.dhmmusicdesign.com**

Copy Notes: This is a typical corporate marketing project that demonstrates how a good voice-over delivery can make even dry copy interesting. The script is loaded with technical terminology and product numbers that only have meaning for those in the business. However, as a voice actor, it is essential that you sound as though you are an expert on the subject. This project is for a company that provides wireless solutions for a specific marketplace. The project's ultimate destination was a Rich Media e-mail that was sent out to a relatively small list of potential Covigo clients.

Flashpoint's client was looking for a specific "sound" for both the music and the voice. Covigo wanted something that sounded corporate and professional, yet hip enough to keep people's interest and appeal to a younger demographic as well. Since the audience would range from "20 somethings" to middle-aged "IT guys," it had to be attention grabbing and energetic, but not too over the top. The client thought the project did a great job of keeping extremely dry material lively and attention retaining.

The script included here is formatted just as you would see it during a session. The bolded items in brackets refer to visuals that will be added after the voice track is recorded and mixed with the music. Notice that there are sections of the script that are divided by visual notations. As a voice actor, you will need to work around the visual cues and only read the voice copy, yet maintain a smooth and consistent delivery.

As you listen to the CD, you will notice that there are what appear to be long sections of music. These long pauses are not recorded during the actual voice session. During the voice session, the script would be read in its entirety, with many stops and starts to get exactly the right delivery for each section. Only after the best takes are chosen will the voice track be mixed with the music and timed to match the desired video.

One other thing to listen for is the clarity of Stephanie's delivery and the pacing of her delivery. Remember, this project was intended to be played back from an e-mail, so it will be heard on computer speakers, which are not the best in the world. For a project like this, it is absolutely imperative that every word be clearly understood.

Introduction

[Covigo's logo - Who we are]
Covigo enables businesses to quickly adapt to the changing wireless world.

Our unique <u>user-centric process modeling approach</u> separates business logic from presentation design and data source integration. Based on this approach,
[lifecycle slide – What we do]
we provide businesses with complete lifecycle management of mobile applications, from design and deployment, to management and analysis. Our product suite consists of

[lifecycle slide - studio]
Covigo Studio,
  [lifecycle slide - engine]
Covigo Engine,
  [management console]
Covigo Console,
  [lifecycle slide - insight]
and Covigo Insight.

Studio: Design

  [highlight design on lifecycle slide & place "Covigo Studio" next to it]
Build applications using Covigo Studio,

  [Shot of completed Studio project]
…a team-based, visual programming environment. Covigo Studio facilitates rapid development and deployment of integrated data and voice applications. You can
  [highlight application flow - top half of screen]
visually model an application flow,
  [highlight interface designer - bottom right of screen]
define its user interface,
  [highlight integration designer - bottom left of screen]
and integrate it with existing applications and data sources.

  [Shot of completed Studio project]
Covigo Studio separates business processes from both presentation design and data source integration. Leverage existing IT investment by importing and extending Enterprise Java Beans and other Java objects.

Deployment: Engine

  [click on deploy button]
Instantly deploy your newly created applications to the Covigo Engine.

  [highlight design on lifecycle slide & place "Covigo Engine" next to it]
The Covigo Engine is a robust and highly scalable run-time environment for executing mobile applications.

  [Covigo engine architecture slide]
Based on XML and J2EE standards, the Covigo Engine is built with a modular architecture to easily integrate with existing enterprise infrastructure. You can deploy the Covigo Engine on any J2EE-compliant application server. It also supports interfaces to third-party services and technologies, such as SMS and location-based services.

Management: Covigo Console

[Lifecycle slide - manage]
Proactively manage live mobile applications after deployment, using Covigo Console.

[console shots with blinking lights and error state]
Covigo Console enables you to securely and remotely configure the runtime environment. It can also monitor all applications by periodically running diagnostic tests, alerting you if problems are detected.

Analysis: Insight

[highlight design on lifecycle slide & place "Covigo   Insight" next to it]
And lastly, for comprehensive data tracking and analysis, Covigo Insight provides powerful reporting tools for gathering business intelligence from mobile applications.

[Shots of Insight data]
Track how users navigate your mobile site and analyze user behavior at specific stages in the application. Use this information to make adjustments and enhancements accordingly.

Product Advantages

[Slide of platform advantages]
The Covigo Platform offers businesses three unique advantages:
[first advantage appears]
First, we offer a rapid development and deployment environment that separates business logic from presentation design and data integration.
[second advantage appears]
Second, we enable integrated voice and data applications.
[third advantage appears]
Lastly, we support end-to-end secure transactions.

Closing

[Covigo logo & tagline]
Thank you for your interest. Please visit covigo.com for more information.

THE POWER OF YOUR THOUGHTS — (CD track 27)

Title: "Passion, Profit & Power" — audio training program
Agency: Mind Power, Inc.
USP: "Reprogram your subconscious mind to create the relationships, wealth, and well-being that you deserve"
Target Audience: Self-motivated people who desire to improve their life
Style: Friendly, professional, expert
Characters: Author/expert
VO Talent: Marshall Sylver — **www.sylver.com**
Copy Notes: Marshall Sylver is a motivational speaker, professional hypnotist, and an expert in the area of subconscious reprogramming. This excerpt from his program "Passion, Profit and Power" is an excellent example of taking the words "off the page." Many professional speakers will produce an audio version of their seminar, or a training program. For studio recordings such as this, the material is scripted in advance and read during the recording session. The challenge for the presenter is to sound as though the words being spoken are coming off the top of the head. They must sound completely natural, very conversational, and be absolutely comfortable with the complexities of their topic — yet it is totally scripted.

With this sort of material, it is very easy to fall into a "read-y" narration style that can sound more like a lecture than a conversation. As an experienced motivational speaker, Marshall delivers his message in an intimate style that presents him as a knowledgeable expert. Notice how effectively he uses many voice-acting techniques like sense memory, pulling lines, pacing, and physicalization just to mention a few. Also notice how you, as a listener, are affected by the way in which Marshall tells the story. He draws you into what he is saying, and keeps you listening by presenting a skillful blend of intellectual and emotional content.

As you listen to the CD, observe the variety in Marshall's delivery; the way he adjusts his pacing to emphasize a point, the way he changes the pitch of his voice, and the way he creates a vivid image in your imagination. Also listen for changes in his delivery that are affected by physical alterations of his body, arms, and face.

As you work with this script, keep in mind that as a voice actor you are both a communicator and a storyteller. Notice that there are several lists in this story, as well as lots of vivid imagery. Use the techniques you've learned in previous chapters to determine your audience, back story, and character so you can create a powerful interpretation. Use sense memory, visualization and physical movement to create a totally believable experience in the imagination of your audience.

This story is excellent for stretching your performing abilities. Become familiar with the basic story, and then tell it to different groups of friends in different ways — for one group simply tell the story without much emphasis or feeling; for another group, pull out all the stops. Notice how much more effective and real the reaction will be for the second group.

Passion, Profit & Power:
The Power of Your Thoughts

Every single thought that you can have possesses the ability to psychosomatically affect you. What this means is that every thought has a response in the physical body. In a moment I'm going to cause your body to respond to something simply by the thought of it.

Recently, I was driving through a citrus orchard near my home, and as I looked around me I saw thousands and thousands of totally ripe lemons. If you've ever driven through a citrus orchard, the first thing you'll notice is the scent . . . it smells like "sweet tarts." As I was driving through the citrus orchard, and looking at these juicy, plump, ripe lemons, I couldn't resist. I pulled my car off to the side of the road and I got out. And I walked up to the nearest tree that was laden full and heavy with the juiciest, plumpest, biggest, sour lemons I'd ever seen in my life.

I couldn't resist. I reached up to the tree . . . and I plucked the biggest, juiciest lemon I could find . . . and when I did, I smelled that scent, popping as the stem burst away from the fruit. That sour, tangy, juicy citrus scent from the lemon. I couldn't resist any more. In that moment, I reached into my pocket. I pulled out my pocket knife, and I pressed the shiny metal blade of the knife against the smooth, juicy flesh of this yellow lemon. And I began to slice through this juicy, tangy, tart, sour lemon . . . and as I did, the pulp and the juices from the lemon ran down the knife blade and across my hand. I put the knife aside, and I took my thumbs and I pressed them between the halves of this juicy, sour, tangy, tart lemon – and I split them apart. It was like sunshine in both hands! I couldn't wait – I tipped my head straight back – and I began squeezing half the lemon into my mouth. The sour juices, dripping, running down my chin, going back into my mouth. I couldn't wait any more . . . I took the other half of the lemon and I bit into it fully . . . tasting the sour, juicy, tangy lemon. And when I did, my jowls tightened, just like yours are tightening now.

Every thought has a psychosomatic response in the body. By virtue of the fact that you think it – you'll telegraph to your body to respond to that thought as if it were true. What you believe is true for you. Nothing else.

13

Your Demo Tape

Your demo tape is your best first opportunity to present your talents and abilities to talent agents, producers, and other talent buyers. Many times, you will be booked for an audition or for a session simply based on something the producer hears in your demo. The purpose of a demo tape is to get you work!

Your Professional Calling Card

In the world of voice acting, your demo tape is your calling card. It is your portfolio. It is your audio résumé. It is your letter of introduction. It is the single most important thing you *must* have if you are to compete in the world of professional voice-over.

Since your demo tape may directly result in bookings, it is extremely important that you be able to match the level of your demo performance when under the pressure of a session. It is quite easy for a studio to create a highly produced, yet misrepresentative, demo that gives the impression of an extremely talented and polished performer. If the performer's actual abilities are less that what is depicted on the demo, the shortcomings will be quickly revealed during a session.

I know of one voice actor who was booked through an agent based solely on the demo tape. The tape sounded great and had logos of major television networks and other advertisers on its cover. The impression was that this performer had done a lot of work and was highly skilled.

The performance was recorded during an ISDN session in San Diego with the performer in a New York studio. A few minutes into the session, it became apparent that the voice actor could not take direction and would not be able to perform to the caliber of the demo. The producer gracefully ended the session and a different voice actor was hired to complete the session the following day. The producer refused to pay the talent agency's commission because she felt the talent agency had misrepresented the voice actor's abilities. The original performer was never told that the session was unsatisfactory and actually sent a nice thank-you note to the producer. The performer did get paid, but the recording was never used.

It turned out that the agent had never worked directly with the performer and, in fact, had not even done a live audition before signing. They had been promoting the person based solely on a highly produced demo. A few days later, it was learned that the performer was actually attempting to memorize the copy due to a problem with dyslexia that made it difficult to perform the lines live, as written.

The talent agent later apologized to the producer and mentioned that this performer had done some excellent self-marketing and presented a very professional image during the agent's interview. The only problem was that the performer had created a demo that clearly exceeded his actual abilities.

Let me say it again: You *must* be able to perform to the level of your demo when booked for a real session.

VERSATILITY IS YOUR SELLING TOOL

A good demo presents the performer in a wide range of styles, including a variety of examples showing different emotions, attitudes, characters, and voices. Good voice actors can do dozens of voices and characters because they are able to find a place in their body from which to center the character and place the voice. It is the range and variety of styles that keep a demo interesting and hold the listener's attention.

Every performer has a unique style, range, and ability. You need to capitalize on your strong points and present them in the best possible manner in your demo. The range of attitudes, emotions, and characters you can express during a voice-over performance is your own *vocal versatility*. Your strongest, most dynamic, and most marketable voice is called your *money voice*. This is the voice that will get you the work and may eventually become your trademark. Your other voices are icing on the cake but are necessary to clearly show your range and versatility.

Demo Tape Basics

Just a few short years ago, the analog audio cassette was the format of preference for voice-over demos. Although cassette tapes are still used, in today's voice-over market the audio CD is preferred by most talent buyers. It's easy to simply drop a CD into the computer CD-ROM drive, and there is never any fast-forwarding or rewinding to find the right spot in the demo. Larger talent agencies will compile their talent demos into a CD format, usually creating separate CDs or sections for male and female talent. Many voice actors will have separate demos that reflect their talents in several areas of voice work — commercial, narration, character, animation, and so on. These may be combined into one demo, but more frequently they are separated into distinct tracks on a CD or separate sides of a cassette: side 1 — commercial (singles, multiples, and character), side 2 — narration.

For most people starting out in voice-over, a combination of CD and cassette demos works best. Mass quantity CD duplication can be quite expensive, but there are many alternatives available for producing short runs, or *one-offs* of CD demos. Many voice-over performers new to the business are burning their own CD's on their home computer and printing their own labels. But a more professional demo will be produced by finding a tape duplication company who does small CD runs and who can imprint the label information directly on the CD.

DEMO DOS AND DON'TS

Plan the content of your demo carefully to include copy you can perform well and that is appropriate for the type of market you want to reach. A demo of commercial copy is not appropriate for a producer of corporate projects, and a demo of character and animation voices is not appropriate for a commercial producer.

Producers often listen to a demo tape with their finger poised on the eject button, ready to toss it in the trash. This is somewhat due to time constraints, but is largely due to the fact that dozens of poorly produced demos cross the desks of producers every day. Remember that producers make their decisions about a voice within the first 15 to 20 seconds of listening to a demo. If you are going to make it past that crucial first 15 seconds, your demo performance must be well presented and highly skilled.

A good demo keeps the producer listening: It has entertainment value with a new surprise, emotional hook, acting technique, vocal variation, or character twist happening about every 5 to 15 seconds. A good demo does not give the listener an opportunity to turn it off.

If you are just starting out, your demo should be focused on the type of voice work you do best. Here are some Dos and Don'ts for your first demo:

- Do include a wide range of variety in style and character. Keep the listener guessing as to what will happen next.

- Do keep each "clip" to only a single, concise statement or few brief sentences. You only have a short time to catch and hold the listener's attention.

- Do focus on what you currently do best. Then revise and prepare new demos as your talent grows and you acquire copies of projects you have worked on (usually once or twice a year).

- Do keep your demo short. If the producer listening to your demo is going to make his or her decision in 15 seconds or less, you would be wise to have your strongest material in that first 15 seconds.

- Do start with just one or two very specific demos.

- Don't do a demo until you are ready. Make sure you have done your homework and have mastered voice-acting skills.

- Don't try to include material from too many different facets of voice work because this only detracts from the effectiveness of your demo.

- Don't think you can put a demo tape together at home and expect it to sound professional. A poor quality demo — in either performance or audio quality — is a waste of time and money.

You will be far better off with a solid 1-minute and 45 seconds of fast-moving, entertaining material than with a slow-moving 2 minutes of uninteresting material lacking variety and range. As you gain a reputation and become more versatile, you may be able to justify a longer demo. A number of voice actors have produced CD demos that include anywhere from 5 to 8 short demos in specific categories. The length of the CDs vary from about 11 minutes to almost 20 minutes, but each category averages just over 2 minutes. Each short demo is well produced, moves quickly, and features a different aspect of these performers' talents. The format of multiple demos on a single CD makes it easy for a producer to quickly find and listen to only the particular style he or she is interested in.

COMMERCIAL DEMOS

There are no hard-and-fast rules for producing a voice demo, but there are certain production techniques that consistently grab and hold listeners' attention. Commercial demos are generally produced on a bell curve with the performer's *money voice* at the beginning and end. In between are a variety of performance attitudes and styles that reflect the performer's range and abilities. Having the same voice at the beginning and end provides a reference point for the listener and gives him or her an opportunity to categorize the performer's vocal age and personality type.

A good demo will begin at a certain pace and pick up speed and intensity as it travels its course. At certain spots the pace should slow again to give the listener a chance to catch his or her breath, and then pick up once again. A demo needs to end on an uplifting, fun, and positive note to leave the listener with a good feeling.

CHARACTER AND ANIMATION DEMOS

Character and animation demo tapes are often structured a bit differently and may include a number of character voices juxtaposed in an incongruous manner, or having a scripted conversation, to hold the listener's attention. For example, one character might have the line: "Our mattress makes all the difference." This might be followed by a totally different character voice saying: ". . . because we do amazing things with rocks and stones."

This form of character demo is called a *concept tape*. A clever scenario is introduced to provide a story or reason for the various characters to converse with one another. As the story continues, there will be changes in attitude, pacing, and character development. Concept demos are challenging to write and must be thought out very carefully. Concept demos fall into one of two categories: extremely good and unbelievably stupid!

The most common method of producing a character demo is to place vocal excerpts randomly to demonstrate the widest possible versatility of vocal talents. A demo of this sort usually has a bell-curve structure similar to a commercial demo with changes of pacing and "wackiness" as it progresses.

Character voice work for animation is probably the single toughest area of voice-over to break into. One of my students, Marc Biagi, chose to concentrate on character voice work, so that was his first demo. He spent several weeks preparing the material and refining the voices for each piece of copy. Marc's original plan was to create a pretty basic demo featuring his wide variety of character voices and attitudes. As we were assembling the demo, we were struck with an idea which instantly created a concept demo and a marketing plan for Marc. One of the tracks featured an Indian voice (as in the country) hosting a food show. We realized that every clip we had recorded could represent a different television station. So I inserted the sound of a mechanical TV channel select knob between every track, and the resulting demo gives the impression of "channel-surfing." Marc's concept demo (along with his constant marketing) resulted in numerous voice-acting jobs for some major video game companies. His first demo (titled "Channels") is track 30 on the CD.

CORPORATE AND NARRATIVE DEMOS

Corporate and industrial demos tend to contain copy that is somewhat longer than the copy in a commercial or character demo. The longer length of copy allows the producer time to more accurately assess your reading and delivery skills. It also gives them an opportunity to hear how you handle complex words, concepts, and sentences. As with the other types of demos, your money voice and strongest material should lead the demo, followed by a variety of styles, range, and versatility. Narrative demos offer a good opportunity to use various microphone techniques, a range of delivery speeds, and storytelling techniques to good advantage.

Ideally, your demo should be compiled from actual projects you have worked on. However, for the person just starting out, this is not possible. You will need to create your own copy and design a demo that will catch the listener's attention and hold it. Even working professionals sometimes need to make up copy to create a demo that really puts their voice in the spotlight. This can be a challenging task, but it can pay off big. The rest of this chapter and the next chapter will cover everything you need to know about creating your demo, from finding the copy to getting your demo recorded, to getting it duplicated. You will also learn how to create your marketing campaign and get your demo into the hands of agents, producers, and other talent buyers.

Don't Do a Demo Until You Are Ready

Producing a demo before being ready is one of the biggest mistakes many people make when they are eager to get started in voice-over. Producing your demo too soon may result in difficulty finding an agent who will represent you. Not to mention the fact that the presentation and performance quality is likely to be much less than is needed to be successful in this business. Producing your demo too soon is simply a waste of time and money, and can potentially affect your credibility as a performer later on. Remember the story of the dyslexic performer who had a wonderful demo, but who was unable to perform under the stress of a session.

Before you even think about having your demo produced, make sure you have acquired the skills and good performing habits necessary to compete in this challenging business. Remember that there are a lot of other people trying to do the same thing as you. Anything you can do to improve your abilities and make your performing style just a bit unique will be to your advantage. Study your craft, learn acting skills, and develop a plan to market yourself *before* you do your demo. Take classes — lots of classes!

Your demo should be professionally produced by someone who knows what they are doing. Don't think you can put a demo together at home and expect it to sound professional. Even if you have a home project studio, a sophisticated computer system, or a friend who has a home studio, you still need the assistance of a good director. It is extremely difficult for one person to deal with both the engineering and performing aspects of producing a demo at the same time. You need to be focused on your performance and not dealing with any equipment.

You need a director to listen to your performance objectively, help you stay focused, and help get you in touch with the character in the copy. Performing effectively without a director, or by directing yourself, is very challenging. Although many professional voice actors believe they don't need a director, all voice actors do, in fact, need a director to bring out their best work. The top professionals will tell you that they perform much better when they have a good director to guide them through their performance.

When you go to the studio to produce your demo, you should consider the session to be just like a real commercial recording session. You need to be able to get a good performance, in three or four takes. If you need more than six or seven takes to get the right delivery, you may not be ready.

Become an expert at communicating with drama and emotion before you have your demo produced. Here are some of the things you need to keep in mind:

- **Study acting.** Acting is the key to an effective performance. Learn how to act and learn how to use your voice and body to express drama and emotional tension.

- **Do your exercises.** Set up a daily regimen for doing your voice exercises. Get into the habit of keeping your voice in top condition. Your voice is the "tool" of your trade — take care of it.

- **Take classes and workshops.** Have an attitude of always learning. You will learn something new from each class and workshop you take or repeat. The voice-over business is constantly adapting and new trends become popular each year. You need to be ready to adapt as new trends develop.

- **Read other books about voice-over.** Every author on this subject presents his or her material in a slightly different manner. You may also learn new techniques or get some fresh ideas from reading a variety of books on the subject.

- **Practice your skills and techniques.** When you are working on a piece of copy, rehearse your performance with an attitude of continually perfecting it. Have a solid understanding of the techniques you are using and polish your performance in rehearsal.

Producing Your Demo

Remember, doing your homework before going to the studio to produce your demo will save you time and money. Rehearse your copy with a stopwatch, and know how you want to deliver each script. Do a complete script analysis for each script. Make notes on your scripts about the character, attitude, and emotional hooks, as well as ideas for music style and sound effects if appropriate. Consider mic placement for each script. Mark off what you believe to be the strongest :10 to :15 of each script and consider a possible sequence for the demo. Be flexible enough to understand that this will probably change.

Ideally, you should find a director who can assist you with the production of your demo. Hiring a director will allow you to focus on your performance so you will not have to worry about the technical details of the session. Many recording studios have engineers experienced in directing voice-over.

Above all, when you are in the studio recording your demo, have fun and enjoy the experience! I encourage you to stay through as much of the process of producing the demo as you possibly can. This is your primary tool for establishing yourself in the business. Your input will be important for the engineer to create an effective demo. You take a great risk if you simply go in and record your tracks, then leave the production up to the engineer. Through the process of producing your demo, you will learn a lot about what really goes on behind the scenes in a recording studio.

HOW LONG SHOULD MY DEMO BE?

Your demo tape should be approximately 2 minutes in length. This doesn't sound very long, but remember that the person listening to your tape usually decides if your voice performance is right for them within the first 15 to 20 seconds.

You should include about 12 to 20 short excerpts demonstrating your range and talents. The length of each clip will depend on its content, but on average should be between 6 and 15 seconds. The length of clips for narrative demos should be a bit longer (15 to 20 seconds) to provide a better presentation of long-form copy. The engineer or producer you hire to put your demo together should be able to sequence the clips into a logical order that will hold the listener's attention and offer plenty of variety.

The clips in your demo do not need to mention any product names, but should demonstrate your ability to communicate emotionally with a variety of styles and attitudes. There are actually two schools of thought on this. Some agents and producers believe that including product names lends credibility to the performer (especially if the spot is one that the performer actually worked on) and that they give a good opportunity for the producer to hear how the performer "sells" the client, or puts a spin on the product name. Other producers feel that the most important aspect of a demo is the performer's talent and ability to communicate effectively on an emotional level, and that product names can actually become distracting.

It would probably be a good idea to include a few product names in your first demo just so you can demonstrate how you can sell the client or product. If you have not done any real sessions, and you are producing your first demo, change or make up the product names to avoid any confusion or misrepresentation. As you acquire copies of projects you have worked on, you should include several product names from actual spots in your updated demos. When using product or service names, be careful that you do not misrepresent yourself by implying, either on the demo or its packaging, that spots on your demo actually aired if, in fact, they have not.

WHERE DO I GET THE COPY FOR MY DEMO?

There are several approaches to obtaining copy for a demo. Some demo studios provide the copy and handle all the production. This is fine if you don't mind taking the chance of other people in your market having the same copy on their demos. The only real advantage of having the studio provide the copy is that your demo session becomes more like a real recording session; that is, you won't have the opportunity to see the copy in advance. The downside is that your session may take considerably longer because you will be working the copy cold and relatively unrehearsed. You might also feel rushed when you are "on the clock" to get through all the copy necessary, which could easily affect the quality of your performance.

However, the major problem with the studio providing the copy is that you can easily end up using copy that is not right for your performing style. The purpose of your demo is to present your talent in the best possible manner. Performing copy that is not right for you can only work against you, no matter how well the demo is produced.

A much better approach to finding copy for your first demo is to listen to radio and TV commercials and browse through magazines. By listening to commercials on radio and TV, you can find copy that matches your style and abilities. Record commercial breaks on audio cassette or on your VCR and transcribe the ads that fit your abilities, putting each script on a separate piece of paper. Transcribe the entire commercial even though you may end up using only a small portion if that script makes it into the demo. Having the entire script in front of you will help you discover the emotional content of the commercial and the target audience.

Also, when browsing through magazines, look for ads that include a lot of copy. Technical, news, travel, and women's magazines frequently have ads that can be easily adapted for voice-over. Most print ads are written for the eye, designed to be read, and include a lot of text that may not be appropriate for voice-over. Look for ads that target specific audiences: men, women, young, older adults, and so on. Look for products or services that will allow you to perform the copy in a variety of styles: serious, humorous, hard-sell, soft-sell, dynamic, emotional, and so on. Look for key phrases and sentences that have emotional content — these will be your keys to an effective performance. Since print copy is written to be read silently, you may need to rewrite the copy somewhat so that it can be used for voice-over. You don't need to completely rewrite a print ad; just take the strongest sections and rework them so that they make sense as a voice performance.

Another possibility for obtaining copy is to call advertising agencies in your area. Advertising agencies have files of old scripts and might be willing to let you use some of them for your demo. If you take this approach, try to get a variety of scripts from several ad agencies so that you will have an assortment of writing styles and attitudes. You might also try contacting radio and TV stations or recording studios in your area; try to get connected with a producer who might have some old scripts you can use. Recording studios usually throw out scripts when a session is finished, but they might be able to give you a lead to a producer or ad agency that would be willing to give you some old scripts.

Obtain as much copy as you can and narrow the scripts down to about 30 to 40 different ads from radio, TV, and magazines. Also find several brief passages from technical journals, magazine articles, or other suitable corporate or narrative copy. Make sure the copy you gather includes a variety of styles that will reveal your full range of capabilities: slow, fast, dynamic, emotional, character, and so on.

Be prepared to perform the entire script at your demo session. The reason for this is that you may actually end up with an extremely effective delivery on a segment of the script that you may not have expected. If you only rehearse portions of your scripts, you might overlook an opportunity for a perfect transitional element in your demo, or an especially emotional performance. Your director or engineer can help you do your best performance for each script and you may end up actually only recording a small portion of the copy.

Make sure you have at least three clean copies of each script when you go to the studio: one copy for yourself, one for the engineer, and the third for your director (with your notes and delivery ideas).

WHAT ABOUT DIALOGUE, MUSIC, AND SOUND EFFECTS?

You might be inclined to include a dialogue spot on a demo. For your first demo, this may not be a good idea. The purpose of a demo is to feature *your* voice-acting performance. Including other voice-over performers should be done judiciously. If you include a dialogue spot, make sure that yours is the featured performance and that the other voice is of the opposite gender. This may seem obvious, but you'd be surprised at the number of demos there are that have two voices that are hard to tell apart. Also be certain that the other performer knows how to act and work dialogue copy. You can't imagine how many demos I've heard that include a dialogue spot where the second player showed little or no acting ability. Of course, if you are talented at performing a variety of character voices, you might want to include a dialogue spot in which you perform all the voices.

As you prepare your demo copy, make notes on your scripts if you have an idea about music style or sound effects, but don't worry about finding them. The engineer will handle that at your session. What you need to focus on is finding copy you can perform effectively. You have the luxury of being able to prepare for your performance. Take advantage of it! You will not have this luxury in a real-life studio session.

Do an appropriate script and character analysis for each piece of copy, making notes on the scripts. Practice your performance for each script just enough to become familiar with it. Be careful not to get yourself locked into any specific attitude or character. Keep in mind that your session engineer might direct you into a performance completely different from what you had decided on. If that happens, you need to be able to adapt to the direction. If you can't, or if you find yourself getting stuck in the same delivery for each take, then you are not ready to have your demo produced.

HOW MUCH WILL MY DEMO COST?

The cost of producing a voice-acting demo will vary from market to market and, to a certain extent, will depend on your performing abilities. For recording studios, time is money, and the faster you can record a high-quality performance (fewer takes), the sooner your demo will be completed and the less it will cost.

Expect to pay anywhere from $500 to $1,000, or more, for the production of your voice demo. Although actual session fees vary, and may be somewhat lower or higher, the following shows how the cost for a typical demo session might break down:

PRODUCTION ELEMENTS	TIME AND FEES	SUBTOTALS
Studio time (voice recording)	1.5 hours @ $100/hour	$150.00
Postproduction (editing, music)	2.5 hours @ $100/hour	250.00
Track sequencing and/or dubbing	1 hour @ $100/hour	100.00
Music licenses (for music used)	1 blanket license	200.00
Outside producer/director	1 flat fee	200.00
Materials (cassette, CD), including tax		50.00
Total Demo Cost (not including duplication)		$950.00

This example assumes a certain level of competency in the performer. The actual time it takes to record your copy may vary considerably, fees will vary and not all of these items may be required, thus affecting the price.

The cost of studio time varies greatly from city to city and depends on the complexity of your session. Some studios charge a fee for the music used in your demo while other studios will provide the music at no charge. Some studios will charge an hourly rate, while others will charge a flat rate for the production of your demo. In most states, the cost of studio time and music license fees are exempt from sales tax, but the materials and recording media are not. Check with your studio to find out what portions of the session or materials will have sales tax applied.

WHAT DO I NEED TO KNOW ABOUT STUDIOS?

As you prepare for your demo, you will be wearing your producer hat. In that role, you will have already prepared your copy and directed yourself in your performance during practice and rehearsals. Some of your other duties as producer will be to make all the arrangements for studio time, printing, tape or CD duplication, and distribution of your demo.

Most larger cities have at least several recording studios and radio stations. In this age of easily accessible high technology, even many small towns have studios capable of recording a high-quality demo. You will find commercial recording studios advertised in the telephone book. However, there may also be many excellent home-based project studios in your community that are not advertised anywhere. Even though recording services and studios may be plentiful in your area, this does not mean that all studios are able to produce an effective demo tape.

The majority of commercial recording studios are designed to handle music sessions. The engineers at these studios are usually very competent at recording music, but may not know much about producing commercials, directing voice-over talent, or anything at all about voice acting. Home-based project studios are most often designed to handle the recording needs of musicians and composers, but may not be suitable for, or capable of, recording quality voice-over work. Larger recording studios and production houses and even some radio stations are expanding their production capabilities to include a much wider range of services, including voice recording and commercial production.

When you book a recording studio, you may be assigned an engineer who is not interested in demo production. If you are doing the demo on your own, you need to be prepared for this. As the producer of your demo, you need to be ready to guide your engineer through the process and have a good idea of what you want in your demo, including the selection of music and sound effects, and the final sequencing of clips.

After you have selected your scripts, rehearsed them, and are confident that your performing skills are up to par, it's time to start calling the studios in your area to schedule your session.

HOW DO I BOOK A STUDIO?

The following pages contain some questions to ask as you call around looking for a studio to hire to produce your demo, as well as some important basic information about recording studios.

- **Does the studio record radio and TV commercials, or primarily music?** If the studio is primarily a music studio, they may not be capable of handling your needs for a voice-over demo. Look for a studio that is experienced in producing commercials or demos.

- **Does the studio have an engineer who knows how to direct voice-over talent?** Unless you have hired a director, you *will need* an engineer who can direct you as you perform your copy. Many studios have engineers who know how to record the human voice, but don't know the first thing about directing talent for an effective voice-acting performance. When you enter the studio, you need to take off your producer hat and become the performer. Even if you hire a director, you need to find a studio that has an engineer who knows how to produce and direct for voice-over.

- **Does the studio have any experience producing voice-over demos?** You may have this question answered when you find out if the studio has an engineer who knows how to work with voice-over talent. However, even if a studio does a lot of radio commercials, it does not mean that they also produce voice-over demos. Unlike a :60 radio commercial that is a continuous script, your 2-minute demo will consist of anywhere from 12 to 20 very short clips. The sequencing of these clips will play an important role in how the tape is perceived by the final listener. If the studio has produced demos in the past, ask to hear what they have done for others or for the names of other voice performers for whom they have produced demos.

- **Does the studio have session time that will coincide with your availability?** If you can't book the studio at a time when you are available, you need to find another studio. Many recording studios offer evening or weekend studio time, and may either offer a discount or charge an extra fee for those sessions. You may be able to get a reduced fee for late-night sessions, but you may not be able to get an engineer experienced with voice-over.

- **What is the studio's hourly rate for voice recording?** Many studios have a sliding scale of prices depending on the requirements of the project. Other studios book at a flat rate, regardless of the session. Shop the studios in your area to find the best price for your demo production. Find out if there are any price changes between the voice session and the production session. Find a studio that will give you a flat hourly rate for your entire project. Some studios will give a block discount for sessions booking a large amount of time. A demo session probably won't fit this category, but it couldn't hurt to ask.

- **Does the studio use analog or digital equipment?** Some studios may have a higher rate for digital production and a lower rate for analog — or vice versa. The difference between digital and analog production in a recording studio is primarily in the area of editing and post-production. Analog quality in a recording studio is extremely high and should not be a consideration for your demo recording; however, analog production may take some additional time since it usually involves multitrack recording. Digital workstations can reduce the production and editing time considerably because the audio is recorded and edited within a computer. Analog recordings use reel-to-reel tape recorded at 15 ips (inches per second) and cut-and-splice editing or multitrack production, both of which can be very time-consuming. Today, most studios have some form of digital recording equipment and analog tape decks are becoming less popular every year. However, analog audio cassettes are still a popular format for demos and are likely to be with us for many years to come.

- **Does the studio have access to music and sound effects libraries?** Your demo will need music and possibly sound effects to underscore your performance. Many recording studios do not have any CDs of music that can be used in a demo, even though their primary business may be recording music. Find a production studio that has one or more music libraries that can be used to underscore your spots. A music library is a collection of music created by a company that produces CDs of music specifically designed for use in commercial, TV, and film production. As you were preparing for your session, you made some notes on music and sound effect ideas. Discuss your ideas with your engineer at the beginning of your session.

  It is not a good idea to use music from your personal music collection for your demo. Even though your demo is meant for limited distribution and will not be for public sale, the possibility of copyright infringement for unauthorized use of the music does exist. Also, the use of familiar or popular music may create a distraction if it is not used wisely. If you have a specific sound in mind for some of your demo tracks, you might want to take in some examples from your personal collection, but keep in mind that they probably should not be used in the final demo. If you do take in your own music, make sure it is all instrumental and appropriate for the copy.

- **Does the studio have any additional charges for music or sound effects used?** Some studios charge a fee for any music used in your demo, while other studios include the music as part of a package price. If there is a music use fee charged by the studio, make sure it is a *blanket license* rather than a *laser-drop* license. A blanket license covers all music used in a project and is considerably less expensive than several laser-drop licenses. Usually, there is no charge for sound effects. If you provide your own music, there will be no charge, but you take the risk of any problems that might arise from its use.

- **What other fees will the studio charge for materials, including sales tax?** What does the studio charge for cassettes, CD one-offs, digital audio tape (DAT), and any other materials used in the production of your demo? Does the studio have any additional charges for archiving (backing up) your demo project? What portions of the demo production will have sales tax applied? All of these items will affect the total cost of your demo.

- **How much time does the studio estimate it will take to produce your demo?** You should plan on at least six to eight hours for the completion of your demo, although you may be able to have it completed in much less time. The studio's experience in producing demos will be a factor here, as well as your performing abilities. If the studio has experience producing demos, ask for an estimate of production time and an average cost breakdown.

- **What will you take with you when your demo is completed?** In most cases, you can expect to leave the studio with at least two high-quality cassette copies and at least one CD of your demo. Keep one cassette and the CD in a safe place. You will need them later for duplication. Use the second cassette as a backup or to make some interim copies if you have a dubbing cassette deck, but don't plan to send these copies out to agents or clients because the quality most likely will not be up to professional standards.

  Some studios may not have CD capability and will save your demo to DAT (Digital Audio Tape). At one time, DAT was a preferred format for mastering and long-term storage. However, with the advent of workstation CD burners, DAT tape is rapidly fading as a storage medium. If the studio you hire uses DAT for storage, you would be wise to get a copy of your demo on that format, if they should offer. The DAT tape should be kept as a production master that can be used in case your master CD is lost or damaged.

- **What kind of cassette tape should be used for my cassette copies?** Even though your demo is primarily voice, make sure that any cassettes you take with you are on high bias (CrO_2), music-quality tape rather than normal bias tape. The difference in tape quality may not be immediately apparent to you, but it will become apparent later, after duplication. Normal bias tape (voice-quality) has a substantially greater amount of noise, or hiss, than high bias (music-quality) tape. Metal tape is not recommended for a demo master because there is little difference between high bias and metal tape for a voice demo. Also, most cassette duplicators prefer high bias tape.

- **What is this thing called Dolby®?** Another point about the cassette master is to have the tape clearly labeled as to whether it was recorded with Dolby ON or OFF, and if it is Dolby B or C. The Dolby noise-reduction process affects the high-frequency tape noise (hiss) inherent in analog tape by boosting the higher frequencies of the source audio during recording. (Dolby is not a factor with digital recordings.) When a processed tape is played back with Dolby ON, the previously boosted high frequencies are reduced to a normal volume. Since tape hiss is inherent in the tape and is not a part of the recording, when the overall high frequencies are reduced during playback, the hiss volume is decreased proportionally, effectively eliminating hiss and resulting in a very clean sounding recording.

If a tape recorded *without* Dolby is played back with Dolby ON, the unprocessed recording will have its high frequencies reduced, resulting in a "muddy" or "muffled" sound lacking crispness and clarity. On the other hand, if a Dolby processed tape is played back with Dolby OFF, the previously boosted high frequencies will *not* be reduced resulting in a somewhat "brighter" or "crisper" edge to the sound. Ideally, a processed tape should be played back with Dolby ON, and an unprocessed tape with Dolby OFF. However, if there is any question as to how the tape will eventually be played back, my recommendation is to record with Dolby OFF, as this is the most common mode of playback.

- **What about putting my demo on a CD?** Most studios today will give you the option of having your demo recorded directly onto a CD master. This is called a *one-off* CD, and you should definitely have at least one — and two would be better. In today's voice-over market you need your demo on both cassette and CD. If your demo master is on CD, the cassette duplication company usually transfers the CD to a cassette before duplication, or they sometimes use a cassette for direct duplication. The quality of your cassette copies will be higher if you start with a CD. If you do get a one-off CD, handle it carefully. This type of CD is not quite as durable as commercially manufactured CDs and is more susceptible to scratching.

- **How will your demo be backed up?** Some studios offer a choice of backup options such as CD, DAT, minidisk, ZIP drive, Syquest, JAZ, or some other digital format. A backup is different from the master of your session. The *master* is the final version of your demo in a form that will later be presented to an agent or talent buyer. A *backup* is a copy of all the elements of the project, not necessarily in any special order or structure. A digital backup only applies when your session is produced on a digital audio workstation. Even though the backup will contain everything from your session, often including out-takes, it may be in a format that cannot be used anywhere except the recording studio where your demo was produced.

  CD and DAT are the two most universal media for a backup, but regardless of which format you choose, or that the studio has available, you should have your demo project backed up. The backup is usually kept by the studio; however, they should be able to make you a backup for your own files as well, should you feel you need one. Just be aware that the backup format and data may not be usable by another studio unless they are using the same equipment that was used in the production of your demo. In addition, there may be an additional charge for downloading the backup into the studio's audio workstation when you update your demo.

Your Demo Recording Session

If you have practiced and mastered your voice-acting skills and are prepared and ready to work, your demo session can be a lot of fun, and an educational experience. If, on the other hand, you go to your demo session unprepared or without having mastered the necessary skills, your session can be very uncomfortable.

Because you are the producer as well as the performer, you are the one person responsible for making sure your demo is well produced and that it will be a useful tool for marketing your talents. This means you will have the opportunity to supervise the entire process of your demo production. You won't often have this chance when you are doing real-world sessions. Keep in mind, though, that when you are in front of the mic, you need to be focused on your performance, and not on other aspects of your demo. This is where hiring a director or having an engineer who knows how to direct becomes important. Track sequencing, music, sound effects, CD and cassette duplication, packaging, and distribution can all be left for later.

ARRIVE ON TIME AND PREPARED

In recording studios, time is money. If a session is scheduled to start at 10:00 AM and you don't arrive until 10:10, that's at least ten minutes of wasted time and money — probably more, because it takes a certain amount of time for the engineer to prepare the studio. Recording studios will usually bill you for their time whether or not you are there at the scheduled time. The lesson here is to *be on time* for your session! If you live your life in a constant mode of running late, you might want to set your clocks ahead, or do whatever is necessary to make sure you arrive at your session on time, or preferably a bit early. Arriving late for real-world sessions will get you a bad reputation in a hurry, and will cause you to lose work. Arriving late for your demo session will put your performance under unnecessary stress, costing you valuable time and money.

The same goes for being prepared. In real-world sessions, there is little more you need to do than to show up at the studio at the appointed time, ready to perform. However, for your demo session, you are also the producer, and you must be prepared with rehearsed copy and ideas to discuss with the engineer handling your session. If you hire someone to produce or direct your demo you need to make sure that the two of you take the time to rehearse your copy to find the strongest material and that you both have a good idea of what you want to achieve from your demo.

Here are some other tips to make your demo session a productive and pleasurable experience:

- Arrive at your session a bit early.
- Eat a light meal or snack before your session.
- Arrive in good voice, fully warmed up and ready to perform.
- Have a bottle of water with you.
- Do not wait until arriving at the session to rehearse your scripts.
- Make a note of which scripts you think are your strongest.
- Plan in advance for a possible sequence of scripts.
- Plan ahead for music and sound effects.
- Be ready to accept new scripts that the engineer might have available.

WORKING WITH YOUR ENGINEER/PRODUCER

Aside from your director, if you hire one, your engineer/producer will be one of the most important people you work with during the production of your demo. Your director may or may not be the engineer. In any case, it is important that you and your engineer work together as a team on your project. Remain flexible and open to your engineer's suggestions. If you are careful in booking the studio, you will probably have an engineer who knows much more about voice-over work than you do. You can learn a lot from a good engineer and he or she may even become a good contact for work later on.

KEEPING YOUR DEMO CURRENT

Your demo will probably be useful for about six months to a year, although you may actually use your first demo somewhat longer. As you begin doing paid sessions, you will want to get copies of your work and update your demo occasionally. Most voice actors update their tape with fresh material about once or twice a year, depending on how much work they are doing and their marketing plan. Your agent may request an updated demo or a cut-down (shortened) version for inclusion on their house demo CD or website. Each time you update or change your demo, you will need to book a new session. Fortunately, if you are updating your demo, you will probably not need to spend as much time recording new tracks or in post-production. And you will most likely not incur any additional music license fees, especially if you are simply inserting some of your recent work.

Plan ahead by budgeting for the studio time and have a good idea of the tracks you want to include. Send a current demo to people you have worked for. A new demo is a good opportunity to stay in touch with past clients and to inquire about upcoming projects that might benefit from your talent.

14

Your Demo Is Done.
Now What?

You've spent a good deal of time studying your craft, and you have made an investment in producing a high-quality, marketable demo. Essentially, you have set yourself up in business. As you begin making contacts for voice work, you will be speaking to and meeting professionals who may have been in this business for many years. These people have seen it all, and have little time to waste on an amateur trying to break into the business. Your first impression needs to be memorable and professional.

Present Yourself as a Professional

From here on, you need to maintain the level of professionalism you have worked so hard to establish with your demo. Presenting yourself as a professional is important when you submit your demo to agents and talent buyers. A professional attitude and visual appearance, with your printed materials and personal contacts, show that you mean business, and take your career seriously.

YOUR PROFESSIONAL IMAGE AND GRAPHICS LOOK

One of the best ways to create a professional image is to have a coordinated look in print or even a logo. You might use a special graphic design, a clever application of some computer clip art, or simply a unique font style. Whatever you do, it needs to be clean, clearly legible, and professionally presented.

Creating a graphic identity is not always an easy thing to do, and it is something you might not want to tackle yourself. Fortunately, there are quite a few talented graphic design artists in the business who you can hire to assist you. Even if you hire someone to design your graphic image, you still need to provide some input. You might even want your graphic designer to hear your demo to get a better idea of what you do. Graphic designers can get their inspiration from just about anything, so be as thorough as possible when presenting your ideas.

Your graphic look should reflect your individual personality and be consistent in all printed materials. Your visual image is an important part of your marketing campaign.

Many voice actors incorporate a USP, or unique selling proposition, into their graphic design. A USP is what sets you apart from everyone else. It is intended to make a statement about what makes you special, different, or better. A USP can be anything from a single word to a short phrase. Some well-known USPs from major advertisers include: "The real thing" (Coca-Cola), "The king of beers" (Budweiser), "Generation Next" (Pepsi), and "America's truck stop" (Dodge). Although not necessary for successful advertising, a USP can be an important part of a marketing campaign.

Here are just a few USP possibilities taken from current voice-over demo tapes:

- *She just makes cents!* (Penny Abshire)
- *Orchestrate your message!* (James Alburger)
- *Let us speak for you!* (Alburger & Abshire dialogue team demo)
- *Radioactive device* (Ross Huguet)
- *Off the page* (Dave Rivas)
- *Channels* (Marc Biagi)
- *Jump, listen* (Bob Jump)
- *Vocal Magic* (Catheryn Zaro)
- *Brand new spots you've heard a thousand times* (Mike Roth)
- *The voice with a smile* (Paula Hasler)
- *A Classic* (Don Ranson)
- *Your talking head* (Dawn Comer)
- *Voices* (Casey Hayes)
- *Voice Workout* (Bobbi Frant)
- *Straight up or with a twist . . .* (Jim Staylor)

If you have an interesting name that can be adapted to a graphic image, that may be something you can use creatively. Michelle Ruff uses a caricature graphic of a dog in front of a city skyline as her graphic logo. Of course, the drawing of the dog has a text balloon that says "Ruff." Possibilities are limited only by your imagination. Be creative and let your imagination run wild. Come up with as many ideas as you can and narrow them down to a few that work for you. Pick the best one and use it everywhere. If you use a USP, it should be included in every piece of print material.

SETTING UP SHOP

You will probably want to set up some sort of office space in your home, or at the very least keep some records on your computer. Of course, your office can be put together over a period of time, and you may already have much of it in place.

The purpose of setting up a formal office area is so that you can really keep yourself in a mind-set of handling your talent as a business. The record-keeping and organizational aspects of a business become increasingly important as you begin doing sessions and generating income. If or when you join a union, you will want to keep track of your session work and your union paperwork. There are also certain tax advantages to setting up a formal business and you would be wise to consult a tax advisor or accountant on this matter.

Some of the items you might want to consider for your office include the following:

- **An answering machine, voice-mail box, or service** — This is essential for taking calls when you are not otherwise available. Be sure to check for new messages frequently, especially when you get an agent. There are some interesting messaging services beginning to appear on the Internet for free or for a very small monthly charge. One that's been around for a few years is **www.onebox.com**. When you sign up for this free service, you get a special local phone number and mailbox extension that gives you access to voice-mail, e-mail, and fax — all in one place. This service can even "read" your e-mail to you over the phone, and everything is accessible by both phone and over the Internet.

- **A pager or cell phone** — Although these are not as critical as an answering machine or voice-mail box, a pager and cell phone can be useful tools when you are on the road. Please remember to put your pager or phone on vibrate, or turned off, when you are in the booth. Better yet, don't even take them into the booth.

- **Business cards, letterhead and envelopes** — You will be making many contacts as you develop your voice-acting business. As a professional, you should consider each contact as potential work. Your first impression leaves a lasting memory. Professionally prepared and printed business cards and stationery are essential to creating a professional image.

  A business card is an absolute necessity as a voice actor. As part of your personal networking, you will want to let everyone you meet know what you do. Your business card is the first and best introduction to you and your talent, followed closely by your demo tape. Always carry a supply of business cards with you and hand them out every chance you get.

The two most important things on your business card are your name and a telephone number where you can be reached. The most common problem with business cards is that the telephone number is too small to read easily. The second most common problem is too much information on the card.

Figure 14-1: Business card dimensions with sample layout.

The purpose of a business card is to be a reminder of who you are and how you can be contacted. Include only the most important information about yourself on your card. If you are using a USP, that should be on the card as well. Keep the design clean and simple for best results (see Figure 14-1).

- **Thank-you notes** — A frequently overlooked, yet very important, business practice is the thank-you note. A brief note of thanks is often all it takes to leave a good feeling with a producer or client. These little notes can easily be prepared in advance, help generate positive memories of your work, and provide a gentle reminder that you are available.

- **Newsletters and postcards** — Some voice performers send out a brief newsletter on a regular basis to clients and producers. Newsletters can take the form of anything from a simple postcard to a brief letter (mailed in an envelope or simply folded and stapled). Content usually includes a brief description of recent projects and clients and any other interesting information. Of course, your graphic identity should be a part of the newsletter. The purpose of the newsletter or postcard is to keep your name in front of the talent buyer. Keep your copy short, concise, interesting, and to the point. Too much information will result in the mailing being thrown away without even being read. If you have an e-mail address for your contacts, you might compose a brief update on your activities on a monthly basis. The idea is to keep your name in front of the people who book voice-over talent.

Printed Materials

There are several marketing items you will want to consider having professionally printed, including business cards, envelopes, and stationery. For best results, take your layout to an experienced printer. However, if you are on an extremely tight budget and posses the necessary computer skills, you can use a laser printer or high-quality, color ink-jet printer to create some of your own print materials.

Consult with a printing service about paper stock and ink colors. These people are in the business of making printed materials look good and may be able to offer some valuable suggestions. If you do your own printing, a variety of colors for index or cover stock (for J-Card cassette inserts) can be purchased at specialized paper outlets or office supply stores. There are also many types of paper stock for letterhead, postcards, and business cards. You can even purchase sheets of preformatted business cards, cassette labels, and blank J-Cards, ready to be loaded into your printer. However, be aware that business cards printed on the perforated paper (available from Avery) tend to present a less-than-professional image.

PHOTOS

One of the nice things about voice acting is that your physical appearance is far less important than your ability to act. Unless you also intend to market yourself for on-camera work, it is generally not a good idea to include a photo of yourself in your promotion materials. After all, you are selling yourself as a voice that will help your clients communicate their message.

No matter how good your demo might be, a photograph is going to give the talent buyer a face to go with your voice. It is not uncommon for a performer to be pigeon-holed or stereotyped because of the visual image from a photo included in the demo package. Many agents and producers will associate a face to a name before they associate a voice to a name. Although not intentional, this can be a real disservice for the voice actor. However, depending on how you will be marketing yourself, you may want to include a photo. My recommendation for someone just starting in this business is to keep your image clean and simple without photos, and let your voice do the selling. As you build your reputation and a client list, you will be able to afford the additional expense of adding a photo to your marketing materials.

Of course, there are exceptions to not using photos in your promotion. If you are marketing your talents as a model, an on-camera performer, or if you also do live theater, a photo is a must. As a multifaceted performer, a photo can actually work to your benefit because it will tend to associate your versatility with your name in the mind of the talent buyer.

If you decide to use a photo as part of your packaging, it should be a black and white portrait head shot. Hire a professional photographer to take the picture and make sure the photo reflects your money-voice personality. Your photo is an important part of your image and must be of high quality.

Figure 14-2: J-Card dimensions with sample layout.

THE J-CARD

A *J-Card* is the insert inside a hard-shell cassette box (Figure 14-2). It is the first thing people see when they pick up your demo tape. For a voice actor, there are only three things that need to be on a J-Card: your name, your agent's name, and a phone number (your agent's and/or your own). You can also identify what is on each side, and any union affiliation.

Additional information about your demo's contents can be put on the inside of the J-Card. Imprinting only on the cassette is common (no J-Card), but this makes it impossible to refer to the actor's information while playing and it almost guarantees the tape will get lost on the shelf.

The J-Card for your demo should reflect your individuality and unique personality. It should be eye-catching and enticing. It should say to the recipient. "There's something interesting inside that you should listen to." Don't feel limited to a standard type style on white paper. Colored paper, an interesting font, a catchy USP, and a creative layout can all help your demo stand out from the crowd and get listened to.

Your name should be in two places: on the front panel and on the spine. When you do your layout, make sure your name on the spine is facing toward the short flap. Figure 14-2 shows the proper dimensions for a J-Card and a typical layout. The dotted lines indicate folds for the J-Card to properly fit a hard-shell cassette box.

Printing costs vary widely depending on your city and your artwork, but you can plan on spending approximately $150 to $200 for 1,000 J-Cards with black ink. Color increases the cost quite a bit. If you decide to use color for your J-Cards, you might want to consider having them professionally printed — even if you have a high-quality color printer connected to your computer. Remember, you want to present a professional image of yourself, and your own color printer cannot compare to the quality of a professional print shop.

THE CASSETTE LABEL

Just as your cassette box needs a J-Card to identify your demo, so does the cassette need a label to identify the tape. There are two options for labeling cassettes: (1) imprinting the label information on the cassette itself, and (2) printing a paper label that is attached to the cassette.

Imprinting is done by a machine that prints the label information directly to the cassette shell. It is done as part of the cassette duplication process. Cassette imprinting has a professional look, but you will be limited to only a few possible ink colors, and only one color can be used. Imprinting is usually less expensive than paper labels because of lower manufacturing costs, less labor, and no additional materials, except for some ink. Another disadvantage of cassette imprinting is that the imprint area is a bit smaller than that of a paper label.

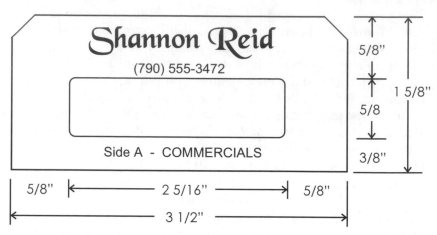

Figure 14-3: Cassette label dimensions with sample layout.

Paper labels are very popular for demo tape labeling probably because they are more versatile (Figure 14-3). Paper labels can use multiple colors and color bleeds to create a very eye-catching tape. With a little creativity, the cassette label and J-Card can be color-coordinated with a matching layout. This makes for a professional look that can attract the attention of someone searching for an interesting demo to listen to. However, imprinted cassettes generally tend to look more professional than paper labels.

CD LABELS

CDs are rapidly becoming the standard for voice-over demos. As with cassette tapes, the way you label your demo CD will reflect your professional image. As with cassettes, you have several options for labeling and packaging your CD demo. Perhaps the most common form of CD packaging is the familiar plastic jewel case. Alternative packaging options include a clamshell case, basic paper or cardboard sleeve, and thin-style jewel case.

Since the purpose of your CD demo is to present your talent in a professional manner so talent buyers will hire you, it is important that they be able to locate your demo quickly when they are in search of the perfect voice. Only the standard jewel case provides easy storage and access to your demo. The thin-style jewel case has no edge labeling, and can be easily lost on a shelf with other demos. The clamshell case and paper and cardboard sleeves all provide no space for anything other than the CD, and are not recommended.

The standard CD jewel case has two areas that can hold labeling and gives you the best possible presentation of your demo. The label for the front clear door is called an *insert*. The label for the back of the jewel case (which has folded portions for the two edge labels) is called a *tray card*. For the "do-it-yourselfer," there are many computer software programs available that include templates for printing both the insert and tray card as well as the round label for the CD. You can find these programs at most office supply stores and many computer retailers. For the most professional results you will probably need to find a graphics designer to do the layout for your CD labels for printing by a full-service print shop.

Your jewel case labels should contain the essential information about your demo: your name, a catchy USP (if you have one), your agent's name, and a contact phone number (yours or your agent's). This information should also be included on both the *insert* and *tray card*. The back should also include the CD contents, especially if there is more than one demo on the CD. You might also include a short bio of yourself or perhaps a brief client list for added credibility. A website and e-mail address might be other items to include, depending on how you are marketing your demo. For example, if you are represented by an agent, it would not be a good idea to put your personal website or e-mail info on the demo CD unless they both direct visitors to your agent. A photo is not recommended, nor is it necessary for a voice-over demo.

Regardless of the outer packaging, the CD itself will need some sort of label. Labeling for the CD comes in two basic forms: a paper label and imprinting on the CD. If you are duplicating your own CDs you will be using paper labels. Some CD duplicators will also use paper labels for short run CD duplication. However, other duplicators will use the more professional-looking process of imprinting your label directly on the CD. Before placing your duplication order, check around for best pricing and labeling format.

Getting Your Demo Out There: Duplication and Distribution

You will need to have your demo tape or CD duplicated and there are a few different ways to approach this. Duplicating tapes yourself is not a good idea. It's a time-consuming process, and will most likely not result in high-quality copies. On the other hand, burning your own CDs may be cost-effective if you have the time to do it and the talent for designing your labels. Of course, you can have your labels professionally printed and ready to insert into the jewel case as you burn each CD. You really want your demo to be of the highest quality possible, so the best approach is to have copies made by a professional duplicator. Look in your Yellow Pages under Recording Services — Sound and Video.

Cassettes and CDs can generally be duplicated in any quantity you need and on relatively short notice. Burning a single CD duplicate is called a *one-off*, and is a perfect copy of the original digital information. Multiple one-offs are made during the process of CD duplication. CD replication is an entirely different process for producing hundreds or thousands of perfect copies. You won't need to worry about CD replication until you are doing mass marketing of your talent on a national level. By the way, the term *burning a CD* comes from the fact that during the recording process, the CD laser literally burns tiny holes (or pits) in the CD media.

There are two basic types of cassette duplication: high-speed and real-time. High-speed duplication may save you a few dollars, but the lower quality may not be worth it. Real-time duplication on high-bias tape is recommended for the highest quality. CD duplication is a digital process that will result in identical copies of your demo whether you do it yourself or have a duplication company do the job. The advantage of having a duplicator do the work is that you may be able to have a much more professional-looking final product. In most cases, your duplicator will be able to help you with different types of labels, or imprinting (on cassettes and CDs), and may even be able to handle J-Card, insert, and tray card printing as well.

You will probably need about 25 copies of your demo to start with, for distribution to the people you contact. I recommend a mix of cassettes and CDs to start with. As you begin marketing your demo, you will quickly discover the most popular media being requested. When you get an agent, he or she will let you know how many copies the agency needs to keep on hand, and in which format. You will also want to keep at least several extras in both formats for your own use.

15

Getting Paid to Play

Acting for voice-over may be one of the best-kept secrets around. You get to be serious, funny, and sometimes downright silly and your voice may be heard by thousands. Working hours can be relatively short, and you get paid for it! In short, you get paid to play!

Well, to be perfectly honest, voice acting can be very challenging at times. There will be moments when you wish you were somewhere else. You will encounter producers and/or directors who do not seem to know what they are doing. You will be faced with cramming :40 of copy into :30 — and the producer will expect it to sound natural and believable. That's show-biz!

Fortunately, the uncomfortable moments are relatively rare, and the majority of voice-over work is enjoyable and often downright fun. If you really enjoy what you do, and become good at it, even challenging sessions can seem like play, although it may appear to be hard work to everyone else. To a large extent, your level of success as a voice actor will depend on your attitude and how you approach your work.

Many successful voice actors do much more than just perform. It is not uncommon to find voice actors wearing many hats — ad-agency rep, copywriter, producer, and performer. As you master voice-acting skills, you may find yourself developing other talents as well. This diversification can provide income from several sources.

Making Money Doing Voice-Over Work

There are only two ways to get paid for voice-over performing: union jobs and nonunion freelance jobs. If you are just starting out, it is a good idea to do as much nonunion work as possible before joining the union. It's sort of like "on-the-job training." You'll have the time and opportunities to get the experience you need and accumulate some tapes of your work.

If you pursue voice-over work as a career, you may eventually join a union, especially if you live in a large market. However, it is not necessary to join a union to become successful. There are many independent voice-over performers in major markets who are earning substantial incomes, even though they are not members of any union. The choice of whether or not to join a union is one that only you can make.

THE UNIONS

This section is not intended to either promote or discourage union membership. However, this is an important decision for anyone pursuing the art of voice acting. If you are just beginning to venture into the world of voice acting, a basic knowledge of the unions is all you need. As you gain experience and do more session work, you may want to consider union membership. Much of the information in this section can be found in the information packet available from your local AFTRA or SAG office[1] or on-line at **www.aftra.com**.

There are two unions that handle voice-over performers: AFTRA (American Federation of Television and Radio Artists) and SAG (Screen Actors Guild). The job of both unions is to ensure proper working conditions, to make sure you are paid a reasonable fee for your work, and to help you get paid in a timely manner and receive health and retirement benefits.

These two performing unions came into being in the early days of film, radio, and later, television. Unscrupulous producers were notorious for not paying performers a decent wage — some not even paying them at all. So, the unions were set up to make sure performers got paid and were treated fairly.

As the unions grew, it was decided that it was unfair for a person just working once or twice a year to have to join the union and pay dues every six months. The result was the Taft-Hartley Act, which made some major changes in labor-management relations. In regards to voice-over, this law gives you (the actor) an opportunity to work under the jurisdiction of the union for 30 consecutive days without having to join AFTRA. You then become "Taft-Hartley'd" and must join the union if you do another union job. What this means is that if you do a lot of freelance work, you can still do a union job without having to join the union or pay union dues. The trick is that the next union job you do, you must join the union, whether it is three days or three years after your first union job. Immediately after the 30-day grace period you have the option to join or not join the union.

One of the advantages of being in the union is that you are more likely to be paid a higher fee, or scale, than if you did the same job as a freelancer — although, in some situations, you can actually negotiate a higher fee as a freelancer. Union *scale* is the fee set by the union for a specific type of work. By the time you reach the level of skill to have been hired for a union job, you will most likely be ready to join the union.

AFTRA is an *open union*. Anyone can join by simply paying the initiation fee and current dues. SAG works a little differently in that you must be hired for a union job in order to join the union, and you must join the union when you are hired for a union job. It used to be that you had to somehow get a union job to join SAG. However, today you can join SAG if you are a paid-up member of AFTRA or another affiliated union for one year, and have worked at least one job as a principal performer during that time in that union's jurisdiction.

AFTRA and SAG cover different types of performing artists and do not duplicate the types of performances covered. Certain types of voice-over work are covered by AFTRA (radio, television, and sound recordings), while other performances are covered by SAG (film and multimedia). For example, if you were hired to work voice-over for a CD-ROM interactive program, you probably would be working a SAG job (although some interactive work is covered by AFTRA). A radio commercial or corporate video would be covered by AFTRA. There are some gray areas, but if you are a member, the union office will help sort out the details. Although separate unions, AFTRA and SAG work closely together and even share office space in many cities.

Both unions have a one-time initiation fee to join and semi-annual dues. Joining AFTRA and SAG requires payment in full of the initiation fee and current dues. The initiation fee and dues charged by AFTRA and SAG vary from city to city, based on market size, and are adjusted regularly. Call the AFTRA or SAG office in your area for current fees. New member information packets, which will answer most of your questions about the unions, can be purchased for a nominal fee. You can also ask the union what the current scale is for the type of work you are doing (commercials, industrial, etc.) and you can find current talent rates for most types of voice-over work on-line at **www.aftra.com**. The staff at the AFTRA and SAG offices are union members and will be happy to answer your questions.

One function of the unions is to protect your rights as a performer. A recording of your performance can be used for many different projects, and unless you are a union member, there is little you can do to protect yourself. A voice-over performance for a radio commercial can also be used in a TV spot or for an industrial video. There are some 400 different AFTRA and SAG agreements for different types of projects, each of which has a different pay scale. Radio and TV commercials are paid based on the market in which they air and how long they will be aired. Industrial videos and CD-ROMs are handled in other ways. Without the union you are potentially at the mercy of the person hiring you, and your voice may end up being used for projects you never agreed to.

A union member working in a nonunion production cannot be protected if the producer refuses to pay, pays late, makes unauthorized use of the performance, or in any other way takes advantage of the performer. Any legal action taken by the performer is at the performer's expense, and the union may actually discipline the member with fines, censure, suspension, or even expulsion.

As a member of AFTRA, you are free to audition for any job, including nonunion jobs. If you are hired for a nonunion job and the employer is not a signatory, the union may contact the producer and have him or her sign a signatory agreement before hiring you. If you are a union member, and are not sure about your employer's status with the union, call the union office in your area.

One way for a union member to work a nonunion job is a waiver called a *One Production Only* (O.P.O.) *Limited Letter of Adherence*. This waiver is good for one job only, and the work you do on that job is considered union work. The advantage is that the nonunion producer agrees to the terms of the union agreement, but does not have to become a union signatory. The O.P.O. contract must be signed before any sessions.

There are producers who, for one reason or another, will not work with union performers. Money is usually not the reason. It may be unrealistic demands from an agent, company policy to work only with nonunion talent, or simply a dislike of the paperwork. To get around the paperwork and other issues, some agents and production companies will work as a union signatory effectively separating a nonunion producer from the union. This is a win-win situation — because the producer does not have to deal directly with the union, the quality of the talent remains high and union performers have the opportunity to work for a greater variety of clients at a fair level of compensation. Some voice-over performers operate their own independent production companies as signatories and essentially hire themselves. It is also possible for you, as a union member, to handle the paperwork, thus making it more attractive for a producer to hire you.

It is generally a good idea to put off joining AFTRA until you have mastered the skills necessary to compete with seasoned union talent. Producers expect a higher level of performance quality and versatility from union performers and it takes time and experience to master those skills. Joining AFTRA too soon not only may be an unwise financial expense, but could have the potential for adversely affecting your voice-acting career.

Here are some reasons to consider union membership when you feel you are ready, or when you begin getting calls for union work:

- Union membership is considered an indicator of professionalism and quality. Producers know they will get what they want in 2 or 3 takes instead of 20.

- Your performance is protected. Union signatories pay residual fees for use of your work beyond the originally contracted period of time. The usual life span of a radio or television commercial is 13 weeks.

- You will also be paid for any time over one hour on first and second auditions, and paid a fee for any additional callbacks.

WORKING FREELANCE

Nonunion, freelance work is an excellent way to get started in the business, and there are lots of advertisers and producers who use nonunion performers. As a nonunion performer, you negotiate your own fee, or take what is offered — the fee will be a one-time-only *buy-out* payment. There are no residuals for nonunion work. The going rate for freelance voice work can be anywhere from $50 to $250 or more depending on the project, the market, your skill level and what you can negotiate. For nonunion work, or work booked without representation, the negotiated terms are between you and the producer.

If a nonunion producer should ask your fee, and you are not sure what to say, the safest thing to do is to quote the current minimum union scale for the type of project you are being asked to do. You can always negotiate a lower fee. If you have an agent, the correct thing to do is to ask the client to contact your agent.

As a freelance voice-over performer, you need to protect yourself from unscrupulous producers (yes, they are still out there). The best way to protect yourself is to use a simple agreement known as a *deal memo*. The format for this can be as simple as a brief letter or an invoice, to something more formal, such as a contract for services. Keep it as simple as possible. A complicated, legal-sounding document might scare off a potentially valuable employer.

A written agreement is your only proof in the event you need to take legal action to collect any money owed to you, or if your performance is used in a manner that you did not agree to. It's a common practice and should be used whenever possible.

Usually, you will want to arrange for payment at the end of a freelance session. If you agree to payment by mail, you should create a simple invoice for your services, or modify your deal memo to reflect the arrangement. When you agree to payment by mail, you might want to have the producer sign your copy of the invoice or deal memo *before* you start the session.

Getting the paperwork out of the way before the work begins is a good way to make sure that the terms of your performance are understood by all parties and that the producer doesn't try to change the agreement after you have done the work. If you are booked early enough, you might want to fax a copy of the agreement to the producer in advance. But you should still plan on having two copies with you when you arrive for the session — the producer is probably not going to bring his copy. Leave one copy for the producer and make sure you have a signed copy before you leave the studio.

The following is an example of a simple deal memo letter. This deal memo includes all the necessary information to confirm the agreement, yet it is presented in a nonthreatening and informal manner.

Mr. Producer
The Big Store
1234 Fifth Ave.
This City, TS   12345

Dear Mr. Producer:

Thank you for booking me to be the voice for The Big Store's new radio commercials. As we discussed on the phone today, I will be doing (4) radio commercials (including tags) for $150 per spot as a buy-out for radio only. If you later decide to use my voice for television spots or other purposes, please call me to arrange for a new session. You have also agreed to provide me with a CD or a DAT recording of the final commercials. I'll call you next week to arrange to pick it up.

I will arrive at Great Sound Recording Studios, 7356 Hillard Ave. on Tuesday the 5th for a 10:00 AM session.

For your records, my Social Security Number is 123-45-6789. Please make your check in the amount of $600.00 payable to My Name so I can pick it up after the session.

I look forward to working with you on the 5th.

Sincerely,

Some larger companies, such as major radio and TV stations, will not accept or sign a performer's deal memo or contract. These, and other reputable businesses, usually have their own procedures for ensuring payment. You will be asked to provide your social security number and sign their document before you can be paid. If you are not offered a copy, you should request one for your own records in case payment is delayed. You usually will not be paid immediately after your session, but will receive a check in the mail within four to six weeks. If you have representation, this detail will be handled by your agent. However, if you are working freelance, some producers and large companies can take advantage of a 30-day payment agreement by basing the payment terms on 30 working days rather than 30 calendar days. This can result in your payment arriving long after you expected it. If you have not received your payment by the agreed upon time, it is up to you to call your client and gently remind them.

Another common problem with working freelance is that you can do a session today and be called back for changes tomorrow, but unless you are redoing the entire spot, the producer may expect you to do the second session for free. Callbacks for changes are common — the callback might be for something as simple as changing a single word or correcting a date to something more elaborate such as redoing a paragraph or two.

When you are called back to fix a problem, the callback session is technically a new recording session. As a union performer, the producer must pay you an additional fee to return to the studio. As a freelance voice actor, it is up to you to negotiate your fee for the second session. This can present an awkward situation, especially if you want to keep a good working relationship with the client. Unless the problem was your fault, you should be paid for the follow-up session. The producer must be made to understand that you are a professional and that your time is valuable. You are taking time away from other activities to help fix their problem and you are entitled to fair compensation. A good producer knows this and the issue of additional compensation is something they will bring up.

Try to find out what needs to be fixed before you begin talking about how much you should be paid to do the new session. If you are redoing most of the copy, you might want to ask for a fee equal to what you charged the first time. If the fix is simple, you might ask for one-half the original session fee. If you are exceptionally generous, and expect to get a lot of work from the client, you might offer to do the new session for free. If you do negotiate a fee for the follow-up session, make sure you get it in writing in the form of an invoice, a deal memo, or a copy of their paperwork.

UNION COMPENSATION

By joining AFTRA and working union jobs, you will be assured of reasonable compensation for your talents and protection from unscrupulous producers and advertisers. Your union-approved agent will normally handle the negotiations for your work and will sometimes negotiate a fee above scale. Regardless of what you are paid, the agent will only receive 10%, and that amount is usually over and above your fee. With AFTRA the "plus-10" (plus 10%) is automatic. With SAG it must be negotiated, or the 10% agent commission will be taken out of your fee. A performer just starting in the business may make less than scale, but the agent's commission will still be added on top of the performer's fee. The signatory also contributes to the union's Health and Retirement (AFTRA) and Pension Welfare Fund (SAG). For many voice-over performers, the health and retirement benefits are the primary advantage of being an AFTRA or SAG member.

Residuals were implemented to guarantee that performers are paid for their work as commercials are broadcast. Each airing is considered a separate performance. Commercials produced by an AFTRA or SAG signatory have a life span of 13 weeks. After the original run, if the advertiser reuses the commercial, a new 13-week life span begins and the performer's fees, agent commission, and union contributions must be paid again. This happens for every period in which the commercial is used. In radio, residuals begin on the date of the first airing. In television, residuals begin on the date of the recording session, or the "use" date.

If an advertiser is not sure whether the company wants to reuse an existing radio or television commercial, a *holding fee* can be paid. This fee, which is the equivalent of the residual fee, will keep your talents exclusive to that advertiser, and is paid for as long as the spot is held. Once the commercial is reused, residual payments are made just as for the original run. If the advertiser decides the spot has lived its life, your residuals end. At that point, you are free to work for a competing advertiser.

Union recording sessions are divided into several fee categories and specific types of work within each category. For radio and television work, the performer's pay varies depending on the type of work and the market size where the product will be aired. The following is a description of the basic AFTRA performance fee categories. Although some of the details may change from time to time, this will give you an idea of the broad range of work available in the world of voice acting. Fees are not included here because they will vary from market to market and are constantly being adjusted.

- **Session Fee.** The session fee applies to all types of union voice-over work and will vary depending on the type of work you are doing. A session fee is paid for each commercial you record. For radio and TV commercials, an equal amount is paid for each 13-week renewal cycle while in *use* (being rebroadcast) or if the spot is on *hold* (not aired).

   Session fees for dubbing, ADR, and looping are based on a performance of five lines or more, and residuals are paid based on each airing of the TV program (network, syndication, cable, or foreign).

   Animation voice work is paid for individual programs or segments over ten minutes in length. Up to three voices may be used per program under one session fee. An additional session fee applies for each additional group of three voices, plus an additional 10% is paid for the third voice in each group of three voices performed.

   For off-camera multimedia, CD-ROM, CDI, and 3DO, a session fee is paid for up to three voices during a 4-hour day for any single interactive platform. Additional voices are paid on a sliding scale and there is a one hour/one voice session fee and an 8-hour day for seven or more voices. Voices used on-line or as a lift to another program are paid 100% of the original session fee.

   Industrial, educational, and other nonbroadcast narrative session fees are based on the time spent in the studio. A day rate applies for sessions that go beyond one day.

- **Wild Spot Fee.** This fee is paid for unlimited use of a spot in as many cities, for any number of airings, and on as many stations as the client desires. The Wild Spot *use rate* is paid based on the number and size of the cities where the spot is airing, usually for a 13-week *use*.

- **Tags.** A *tag* is defined by AFTRA as an incomplete thought or sentence, which signifies a change of name, date, or time. A tag can occur in the body of a radio or television commercial, but is usually found at the end. For radio, each tag is paid a separate fee. For television, tags are paid based on a sliding scale whenever two or more tags are recorded.

- **Demos.** These are "copy tests" for nonair use. An advertiser might produce a demo for a commercial to be used in market research or for testing an advertising concept. If a demo is upgraded for use on radio or television, the appropriate *use fee* applies. Demos are paid a fee somewhat less than a regular session fee.

- **Use Fee.** This fee begins when a commercial airs. Voice-over performers for national television spots earn an additional fee every time the commercial airs. A standard of 13 weeks is considered a normal *time-buy* that dictates residual payments. For radio commercials, the cycle begins on the first airdate of the commercial. For television, the cycle begins on the date of the recording session or use date.

PRODUCT IDENTIFICATION

Radio and television commercials are unique in that they both create an association between the performer and the product. This association is used to tremendous advantage by television advertisers when they use a celebrity spokesperson to promote their product. The viewing audience associates the performer with the product, and the advertiser gains a tremendous amount of credibility.

Product identification can, however, result in some serious conflicts, usually for spots airing in the same market. If one of your spots is a national commercial, it may affect what you can do locally. For example, if you performed the voice-over on a national television commercial for a major furniture store, you may not be able to do voice-over work for a local radio commercial for a competing furniture store. You will need to make sure both spots are not airing in the same market, even though one is for radio and the other is for TV. Conflicts are not a common problem, but they do occur from time to time and usually with union talent. As usual, if you have any questions, the best thing to do is to call your union office.

LIMITED RELEASE PRODUCTIONS

Many projects are never broadcast, such as in-house sales presentations, training tapes, programs intended for commercial sale, and point-of-purchase playback. For most of these projects, performers are paid a one-time-only session fee with no residuals, known as a *buy-out*. These projects usually have no identification of the performer with the product or service in the mind of the audience, and therefore present little possibility of creating any conflict. Buy-out fees are usually based on the type of project and its affect on the performer's marketability in other areas.

Casting Agencies, Talent Agencies, Personal Managers, and Advertising Agencies

The jobs of casting agents, talent agents, and personal managers are often misunderstood by people not in the business or just starting out. They all have different functions in the world of voice-over as discussed in the following sections.

THE CASTING AGENCY OR CASTING DIRECTOR

A casting agency is hired by an advertiser or production company to cast the talent for a particular project. They may also provide scriptwriting and some producing services, such as directing talent. They may even have a small studio where some of the production is done. Casting agent fees normally are charged directly to the client and are in addition to any fees paid for the talent they cast.

Most voice casting agencies have a pool of talent that covers all the various character styles they use. Talent from this pool is used for all projects they work on and they will rarely add a new voice to their pool unless there is an opening or special need. The talent in their pool may be represented by several talent agents. Other casting services will hold open auditions to cast for the projects they are working on.

THE TALENT AGENCY

The talent agent is the direct representative for the performer. Talent agencies are licensed by the state and must include the words "Talent Agent" or "Talent Agency" in any print advertising, along with their address and license number. The talent agent works with advertising agencies, producers, and casting directors to obtain work for the performers they represent.

A talent agent receives a commission of 10% to 25% based on the scale they negotiate for their performer and whether their performer is union or nonunion. For AFTRA work the commission is above and beyond the performer's fee (scale plus 10%). In some cases, the commission may be taken out of the talent fee, especially for freelance work obtained by an agent. For talent agencies to book union talent, they must be franchised by the local AFTRA and SAG unions. Contact the union office in your area for a list of franchised talent agents.

Unfortunately, this is not a perfect world, and there are many unscrupulous agents who will attempt to relieve you of your money. If anyone asks you for money up front to represent you or get you an audition, he or she is trying a scam. Period! The same is true for 1-900 numbers that charge a fee for information on auditions and casting. Most of the information is available elsewhere, either for free or a minimal charge. The best thing to do is find a reputable agent and stay in touch with him or her. Even if you are freelance and must pay your agent a 25% commission, the advantages of representation may well be worth it.

THE PERSONAL MANAGER

A personal manager is hired to manage a performer's career. The personal manager attempts to get the talent agent to send the performer out on auditions, and encourages the agent to go for a higher talent fee. Managers usually work on a commission of up to 20% of the performer's fee, which is taken out before payment to the performer and in addition to the agent's commission. Some managers may work on a retainer. Either way, a manager can be expensive, especially if you are not getting work. Personal managers are fairly rare in the world of voice-over.

HOW ADVERTISING AGENCIES WORK

Advertising agencies work for the companies doing the advertising, coordinating every aspect of an advertising or marketing campaign. They write the scripts, arrange for auditions, arrange for the production, supervise the sessions, handle distribution of tapes to radio and TV stations, purchase air time, and pay all the fees involved in a project.

Ad agencies are reimbursed by their clients (advertisers) for production costs and talent fees. They book airtime at the station's posted rate and receive an agency discount (usually about 15%). They bill their client the station rate and get their commission from the station as a discount. If the advertising agency is an AFTRA or SAG signatory, they will also handle the union fees according to their signatory agreement. Since the ad agency books all airtime, they also handle residual payments, passing these fees on to their clients.

Most advertising agencies work through production companies that subcontract everything needed for the production of a project. Sometimes the production company is actually a radio or TV station that handles the production. In some cases a casting agent might be brought in to handle casting, writing, and production. Some larger ad agencies, with in-house facilities, may work directly with talent agents for casting performers.

Ad agencies can be a good source of work. Your agent should know which agencies use voice-over and will send out your demo accordingly. You can also contact ad agencies directly, especially if you are nonunion. Phone ad agencies and let them know who you are and what you do. You will find many ad agencies work only in print or use only union talent. When you call, ask to speak to the person who books voice-over talent.

The ad agency assigns an account executive (AE) or on-staff agency producer (AP) to handle the account. Sometimes both an AE and AP are involved, but it is usually the AP who knows more about the production than the AE. The AE is more involved with arranging the schedules for airtime purchases. The AP is the person who is generally in charge of selecting talent. The AE is less involved, but often approves the AP's talent choices.

Either the AE or AP may be present during auditions and one or both is almost always present at the session. If the ad agency is producing the spot, they will want to make sure everything goes as planned. If the spot is being produced by a casting agency, someone from that company may also be at the session. Casting agencies are more common for television on-camera productions than for voice-over, but a casting agency rep may be present at an audition or session if their agency is handling the production. And, of course, advertisers are very likely to be at the audition and session to provide their input.

Finding and Working with an Agent

You will probably get your first few voice-over jobs through friends, networking or some other contact you make yourself. As you begin working, your skills will improve, producers will begin to know about you, and your talents will become more valuable. When you reach the point where you are confident with your abilities and want to get more work, it's time to find an agent. Remember, most working pros have an agent. To present yourself with a professional image, you should too. Keep in mind, though, that you don't need an agent to be a successful voice artist. In less than two years of self-promotion, one of my students is now doing lead character voice-over for some major video game producers — and he is only now beginning to submit himself for representation. So, how do you go about finding an agent?

The first thing to understand is that your agent works for you! Some performers just starting out think it's the other way around. Many agents are very selective about who they represent, and even may give the false impression that the performer is working for them. It is their job to get you work by sending you out on auditions and connecting you with producers who will hire you. Once on the audition, it becomes your job to perform to the best of your ability. Your agent only gets paid when you do. Your agent will also send your tape to casting directors, advertising agencies, and production companies. Once a job is booked, the agent negotiates your fee.

As you begin your search, you will find that no two agents are alike. Some handle the paperwork for the union, while others want the client or performer to handle the paperwork. Talent agents in a large market, like Los Angeles, run their businesses totally differently from a talent agent in a smaller market in the Midwest. As with much of the voice-over business, there are no hard-and-fast rules. The most important thing is that you are comfortable with your agent, and that your agent is comfortable with you.

SEARCHING FOR AN AGENT

One way to find an agent in your area is to contact your local AFTRA office. Even if you are not a union member, they will be able to provide you with a list of all franchised agents in your area. Many agents work exclusively with union talent, although some work with both union and nonunion talent.

Blindly sending out your demo tape can be both expensive and unproductive. Most agents and producers will not even open or listen to an unsolicited demo. You will have much better success finding an agent and finding work if you spend some time on the phone first. It may take a little research on your part, but the time you spend talking with agents and producers on the phone will pay off later on. Don't expect to get results on the first call. Marketing your talent is an ongoing process and results often come weeks or months later.

You can start your search for an agent by looking in the Yellow Pages of your local phone book under "Talent Agencies." Yet another way to find an agent is to go to a theatrical bookstore. In Los Angeles, an excellent theatrical bookstore is Samuel French, Inc. (7623 West Sunset Bl., Hollywood, CA, (213) 876-0570), **www.samuelfrench.com**. Check the reference section for a book titled *The Agency Guide*. This book includes a brief description of every franchised agent in the Los Angeles area, how long they have been in business, the types of talent they represent, who to contact at the agency, and a wealth of other information. Samuel French also carries preprinted address labels for the Los Angeles talent agencies, which can save you time later on.

While on your search for an agent, you can also call recording studios, TV stations, and production companies in your area. Ask for the production manager. Let this person know you are available for voice-over work, and that you are looking for an agent. Ask for the names of the talent agencies he or she works with. Let them know your union status. If the company is a union shop (an AFTRA or SAG signatory) and you are nonunion, it will not be able to hire you, but may be able to give you some good leads. Don't forget to let companies you contact know that you have a demo you can send to them. Follow up all phone contacts with a thank you letter.

Many talent agents specialize in certain types of performers, such as modeling, on-camera, voice-over, music recording, theatrical, and so on. You can call the agent's office to find out if they represent voice-over talent and if they are accepting new performers. Keep this initial call brief and to the point, but be sure to get the name of someone to send your demo to if the agency expresses any interest.

Proper phone etiquette is important when calling an agent. Agents are busy people and will appreciate your call more if you are prepared and know what you want. Here's an example of an ineffective call to an agent:

AGENT: Hello, Marvelous Talent Agency.
ACTOR: Hi, uh, is there somebody there I could talk to about doing voice-over?
AGENT: Who's calling?
ACTOR: Oh, yeah. My name is David Dumdum, and I'd like to talk to someone about doing voice-overs.
AGENT: This is a talent agency. We don't do voice-overs, we represent talent.
ACTOR: That's what I mean, I want to talk to somebody about representing me.

This kind of call not only takes a long time to get anywhere, but the so-called actor is not at all clear about what he wants to discuss. Even if this performer had a decent demo tape, the chances of getting representation are poor simply because of a nonbusinesslike presentation. Here's a much better way to approach a call:

AGENT: Hello, Marvelous Talent Agency.
ACTOR: Hi, this is Steven Swell. I'd like to know if your agency represents voice-over talent.
AGENT: Yes we do.
ACTOR: Great! I'd like to speak to someone about the possibility of representation. Are you taking on any new performers?
AGENT: We are always interested in looking at new performers. If you'd like to send us a copy of your demo tape and a résumé, we'll give it a listen and one of our agents will give you a call in a few days.
ACTOR: That's terrific. I'll get a copy to you in today's mail. Who should I send it to?

This performer gets to the point of his call quickly and effectively. He is polite, businesslike, and keeps an upbeat, professional attitude throughout the call. Even though he didn't connect with an agent on this call, he did get a name and there is now a clear process for getting his demo into the agency.

Narrow down the prospective agents in your area. You can immediately eliminate those who represent only models, print, or on-camera talent. The Los Angeles area has more than 250 franchised agents, so in a larger market, you must be very specific in targeting potential agents before sending out your demo and résumé. Smaller markets can have zero to several talent agents, depending on the market size. Representation by a small talent agency in a small market can be an excellent way to break into the business of voice-over.

Prepare a brief and to-the-point cover letter that will accompany your demo. This is not the place to give your life history — keep it to no more than three short paragraphs. This is a business letter intended to introduce you to the agency. Simply state that you are a voice-over performer and that you are interested in discussing the possibilities of representation by the agency.

Each letter you send out should be an original, and should be addressed to the person whose name you learned during your research. The address on the envelope should be either typed or printed by a computer. If you have any other experience that is relevant, you should also prepare a résumé and include it in the package. Most agents require a demo tape and a résumé from any talent they are considering. Here's an example of a good cover letter:

Dear Mr. Agent:

Thank you for your interest in my demo. As I mentioned on the phone, I am a voice actor seeking representation. I have been booking myself as a freelance performer for the past year or so and have had several successful commercials on the air.

My background, training and additional information are on the enclosed résumé. A copy of my current demo tape is also enclosed.

I believe I can be a valuable asset to your agency. I look forward to hearing from you so that we can arrange for a meeting to further discuss representation by your agency.

Sincerely,

This letter is short, to the point, gives some important basic information, and suggests the performer's potential value to the agency. The letter concludes by requesting action from the agency to arrange an interview.

If you call to see if your tape was received, it will often do you no good, and may even irritate some agencies. It will also do you no good to call to get a reaction to your tape — and don't expect to get your demo tape back. Talent agents know you send out demos to other agencies in the area. If they hear something they like, agents will call you. If you are good, the agents will call quickly, simply because they don't want to miss out on representing a good performer by not getting back to you in time.

Don't get discouraged if you are declined for representation. It only means that either the talent agent has a full roster of talent, they may have other voice talent with a similar style as yours, or they may simply feel you are not ready. Don't expect or ask for a critique of your tape. If an agent is kind enough to critique it for you, use that information to learn how to improve your skills and create a better demo. You might even think about taking some more classes. I've known some voice artists who produced 3 or more demos before landing their first agent.

Sooner or later you will find a talent agent who is interested in talking to you. The agent's interest does not mean you have representation. It only means that he or she is interested in learning more about you and your talent.

INTERVIEWING AN AGENT

When you get a positive response, you will be asked to set up an appointment to meet with the agent. This can be quite exciting. What will you wear? How should you act? What will you say?

Handle this interview just as you would an interview for a new job. Dress nicely, and present yourself in a businesslike manner. Be careful to wear clothes that do not make noise. You may be asked to read a script as part of the interview. Enter the office with confidence. Play the part of the successful performer. Create your character for the interview just as you would for a script, and act as if you are a seasoned pro and already represented. Your chances of signing with an agent will be much better if your first impression is one of a skilled and professional performer.

Interview all your prospective agents as thoroughly as possible. Don't be afraid to ask questions at any time. What types of work have they booked in the last month? What is the average scale they get for their performers? What is their commission? Is their commission added to the performer's fee, or taken out? How many voice-over performers do they represent? How long have they been in business? You can even ask whom they represent and for a list of some performers you can contact.

During your meetings with agents, you may talk about everything except your voice-over work. They will want you to be comfortable so that they can get a sense of you as a person, and you will want to get to know them a bit. You need to decide if you like them and have confidence that the agency will be able to get you work.

Take your time. Don't rush to sign up with the first agent who offers to represent you. Also, if any agent gives you the impression that you are working for him or her, you might want to consider eliminating that person from your list. The agent works for you — not the other way around.

When you sign up with a talent agency, normally you will sign a contract for one year. Some agencies request a multi-year agreement, but this can cause problems if your agent doesn't promote you, and you don't get work. It is generally a good idea to renegotiate with your talent agent every year.

A large agency may have many people in the office and represent a large talent pool. A small agency may have only one or two people handling the entire business. It is easy to become a small fish in a big pond if you sign with a large agency. On the other hand, most large talent agencies sign only voice-over performers with years of experience and a solid track record. Your first agent most likely will work for a smaller agency that can give you more attention and help guide your career.

WORKING WITH YOUR AGENT

Once signed, you should keep your agent up to date on your work. Let him or her know how an audition or session went, and keep the agent current with an updated demo as needed. Calling your talent agent once a week should be adequate, unless he or she requests you call more or less frequently. Your agent can also be a very good indicator of the areas you are weak in, and may recommend classes and training if necessary. The key to working with an agent is to stay in touch and ask for advice.

When someone approaches you for work, refer the company or person to your agent, especially if you are a union member. As a professional performer, your job is to perform. Your agent's job is to represent you and negotiate for the highest fee. Although it is generally wise to let your agent handle the negotiations, there may be some situations where it might be best for you to handle the money talk yourself. If you have a good relationship with your agent, and the situation warrants, you might just save the job.

I know one voice actor who auditioned for a CD-ROM game and noticed that the other voice actors who said they had an agent were being passed over for callbacks. After noticing this, he called his agent to discuss the situation. Their mutual decision was that the voice actor would avoid any mention of representation until after he was booked. He handled the negotiations himself and actually managed to get a higher fee than most of the other voice actors booked for the project. Even if you are an accomplished negotiator, your agent is your representative. Generally, it is not a good idea to take things into your own hands until you have talked things over with your agent.

As a career grows, it is common for performers to change agents several times. A word of warning, though: Changing agents can be traumatic. You are likely to have a case of the "guilts" when leaving an agent, especially if the person has done a lot to help promote you and develop your career. When this time comes, it is important to remember the reasons why you must change agents. You may have reached a level of skill that is beyond your agent's ability to market effectively, or you may simply be moving to a new part of the country. On the other hand, you might be changing agents because your current agent is simply not getting you the kinds of jobs you need.

Promoting and Marketing Yourself

Getting voice-over work is a numbers game: The more you hustle, the more contacts you will make. The more contacts you have, the more you will work. The more work you do, the better known you will become. The better known you become, the more people who want to hire you, and you get more work. It's not quite that simple, but you get the idea.

Again, the voice-over business is a numbers game. Having an agent working for you is definitely to your advantage; however, that does not mean you can relax and just wait for the work to come in. It is important for you to network constantly and let your talents be known. Networking with other voice-over performers keeps you up on current trends, and, if you are nonunion, you may get a better idea of the fees other performers are earning. Always keep a few demos and business cards with you and be ready to pitch yourself when the opportunity arises. Remember, always present yourself professionally. It's a subtlety, but maintaining an attitude of professionalism communicates credibility and integrity.

Your agent, if you have one, will be pitching you to ad agencies and other producers in your area. Before embarking on an all-out promotion campaign for yourself, discuss your ideas with your agent. The agent may be able to recommend specific places for you to contact, or ask that you let the agency handle all your promotion. If you agree to let the agent do all the work, set a time limit of perhaps a few months to see how many auditions you are booked for. Working with your agent is the best way to have an organized and consistent promotion campaign for your voice-over talents.

If you do not have an agent, and are not planning to get one in the immediate future, you are on your own. If you expect to get any auditions or any work, you must devise your own promotion and marketing campaign and do all the legwork. This can be a time-consuming process, but you can make it go a bit easier if you take it in stages. As you create your promotion campaign, remember why you are doing it, and keep polishing your acting techniques.

There are many good books on marketing and advertising from which you can gain a tremendous amount of information. You can also learn a great deal by taking an adult education or college extension advertising and marketing course. Not only will you learn some good ways to promote yourself, but you will also learn some of what goes into creating the copy that you work with as a voice-over performer.

When you promote and market yourself, you are your own agent and ad agency. These simply become additional aspects of your business and you must become familiar with them if you are to be successful. There are three basic parts to the promotion of your voice-over work: the demo tape, making contacts, and follow-up.

A BUSINESS PLAN FOR VOICE ACTOR YOU, INC.

You have probably heard the phrase: "If you fail to plan, you are planning to fail." This is as true in voice-over as it is for any other business. You need to have a vision of where you want to be and you need to have some sort of plan as to how you will get there. If either of these is missing, chances are you will not be as successful as you hope to be as quickly as you would like to be. Things will get in your way from time to time, and you will be distracted by just living your life. However, if you have a plan, you will be prepared to work through those obstacles when they jump in front of you.

As an independent professional, you need to look at what you do as a business. With that in mind, my speaking partner, Penny Abshire, adapted a simple business plan that you can use to develop focus on the business side of voice acting. You will wear many "hats" as you operate your business. You are the CEO, CFO, Sales Manager, Marketing Director, Director of Education, and finally, a performer. It is critical to your success that you understand what you are doing for each of your duties and that you have a direction in which you are moving. The "Business Plan for Voice Actor You, Inc." (pages 218-221) is something to which you should really give some serious attention. Don't just skim through this and forget about it. Set aside a few hours to think about how you will plan your career, market yourself, sell your services, learn new skills, and protect your future. Some of the questions will be fairly easy to answer, while others may take a great deal of thought.

The time you spend preparing your plan will be time well spent. Refer to your plan on a regular basis and review it about every six months, or at least once a year. Things do change, and your goals and objectives may change. Your business plan is intended to be a guide to keep you on track for your career.

Should you want to take your business plan further, there are many good computer programs on the market that will help you prepare the ultimate business plan for "Voice Actor You, Inc."

YOUR DEMO

This is your résumé and your product (at least at this point in time). Your demo is what your potential employers (your customers) will use to judge your talent as it applies to their projects. Your demo is your primary marketing tool. You will need a high-quality demo to market your talent and sell your services. Chapter 13, Your Demo Tape, covers this subject in detail.

Business Plan for *Voice Actor You, Inc.*

This simple business plan is designed to help you focus on your business and propel you in the direction you want to go. Give each question some serious thought before answering and review this at least once or twice a year.

1. As **Chief Executive Officer,** what is your vision or plan for a career as a voice actor, which is specifically designed to ensure your growth, profitability, and financial gain?

    _____

    _____

    _____

    What change(s) must take place to bring this plan to fruition?

    _____

    _____

2. What strategic alliances are you forming to ensure the achievement of the vision or plan of **VOICE ACTOR YOU, INC.?**
    a) With whom are you aligning?

    _____

    b) How will this be beneficial?

    _____

3. As **V.P. of Quality Control**, what are you *specifically* doing to ensure and/or improve the quality of the service provided by **VOICE ACTOR YOU, INC.?**

    _____

    _____

    _____

4. As **Chief Financial Officer**, what plans must be made to accommodate the financial and marketing continuity of **VOICE ACTOR YOU, INC.**?
    <u>Current Strategy</u>:   <u>Anticipated Cost</u>:

    _____

    _____

    _____

    a) Alternative sources of revenue?

    _____

    b) Probability of primary revenue continuation over next 5 years?
        Excellent____   Very Good _____   Fair____   Poor____

c) Back-up strategy:

_____

_____

5. As **V.P. of Marketing**, what steps are you taking to seek new or additional target markets for your services?

_____

_____

_____

a) Local markets?

_____

_____

b) Other markets?

_____

_____

_____

6. As **V.P. of Promotions**, what steps are you taking to complete the following:
   a) Seek representation?

_____

_____

   b) Collect materials and prepare for demo tape?

_____

_____

   c) Demo tape/CD production?

_____

_____

   d) Graphic design (logo, U.S.P., business cards, stationery/thank-you cards, etc.)?
      Design _____
      Printing _____

7. As **V.P. of Sales**, what is the projected revenue for year end?
      $_____
   a) Is that enough to cover company expenses? ___yes ___no
   b) What about expected revenue growth for next year?
      $_____

8. As **V.P. of Education**, what is the training plan *specifically designed* to ensure the services offered by **VOICE ACTOR YOU, INC.** are equal to, or exceed, industry standards?

_____

_____

_____

_____

What is the time line for implementation of the training program?

By _____ I will be enrolled in _____ Completion Date: _____

By _____ I will be enrolled in _____ Completion Date: _____

By _____ I will be enrolled in _____ Completion Date: _____

By _____ I will read _____ Completion Date: _____

By _____ I will read _____ Completion Date: _____

By _____ I will read _____ Completion Date: _____

By _____ I will study and/or research _____

_____ Completion Date: _____

By _____ I will study and/or research _____

_____ Completion Date: _____

By _____ I will study and/or research _____

_____ Completion Date: _____

9. As **V.P. of Human Resources**, what will you do to protect the mental, physical, and spiritual health of the primary employee (*you*)?

_____

_____

a) Vacation allotment, family leave, and general mental health maintenance?

_____

_____

b) Maintaining connection with corporate stockholders? (*family*)

_____

_____

c) Your spiritual health?

_____

_____

10. As **Director of Maintenance**, what improvements should be made to improve the visual appearance and physical health of the primary employee (*you*), the product, or service?
   a) What do you plan to do?

   _____

   _____

   _____

   _____

   b) When will you get started - *specifically?*

   _____

11. As **Chief Benefits Officer**, what financial planning is in place to ensure your future financial security (*i.e., retirement*)?
   a) What do you plan to do?

   _____

   _____

   _____

   b) When will you get started?

   _____

   _____

   _____

12. As **Accounting Department Head**, what steps are you taking to maintain accurate invoicing, record keeping, and IRS accountability?

   _____

   _____

   _____

   _____

   _____

   _____

   _____

MAKING CONTACTS

You will need to spend a fair amount of time on the phone, contacting potential talent buyers. Before making any calls, you must be prepared, and know what you want to discuss. Be specific about the type or types of voice-over work you are promoting. If you are trying to get into animation voice-over, you don't want to call ad agencies.

When making your calls, be ready to provide the names of any producers you have worked for and some of the projects you have done. Have some prepared notes to look at so that you don't forget anything important during your call. Needless to say, your stationery should be printed, and your demo tape should be produced and ready to mail out before you begin making calls.

Remember, you need to talk to someone who is directly responsible for hiring voice-over performers for commercials, sales presentations, and in-house video projects. If you do not have a contact name already, tell the receptionist the purpose of your call, and she will most likely direct you to the person you need to speak to, or refer you to someone who might know to whom you should speak. If you can't get connected right away, get a name to ask for when you call back. If you get voice-mail, leave a clear and concise message that includes your phone number at the beginning and end.

Be brief and to the point. State who you are and briefly describe the purpose of your call. Find out if the company uses voice-over performers for any of their advertising, promotional, or marketing needs, and if they use in-house talent, union talent, or freelancers. You probably will find some companies that have not even considered hiring an outside professional for their voice-over needs. Undoubtedly, you will also find many that are not even interested. Remember, this is a numbers game, so don't let yourself get discouraged.

Offer to send a copy of your demo to those who are interested. Follow up by mailing your demo with a letter of introduction. It is amazing how many people never follow up a lead by sending out their promo kit. You will not get any work if you don't follow up.

FOLLOW-UP

You will need the following basic items for follow-up:

- A cover letter on a professional-looking letterhead
- Business cards
- Labels or envelopes capable of holding your print materials and demo
- A voice-over résumé detailing any session work you have done
- Your demo tape

With appropriate computer software and a laser or ink-jet printer, you can design a simple form letter that can be adapted to your needs. If not, most quick-print companies can provide inexpensive letterhead and business cards. Don't use an old dot matrix printer — the quality just does not look professional by today's standards. First impressions are important, and the more professional you look in print, and sound on the phone, the more your prospect is likely to consider you for work.

You will need several different versions of your letter of introduction, depending on whether you are following up from a phone call, or if the follow-up is from a personal meeting.

Keep your letter to no more than three or four short paragraphs in a formal business style. Personalize the heading as you would for any business letter. Thank the person you spoke to for his or her interest, and for the time spent talking to you. Remind them of who you are and what you do. Let the company know how you can help them and how they can contact you. Also, mention in the letter that you are enclosing your demo. The following is an example of a typical follow-up letter:

Mr. Charles Client
5007 Santa Monica Bl.
New Town, CA 80750

Dear Mr. Client:

Thank you for taking the time to speak with me yesterday, and for your interest in my voice-over work.

As I mentioned during our conversation, I am available to help your company as a voice-over performer for in-house training tapes, marketing presentations and radio or television commercial advertising. I am enclosing a list of some recent projects I have done, which have been used successfully for in-house productions and on-air commercials. I am also enclosing a copy of my demo, which runs approximately two minutes. This will give you a good idea of the types of voice-over work I do that can be of benefit to you.

Should you be in need of my services, please feel free to call me anytime at the phone number above. I look forward to working with you soon.

Sincerely,

You might include a copy of your voice-over résumé, provided you have some experience. If you have an agent, include the agent's name and phone number in the letter. In larger markets your agent's number should be the only contact reference. In smaller markets you may want to include your own number as well as your agent's. (NOTE: Your agent's name and phone number should be on your demo, but mention it in the letter as well.)

Two things you *do not* need to mention in your follow-up letter are your union status and fees. Your union status should have been established during your phone call, if that was an issue, and it should be noted on your demo label. Your fees are something to be negotiated either by your agent, or by you, at the time you are booked. If it comes up in a conversation, just tell the person that your agent handles that, or that you cannot quote a rate until you know what you will do. If they insist, quote the current AFTRA scale for the type of work they are asking about. At least that way you will be quoting a rate that will be close to any union talent interviewed later on. If you are booking yourself as nonunion, freelance talent, you might want to let your contact know that your fees are negotiable.

After sending your follow-up letter and demo, wait about a week, then call your contact again to confirm that the package was received. This helps to maintain your professional image and serves to keep your name on their mind. Don't ask if the person has listened to your tape. That's not the purpose of your call. If they bring it up, fine, but you should not mention it.

Before completing your follow-up call, ask if there are any projects coming up in the near future that might take advantage of your talents. If so, and if the company is considering other voice-over talent, be sure to make yourself available for an audition. Phrase your conversation in such a way that it seems like you are offering to help them. This puts you in a position of offering something of greater value to your potential employer, rather than just being someone asking for work.

Once you have established a list of possible employers, you will want to stay in touch with them. Consider sending out a brief note or postcard every six months or so and on holidays. The purpose here is to keep your name in front of the people who book talent. You can even include a list of recent projects, and enclose a reply card, or offer to send a current demo.

Perhaps the only rule for follow-up is to be consistent and persistent. Maintain a professional image, keep your name in front of your prospects, and you will get more work. Here are some ideas for follow-up reminders:

- Thank-you card (after session, meeting, or conversation)
- Holiday and seasonal cards
- Birthdays and anniversaries (if you know them)
- Current projects you have done
- Generic reminder postcard
- Semi-annual one-page newsletter updating your activities
- Special announcement about upcoming projects

REACHING THE PEOPLE WHO BOOK TALENT

Many large companies have in-house production units, while others hire outside production houses and work with agents. There usually will be someone who is in charge of coordinating promotion and advertising that may require the use of voice-over performers.

One problem in reaching people who use voice-over talent is figuring out which companies are likely to need your services. Here are some possibilities:

- **Watch local TV and listen to the radio.** Look for local advertisers who are doing commercials with voice-over talent.

- **Call advertisers and ask who coordinates their radio and TV advertising.** Radio stations frequently use station staff for local commercials, and will not charge their advertisers any talent fees. You need to convince these advertisers why they should pay you to do voice-over work when the radio station does it for free. When talking directly to radio advertisers, you need to put yourself in a class above the radio DJ. Some advertisers like the radio station tie-in by using station talent. Other advertisers may simply prefer to spend as little as possible on advertising. You *can* get work from these people, but it will be an educational process to get them to understand the value of using you instead of doing it themselves or using a DJ for their commercials. You may find that they have other uses for voice-over talent for which you would be far more qualified than a DJ.

- **Contact the local chamber of commerce.** Get a list of the largest companies in your area. Many of them will use voice-over performers and some will do in-house production.

- **Check the local newspapers.** Call advertisers that you think might be likely prospects.

- **Use resource directories.** Many cities have a resource directory or a service bureau that can provide you with specific information about businesses in the area. Or, your chamber of commerce may be able to provide this information.

When you contact a nonbroadcast business that has a production unit, start by asking to talk to the creative, promotion, or marketing department. You should talk to a producer, director, or writer. Don't ask for advertising or sales, or you may be connected to a sales rep. If you ask for the production department, you may end up talking to someone in charge of an assembly line.

Television stations can be a good source for bookings. They use voice-over for all sorts of projects, many of which are never aired. At a TV station, the production department handles most audio and video production. Some TV stations may even have separate production units for commercials, station promotion, and sales and marketing projects. Start by asking to talk to the production manager, an executive producer, or someone in creative services. You may end up talking to someone in the promotion department, because a promotion producer frequently uses more voice-over talent than anyone else at the station.

Recording studios usually will not be a good source for work, simply because most recording studios specialize in music recording. Usually, those that produce a lot of commercials work with performers hired by an ad agency or client. Some studios do a limited amount of producing and writing, and may book their voice-over talent from a pool of performers they work with regularly. In most cities, there are at least one or two studios that specialize in producing radio commercials. Use good judgment when sending your demo to recording studios. You might be wasting your time, but then, you never know from where your next job might appear.

Of course, contacting advertising agencies directly is another good way to reach the person who books talent. At an ad agency, the person you want to reach is the in-house agency producer (AP). Some ad agencies may have several in-house producers, and some agencies have account executives (AE) who work double duty as producers. If there is any doubt, ask to speak to the person who books or approves voice-over talent.

There are no hard-and-fast rules here. As you call around, you just need to try to find the correct contact person. Once you connect, use the basic marketing techniques described in this chapter to promote yourself.

KEEPING RECORDS

As an independent businessperson, whether you have an agent or are working independently, you need to keep complete and accurate records of income and business-related expenses. This is not just for your tax records, but also so you have a way of tracking your career as a professional voice-over performer. Consult a tax advisor as to the best way to set up your recordkeeping or refer to some of the many books on the subject.

You will want to keep records of clients you have worked for, what you did for them, and when you did it. When you get called by a producer you worked for last year, you can avoid undercharging by checking your files to see what your fee was last time. You can also use these records for future promotion and reminder mailings. A simple scheduling book can serve the purpose nicely, or you can even set up a database on your computer. Personal money management computer programs are another excellent way to keep records. Most range in the price from $30 to $75.

Under the current tax code, just about any expense you have that directly relates to your business can be deducted as a business expense. Even if you work another full-time job, you can still deduct expenses that directly relate to your voice-over business. Depending on your situation, you may want to obtain a business license in your city, and eventually may want to incorporate. Setting up a legitimate business entity may have certain tax advantages. A tax advisor can help you with these decisions.

Voice-Acting Expense Report

Use this expense report on a weekly basis to track round-trip mileage for classes, sessions, errands, and other business-related expenses.

WEEK OF: _____

DATE	DESCRIPTION	START MILEAGE	END MILEAGE	MEALS	OTHER	TOTAL

ENTERTAINMENT:

DATE	PERSON(S) ENTERTAINED	BUSINESS PURPOSE	PLACE	TOTAL

NOTE: Attach all receipts to this expense report.

The following are some of the things you should keep records of:

- **Income** — Keep separate account categories for income from all sources, and anything deducted from a paycheck: income received, income taxes deducted, social security taxes deducted, Medicare taxes deducted, state disability taxes deducted, union fees deducted, and any other deductions from a paycheck.

- **Expenses** — The costs of doing business.
  Demo production: Keep track of payments for studio time, costs and materials, duplication, printing, letterhead, business cards, envelopes, postcards, résumés, J-Cards, and CD/cassette labels.
  Telephone: Keep track of phone calls made to prospects or your agent, especially any long-distance charges. You might consider a separate phone line to use exclusively for your business. If you have a cell phone or pager, these costs are deductible as well.
  Transportation: Keep a log book in your car and note the mileage for all travel to and from auditions and sessions. Include parking fees. (see the "Voice-Acting Expense Report" on page 227.)
  Other business expenses: Keep track of postage, office supplies, office equipment, computer equipment, and other supplies. The IRS tends to view computers as personal equipment, rather than business equipment, unless the use is well documented.
  Classes, workshops, and books: Classes and books may be deductible as expenses for continued education and training in your chosen field.
  In-home office: Deducting a portion of your mortgage or rent, and utilities for an in-home office, although legal, may trigger an audit by the IRS. Consult a tax advisor before taking this deduction.

You may want to set up a separate checking account for your voice-over business and perhaps use accounting or money management software on your computer. This can help to keep all the financial aspects of your business in one place. The bottom line is that, as a professional voice actor, you are in business for yourself whether you work another job or not. As a business person it is important that you keep accurate records of your business-related income and expenses.

---

[1] AFTRA-SAG Information Packet, 1997.

16

Auditions

Auditions may seem frustrating and nerve-wracking, but they are an essential part of the voice-over business. Without auditions, it would be very difficult for performers to get exposure to producers and ad agency talent buyers.

If you are a union performer, there are specific rules regarding compensation for auditions and callbacks. I know of some high-priced voice performers who demand $1,000 for an unsupervised and undirected audition. This is an extreme case, but it makes the point that if you are very good and in demand, you will be paid what you are worth.

The Audition Process

The audition process is the most efficient way a producer or advertiser has of choosing the best performer for a project. The process actually begins when the copy for a project is first written. Quite often a script is written with a particular attitude in mind, and sometimes even with a specific performer in mind.

Once a script is written, copies are sent out to talent agents and casting directors. Specific performers or character types may be requested for an audition, but usually the talent agent and casting director select performers from their talent pool that they feel will work best for the project being submitted. If a specific voice actor is requested, the talent agent will attempt to book that performer.

You, the *talent*, are then called and scheduled for an audition. If you are just starting out, chances are you will get the call from one of your contacts, through classes, recommendations, friends, networking, or sending out your demo. You may receive the call several days in advance, the day before, or even the day of an audition.

The audition could be held anywhere. Some ad agencies have a recording booth for handling voice auditions. Sometimes auditions are held at a recording studio, the client's office, a radio or TV station, or even at a hotel conference room.

You will be given a time and location for your audition, but usually you will not be asked when you are available, although you often can arrange a mutually agreeable time. Auditions are generally scheduled over one or two days, every 10 to 20 minutes and, depending on the scope of the project, there may be dozens of performers auditioning for the same roles.

You may or may not be told something about the project, and you may or may not receive the copy ahead of time. I've actually done auditions while on my cell phone after the casting person dictated the copy.

Once scheduled for an audition it is your responsibility to arrive at your scheduled time, prepared to perform. Only if you absolutely cannot make the scheduled appointment should you call the casting agent to let him or her know. The agent may, or may not, be able to reschedule you.

In this day of electronic communication, a variety of other types of auditions are becoming popular. You might receive a script by e-mail or fax with instructions to call a phone number to leave your audition. Or, if you have your own recording equipment, you might be asked to record your audition and e-mail it as an MP3 file or possibly upload your file to a website.

Regardless of the process, a successful audition is critical to getting the work. Always be professional, be prepared, and do your best.

Preparing for Your Audition

You most likely will feel a rush of excitement when you get the call for an audition. That excitement could quickly turn to panic if you let it. Don't let yourself get caught up in the excitement. Focus on the job before you and keep breathing. Approach the audition with a professional commitment to do your best.

WHERE DID THOSE BUTTERFLIES COME FROM?

As soon as you get the call for an audition, you will probably begin to feel butterflies in your stomach. This is a good time for you to practice some relaxation exercises. You need to prepare yourself mentally and physically for the audition. Just the fact that you were called to audition is a good sign, so keep a positive mental attitude. After all, you have been invited to be there.

THE DAY HAS ARRIVED

On the day of the audition, loosen up with some stretches and voice exercises. Dress comfortably, yet professionally. Be careful not to wear clothing or jewelry that will make noise when you are on-mic. If your audition is close to a meal, eat lightly and avoid foods that you know cause problems with your performance.

Plan to arrive at your audition about 15 to 20 minutes before your scheduled time. Make sure you leave enough time to allow for any traffic problems and for parking. If you are not on time, you may arrive too late to read for your part, especially for multiple-voice auditions. When in your car, continue with some warm-up exercises and listen to music that will put you in a positive frame of mind. Sing *loudly* to songs on the radio to loosen up your voice and relax your inhibitions, but don't overdo it.

Always bring several sharpened pencils for making copy notes and changes and a bottle of water. A briefcase containing your supplies, business cards, and several copies of your demo tape can add that extra touch of professionalism to your image. Don't plan on giving tapes or business cards to the people you are auditioning for, unless they request them — they already know who you are. These are for other people you might meet whom you did not expect to be there.

Act as if you know what you are doing, even if this is your first audition. Watch others, follow their lead, and keep a positive attitude.

KEEP TRACK OF THINGS

Under current tax laws, any expenses you incur that directly relate to earning income are deductible, including travel expenses to and from auditions and parking fees, whether or not you get the job. It's a good idea to keep a journal with you so that you can itemize your mileage and expenses. You also may want to keep a record of auditions you are sent on, who the casting people are, where the audition was held, and how you felt about it. You might include names, addresses, and phone numbers to add to your follow-up mailing list.

What to Expect, and What's Expected of You

When you arrive at the audition, you may find several other performers already there. Also, you may find that several auditions are being conducted at the same time, with different copy for a variety of projects. Find the correct audition and pick up your copy. If the audition is for a large account, someone may be "checking-in" the scheduled performers. In most cases, there will simply be a sign-in sheet at the door and a pile of scripts. Once signed in, you are considered available to audition and may be called at any time. If you are early and want to take some time to study the copy, wait a few minutes before signing in.

In many cases, you can expect to see the copy for the first time only after you have arrived at the audition site. However with e-mail, fax, and on-line casting services, it is becoming more and more common for audition scripts to be delivered to the talent ahead of time. On some occasions, for reasons only the producer can understand, you will have to wait until you are *in* the booth before you know what you are doing. I've even heard of auditions where there is no formal script and the performers are simply asked to improvise on lines or props provided by the producer. Fortunately, this is rare, but it does happen.

BE PREPARED TO WAIT

Even if the audition starts on schedule, chances are that within a short time, the producers will be running late. Have something to read or do while you wait for your turn at the mic. Stay relaxed and calm, and keep breathing. This is a good opportunity to get to know some of the other performers who are there, if they are willing to talk to you. Many performers prefer to keep to themselves at an audition in order to stay focused or prepare themselves. Always respect the other people who are auditioning. You may end up working with them some day. If the opportunity arises to get to know someone new, it might be in your best interest to take advantage of it.

Remember, networking can be a valuable tool — it's often not what you know, but who you know that gets you work. Even though these people may be your direct competition, you may make a connection for future jobs that would have otherwise passed you by.

If the copy is for a dialogue spot, you may find another performer willing to *run lines*, or practice the copy with you. This can be an advantage for both of you, even if you do not do the audition together. However, be aware that many performers prefer to keep to themselves before an audition and sometimes interaction with the competition can be distracting.

EXPECT TO BE NERVOUS

When you first enter a studio, you will probably be nervous. This is only natural, but it is something you need to control. You must be able to convert your nervous energy into productive energy for your performance. Focus on your acting rather than on the words in the script. Allow a loving and long, deep down through your body breath to center yourself and focus your vocal awareness. Chapter 4, Taking Care of Your Voice, explains how to do this.

You know you are nervous and so do the casting people. Don't waste time trying to suppress or conceal your nervousness. Breathe through it and focus on converting the nervous energy into positive energy.

EXPECT TO BE TREATED LIKE JUST ANOTHER VOICE

At most auditions, the people there really want you to be the right person for the job. However, if the audition is for a major account in a major city, expect the possibility of being treated rudely by people who just don't care and are trying to rush as many performers through the audition as possible in a limited amount of time. If anything other than this happens, consider yourself lucky.

PREPARE YOURSELF

Once you get your copy, use your waiting time to study it for your character, key words, target audience, and for anything that is unclear — especially words you don't understand or don't know how to pronounce. Try to get a feel for what they are looking for. What attitude? What sort of delivery? Most of the time, your choices will be clear. Sometimes, there will be a character description on the copy, or some notes as to what the producers are after. Note the important words to emphasize, the advertiser and product name, what to punch, where to pull back. Mark your copy in advance so that you will know what you need to do to achieve the delivery you want. Read the copy out loud and time yourself. Don't rehearse the copy silently by merely reading and saying the words in your mind. In order to get an accurate timing and delivery, you must vocalize the copy. Make sure you know how you will deliver the copy in the allotted time.

Be careful not to overanalyze. Read the copy enough times to become familiar with it and know what you are doing, and then put it aside. Overanalyzing can cause you to lose your spontaneity. Decide on the initial choices for your performance, and commit to them. But be prepared to give several different variations. Also, be prepared for the director to ask for something completely opposite of what you came up with.

Auditions for a TV spot usually have a storyboard available. This may be attached to the script, or posted on a wall. It may be legible or it may be a poor copy. A *storyboard* is a series of drawings, similar to a cartoon strip, that describes the visual elements of a TV commercial or film that correspond to the copy. If there is a storyboard for your audition, study it thoroughly. Instead of a storyboard, many TV-commercial scripts have a description of the visuals on the left side of the page with the voice-over copy on the right side. The storyboard or visual description is the best tool you have to gain an understanding of a video or film project. If you only focus on the words in the script, you will be overlooking valuable information that could give you the inspiration you need to create the performance that gets you the job.

MAKE A GOOD FIRST IMPRESSION

Greet the producer or host, introduce yourself, shake hands, be spontaneous, be sincere, and be friendly. If you are auditioning near the end of a long day, the people in the room may not be in the best of moods. You still need to be friendly and professional as long as you are in that room. Remember, first impressions are important. Your first impression of them might not be very good, but you need to make sure that their first impression of you is as good as possible. Your personality and willingness to meet their needs will go a long way.

Answer any questions the casting producer, agency rep, or engineer ask of you. They will show you where the mic is and let you know when they are ready for you to begin. Do not touch any equipment — especially the mic. Let the engineer or someone from the audition staff handle the equipment, unless you are specifically asked to make an adjustment.

There will probably be a music stand near the microphone. Put your copy here. If there is no stand, you will have to hold the copy, which may restrict your performance if you need to move your arms or body. If headphones are available, put them on — this may be the only way you will hear cues and direction from the control room. In some cases, you may be asked to read along with a scratch track for timing purposes and you will need the headphones to hear it.

A *scratch track* is a preliminary version of the commercial that is usually produced as a guide for video editing or as a sample for the client. Sometimes, you might be lucky enough to actually have a music track to work against. This can be very helpful, because music is often used to help set the mood for a commercial and can provide clues about the target audience. If you don't have anything to work against, you might ask the producer or director to give you an idea of the rhythm and pacing for the project.

Before you start, the engineer or producer will ask you for a *level*. This is so the proper record volume can be set on the equipment. When giving a level, read your copy exactly the way you plan to when you perform the audition. Many people make the mistake of just saying their name or counting 1, 2, 3, . . , or speaking in a softer voice than when they read for the audition. It is important to give the engineer an accurate level, or your recording may be distorted. Use this as an opportunity to rehearse your performance.

MAKE THE COPY YOUR OWN

Your best bet for getting a job from an audition is to discover the character in the copy and allow that character to be revealed through your performance. Play with the words that are written! Have fun with it! Put your personal spin on the copy! Do not change words, but rather add your own unique twist to the delivery. Use the skills of voice acting you have mastered to make the copy your own. If they want something else, they will tell you.

Making the copy your own is an acquired acting skill. It may take you a while to find your unique personality traits, but the search will be worthwhile. Chapter 7, The Character in the Copy, discusses this aspect of voice-over work.

DO YOUR BEST

You will have only a few moments to do your best performance. Remember, you are auditioning as a professional, and those holding the audition are expecting a certain level of competency. When asked to begin, start by slating your name, then perform as you have planned. To *slate your name*, clearly give both your first and last name, your agent's name, and the name of the project you are auditioning for. You may be asked to give your slate in a specific order or to add additional information. The following is a typical audition slate:

"Hi, my name is Bobbie Wilson. My agent is Cameron Ross and I'm reading for Toasty Magic Squares."

After your slate, wait a few beats, prepare yourself mentally with a visualization of the scene, and physically with a good diaphragmatic breath, then begin your performance.

You may, or may not, receive direction or coaching from the casting person. If you are given direction, it may be completely different from your interpretation of the copy. You may be asked to give several different reads, and you need to be flexible enough to give the producer what he or she wants, regardless of whether you think it is the right way. You may, or may not, be able to ask questions. It depends entirely on the producer.

Don't let yourself get distracted by the people in the room. There may be anywhere from two or three up to several people in attendance. Focus on your performance and don't worry about the people in the control room.

Many auditions are simply intended to narrow down possible voices and the performance is secondary. The copy used in some auditions may not even be close to the final version, while other auditions work with final copy. Either way, you are expected to perform to the best of your abilities. Do your best interpretation first, and let the producer ask for changes after that. It may be that your interpretation gives the producer an idea he or she had not thought of, which could be the detail that gets you the job.

Offering your thoughts and opinions is usually not a good idea at an audition, but it is something you can do if it feels appropriate. Some producers may be open to suggestions or a different interpretation, while others are totally set in their ways. If the producer is not open to it, he or she will tell you. These are not shy people. At other times, the audition producer will be doing little more than simply giving slate instructions and recording your performance.

The casting person will let you know when they have what they want. Two or three reads of the copy may be all the opportunity you have to do your best work. They may, or may not, play back your audition before you leave. If you do get a playback, this is a good opportunity for you to study your performance. Do not ask if you can do another take unless you honestly believe you can do a much better performance, or unless the producer asks if you can do something different. When you are done, thank them, and then leave. Your audition is over. If you like, take the script with you, unless you are asked to return it.

After the Audition

After an audition, and if this is something you have already discussed with your agent, you can call and let him or her know how it went. Most of the time, though, you will simply wait for a call from your agent. If you do not hear anything within 72 hours, you can safely assume that you did not get the job. As a general rule, agents only call if you get the booking or are requested for a callback.

While you are waiting for that call from your agent, don't allow yourself to become worried about whether or not you will get the job. Write your followup letter and continue doing what you usually do. Remember that voice acting is a numbers game, and that if you don't get this job, there is another opportunity coming just down the road.

WHEN THE ACTORS ARE GONE

At the end of the day, the audition staff takes all the tapes and returns to their office. There, they listen to the tapes and narrow down the candidates. They may choose the voice they want right away, or they may decide to do a second audition — called a *callback* — to further narrow the candidates. The audition producer will contact the appropriate talent agents to book talent for a session or callback, or will call independent performers directly. Voice-over audition callbacks are fairly rare, but when they occur, they are usually for a major regional or national account.

If you are scheduled for a callback, you may find there is less pressure and the attitude of the people involved may have changed a bit. At a callback, the producer may say that they really liked what you did on take 3 of the first audition. Chances are, unless they have a tape to play for you, or unless you have an exceptionally good memory, you will not remember what you did on take 3, or any of the takes for that matter. When this happens, all you can do is go for your best interpretation of the copy (which probably changed since the original audition), and use any direction from the producer to guide you.

The simple fact that you are called back for a second audition shows that there is something about your performance that the producer likes. Try to find out what it was that got you the callback. Do whatever you can to stay on the producer's good side and make friends. If for some reason you do not get this job, the producer may remember you next week or next month when another voice-over performer is needed for another project.

After the callback, the audition staff once again takes their collection of tapes (much smaller this time), and returns to their office. This cycle may be repeated several times until the producer or client is satisfied that the right voice is chosen.

BE GOOD TO YOURSELF

You've done a good job! You have survived your audition. Now you deserve a treat. Take yourself out to lunch, buy that hot new CD you've been wanting, or simply do something nice for yourself. It doesn't really matter what you do — just do something special.

When you left the audition, you probably came up with dozens of things you could have done differently. You might even feel like going to your car, winding up the windows, and screaming real loud. Second-guessing yourself is self-defeating and counterproductive. Instead of beating yourself up with negatives, do something positive and be good to yourself.

Demos

Not all auditions are held for the purpose of casting a final project. In some cases, you will be auditioning for a demo. *Demos* are produced by ad agencies as potential commercials that they use to sell an idea to their client. The commercial may never actually be produced for on-air use. Often, the entire concept of an advertising campaign is changed between the time a demo is produced and production of the final spot.

You may be told that the audition is for a demo at the time you are there, or at some time after your audition. Either way, the recording from your audition normally will not be the recording used for the demo. If it is to be used for the demo, you will be compensated for your time at the audition.

AFTRA has a separate rate for demo sessions, which is different from their commercial scale. Demos are usually paid for on a one-time-only fee basis. However, a demo can be upgraded to a commercial if the client decides to use it. In this case, your fee would also be upgraded to the commercial rate. Independent voice actors need to negotiate their own fee for a demo, or let their agent handle it.

Audition Dos, Don'ts, and Common Courtesies

Here are some tips for making your audition an enjoyable and productive experience:

- Do arrange your schedule so that you that you can attend the audition
- Do arrive early — at least 15 to 20 minutes before your audition time
- Do call to let the casting agent know if you absolutely can't make the audition
- Do be prepared to do your best
- Do be spontaneous, sincere, friendly, and willing to adapt
- Do redirect your nervous energy into constructive performance energy — keep breathing and focus on performing, not on the words in the script
- Do stay relaxed and confident of your abilities — remember, you were invited to be there
- Do act as if you know what you are doing — don't let on if this is your first audition
- Do make the copy your own — add your personality and individual "spin" to the copy
- Do keep track of your expenses — the IRS requires detailed records
- Do thank the casting agent or producer when you leave
- Do leave a current demo tape — ask the casting person first if it would be appropriate for you to leave a current demo
- Do make a note of names and addresses and add them to your mailing list for holiday cards, reminders, and follow-up
- Do leave quickly and quietly — when your job is done, make a professional exit
- Do treat yourself to something special — it's a gift from you to you for a job well done — whether you get the job or not

- Do your best — remember that the casting person wants you to succeed and wants you to be the person they are looking for
- Don't touch any equipment (anything on the copy stand is OK); let the engineer make adjustments to the microphone
- Don't ever argue with the casting people about their direction or doing the performance the way they want
- Don't be afraid to let them know if you make a mistake — you can start over
- Don't ask the casting agent when they will know who is hired — they won't be able to tell you anyway
- Don't ask if you can call later — they will call you or your agent if they want you for the job or a callback
- Don't ask for advice or a critique of your work — this is not the time or place
- Don't ask if you can audition again — this is your only chance

The Voice-Acting Survival Kit

As you begin to work voice-over sessions you will find there are certain things you will want to always have with you. Following is a list of items to keep in your "survival kit."

- Water
- Pencil (at least one; mechanical pencils are good because they are always sharp)
- White-out pen
- Small photos (of just one person; to help you with conversational delivery)
- Throat lozenges
- Chap stick or lip balm (to treat dry lips)
- A green apple (to reduce mouth noise)
- A wine bottle cork (for the articulation warm-up cork exercise)
- Business cards
- Demo tapes or CDs
- Blank invoice or agreement
- Other items you'll think of later

You might also want to make a copy of the Quick Reference checklists on page 240. Keep this with you and review it before an audition or session. In no time at all, the tips on this Quick Reference will become second nature.

The Art of Voice Acting

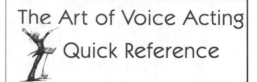

Quick Reference

orchestrate your message!

- ✓ A.B.C.'s of Connecting:
  - Who is the **A**udience?
  - What is the **B**ack story?
  - Who/What is my **C**haracter?
  - What are my **D**esires?
- ✓ Remember to M.O.V.E.®
  - **M**ovement **O**rchestrates
  - **V**ocal **E**xpression
- ✓ Use your face to express emotion
  ☺☻☹☺☺☺☺☻☺☻☺☻☺
- ✓ Commit to your choices
- ✓ Rehearse your lines in character
- ✓ Tell the story to just **one person**
- ✓ Be honest and real in your delivery
- ✓ Get off the page & into the white
- ✓ Use variety to keep it interesting
- ✓ Use sense memory & visualization
- ✓ Emphasize different words to achieve a stronger delivery
- ✓ Articulate to "cut through"
- ✓ Use the "4" & "2" shortcut (#4 for "for," #2 for "to" and "too")

www.voiceacting.com
© 2001 James R. Alburger

The Art of Voice Acting

Quick Reference

Voiceover Session Dos & Don'ts:

- ▲ **Do** confirm date, time, and location (get directions if necessary).
- ▲ **Do** get a contact name & number.
- ▲ **Do** bring water, pencil, small photo, lozenges, white-out pen, business cards, marked script, and your demo.
- ▲ **Do** warm up before a session with favorite tongue twisters & exercises.
- ▲ **Do** dress comfortably.
- ▽ **Don't** wear noisy clothing or jewelry.
- ▽ **Don't** drink coffee, cold drinks, or alcohol – they all affect your voice.
- ▽ **Don't** eat a big meal or dairy products before a session.
- ▲ **Do** leave your inhibitions in the car.
- ▲ **Do** strive to find and reach the producer's vision.
- ▽ **Don't** force or injure your voice.
- ▲ **Do** ask questions if you're not sure.
- ▲ **Do** be cooperative and professional.
- ▽ **Don't** argue with the producer.
- ▲ **Do** your best – then let it go.
- ▲ **Do** complete talent vouchers.
- ▲ **Do** thank everyone at the session.
- ▲ **Do** follow up with a thank-you note.

www.voiceacting.com
© 2001 James R. Alburger

Figure 16-1: The Art of Voice Acting Quick Reference Card

17

You're Hired!
The Session

The recording session is where your voice is recorded and all the pieces of the puzzle are put together to create a final commercial or soundtrack. Besides your voice, the project may include music, sound effects, other voices, recordings of interviews, or other "sound bites," and digitally processed audio. It is the job of the recording engineer to assemble these various puzzle pieces to form the *picture* originally created in the mind of the producer or writer. It can be a challenging process.

A Journey Through the Creative Process

Much of the creative process involves a lot of technology and a high level of creativity from the engineer. As a voice-over performer, there is only a small portion of the recording process that involves you. To give you a better idea of how your performance fits within the whole process, the entire sequence of a project will be explained in this chapter. But first, let's review the creative process and some things you should know about studio etiquette.

THE IDEA

It all begins with an idea! That idea is put into words on a script, which may go through many revisions and changes. At some point during the script's development, thoughts turn to casting the roles in the script. In some cases, a role may be written with a specific performer in mind, but this is usually the exception to the rule. To cast the various roles, the

241

producers listen to demo tapes and hold auditions. The audition process (Chapter 16) narrows the playing field to select the most appropriate voice talent for the project at hand. If your voice is right for the part, and your demo tape or audition was heard by the right person, you could be hired for a role.

IT'S YOU THEY WANT

When you are booked for a studio session, it is because the producer has chosen your voice over all the others that were auditioned. There is something about *you* that the producer believes is right for his or her project. It could be the way you interpret the copy; it could be a quality in your voice; it could be anything. You are the chosen one! You've got the job! Congratulations!

You probably got the call from your agent, or from the client directly if you are working as an independent performer. Either way, you need to make sure you know what your *call time* is for the recording session. You also need to know where your session will be done. If you don't know where the recording studio, radio station, TV station, or ad agency is, get directions.

TIME IS MONEY

Be absolutely certain you arrive *before* your scheduled session time. It is much better to be early and have to wait a few minutes than for you to be late and hold up the session. Recording studios book by the hour, and they are not cheap. Basic voice-over session time can be in the range of $100 an hour or more, depending on the studio. You do not want to be the person responsible for costing the client more money than necessary.

Producing commercials, or any type of audio soundtrack, can be an expensive proposition. So that you are aware of what a producer is dealing with, here are some of the many costs involved in a typical radio or TV commercial:

- Voice-over talent fee (union scale plus residuals)
- Union health, welfare, and pension fees (added on top of the talent fee and agent commission)
- Talent agent commission (10% of talent fee for each performer)
- Casting director fees (if one is hired for the project)
- Writing fees (if an outside copywriter is employed)
- Producing fees (if an outside producer is employed)
- Recording studio time (at an hourly rate — the studio rate could change from the voice-over session to music session and post-production)

- Cost of recording materials (media and tape stock)
- Music licensing fees (charges for licensing the performance of music used)
- Original music fees (composer, musicians, and related union fees)
- Other union charges (meal penalties, overtime, etc.)
- Cartage fees (costs related to transporting musical instruments)
- Duplication fees (cost of making copies of the finished product)
- Distribution fees (cost of distributing copies to radio and TV stations or other end users of the project)
- Airtime (cost of time on the radio or TV station to run the commercial)
- Other fees related to the project

These charges add up quickly and are usually paid by the advertiser. Obviously the advertiser wants to keep expenses to a minimum. Clients are very unhappy when a performer shows up late with an attitude of not caring about how he or she affected the session — or worse, not caring about giving their best performance.

Time is also of the essence when you are in the studio. Things can happen very fast once you are on-mic and recording begins. You need to be able to deliver your best performance within a few takes. If the producer or director gives you instructions, you need to understand them quickly and adapt your delivery as needed.

If you are working a dialogue script with a performer you have never met before, you both need to be able to give a performance that creates the illusion that your separate characters are spontaneous and natural. This is where your character analysis and acting skills really come into play.

WORKING WITH PRODUCERS, DIRECTORS, WRITERS, AND CLIENTS

A voice-actor friend of mine once described a producer/director as "headphones with an attitude." Regardless of the producer's attitude, you need to be able to perform effectively. You must be able to adapt your character and delivery to give the producer what he or she asks for. And you need to be able to do this quickly with an attitude of cooperation.

It is common for a producer, after doing many takes, to decide to go back to the kind of read you did at the beginning. You need to be able to do it. It is also common for a producer to focus on getting exactly the right inflection for a single word in the copy. You might do 15 or 20 takes on just one sentence, and then a producer will change his mind and you will have to start all over.

Every producer has a unique technique for directing talent. You must not let a producer frustrate you. Occasionally, you will work for a producer or writer who is incredibly demanding, or simply does not know what he or she wants. When working for this type of person, just do your best and when you are done, leave quietly and politely. When you are alone in your car, driving down the freeway with the windows rolled up, you can scream as loud as you like.

There are some producers who operate on a principle of never accepting anything the first time — no matter how good it might be. Your first take might be wonderful — hitting all the key words, getting just the right inflection. However, the producer may have you do another 10 takes, looking for something better. When all is said and done, that first good take may be the one used in the final project.

WHO ARE THOSE PEOPLE?

Some sessions may be crowded with many people deeply involved with the project you are working on. Of course, the studio engineer will be present, and there will usually be someone who is the obvious producer/ director. But the client or storeowner may also be there, as well as his wife, their best friend, the agency rep from their ad agency, the person who wrote the copy, and maybe even an account executive from a radio or TV station. All these people have an opinion about what you are doing, and may want to offer suggestions about what you can do to improve your performance. It's a nice thought, but too many directors will make you crazy.

You may actually find yourself getting direction from more than one person. One of the obvious problems with this is that some of the direction from one person may directly conflict with a direction from another. As a performer, you must choose one person in the control room to whom you will listen for direction and coaching. Most of the time this should be the producer handling the session. However, if it is obvious that the producer cannot control the session, you might choose someone else, if you feel the person is a better director.

Once you have made your choice, you must stick with that person for the duration of the session. Changing directors in mid-session will only make your performance more difficult. You don't need to come right out and make a statement as to who you want to direct the session. Simply focus your attention on the person you picked and direct your questions and thoughts to only that person, mentioning him or her by name when necessary.

When someone else presses the talkback button and gives you some direction, you need to bring control back to the person you chose. Allow the interruption to happen, and then refer to your chosen director for confirmation or further comment. After this happens a few times, the would-be director will usually get the hint and let the person in charge handle the session. Future comments will then be routed to you via your chosen producer or director — as they should be.

SESSION DELAYS

Studio time is a valuable commodity. The producer will want your best performance as quickly as possible. In reality, it may take a while to get it. A voice-over session for a :60 radio commercial can take as little as 5 minutes to as much as an hour or longer. A long session for a seemingly simple spot can be the result of one or more of the following factors:

- There may be several voices speaking (dialogue or multiple-voice copy), and it may take some time to get the characters right.

- Microphone placement may need to be adjusted or the microphone may need to be changed.

- The copy may require major changes or rewrites during the course of the session.

- A session being done to a video playback may require numerous takes to get the timing right.

- There may be technical problems with the equipment.

- The voice tracks may need to be inserted into a rough spot for client approval before the performers can be released.

- The session may be a *phone patch* (client is not in the studio, but is listening on a telephone hooked up to the recording console), and he or she may request changes that need to be relayed through the producer or engineer.

- The producer, director, or client may not know what he or she really wants.

- There may be several would-be directors trying to offer their ideas, creating unnecessary delays.

- The voice-over performer may lack experience, and may not be able to give the producer the desired reading without extensive directing.

- An earlier session may have run overtime, causing all subsequent sessions to start late.

Regardless of how long you are in the studio, you are an employee of the ad agency, producer, or client. Present yourself professionally and remain calm. Above all, do your best to enjoy the experience. Keep breathing, stay relaxed, and keep a positive attitude.

Types of Voice-Over Sessions

There are many different types of voice-over projects for which you could be hired. The process in the studio will be basically the same for each, but you should still know the differences between them. For simplification, the various types of sessions are discussed here in terms of a radio or TV commercial.

DEMOS

Demos were discussed briefly in Chapter 16 as they applied to auditions. If you are booked to do a demo session, you can expect to be working on a project that has not yet been sold to the client. It will be a demonstration of what the ad agency is recommending. The client may or may not like it. The ad agency may or may not get the account. A demo is a commercial on spec (speculation).

Mel Blanc, one of the great animation character voices of the 1950s and 1960s, once gave the following definition of working on spec:

> "Working on spec is doing something now for free, on the promise you will be paid more than you are worth later on. Spec is also a small piece of dirt!" (From *Visual Radio,* 1972, So. California Broadcasters Association)

Advertising agencies, television stations, and radio stations often do projects on spec when they are attempting to get an advertiser's business. The potential profit from a successful advertising campaign far outweighs the cost of producing a spec (or demo) commercial — provided the agency lands the account.

Demos will not air (unless they are upgraded by the client), and are paid at a lower scale than regular commercials. In some cases, the demo serves as an audition tape for the ad agency. They may have several different voice-over performers booked to do the demo session. It is not technically an audition, since completed spots will be produced. Instead, demos are intended to give the advertiser a choice of performers for the final commercial. If the demo is simply upgraded, your agent will be contacted and you will be paid an additional fee. If a separate session is booked, you will be contacted, scheduled, and paid an additional fee.

SCRATCH TRACKS

A scratch track is similar to a demo in the sense that it is the preliminary form of a commercial. The major difference is that a scratch track is used as a reference for a commercial that is already in the process of being produced. Scratch tracks are most often used for TV commercials and are produced to give the video editor a reference audio track to edit to. They are often produced with nonprofessional talent doing the voice (often the producer or writer), and the music, sound effects, and other elements of the spot may or may not be in their final placement.

As a voice-over performer, you may be providing the original voice for a scratch track that is being built, or you may be providing the final voice that replaces an earlier recorded voice used on an already-assembled scratch track. Either way, your job will be to perform as accurately as possible to the existing timing for the scratch track. To do this, the engineer will sometimes play the scratch track back to you as you read your lines. This is a process very similar to ADR (Automated Dialogue Replacement) used in the film industry, except that you are working to a previous audio track instead of lip-syncing to a film or video playback.

If the scratch track is on multitrack tape or a digital workstation, the engineer may play back the spot without the scratch voice-over. You will hear the music and effects cues for your timing, but you won't have to compete with the original voice-over. If you are doing the scratch voice, there may only be some elements of the final spot in place, so some of your timing might be guesswork on your part. If you are doing the final voice, the engineer will replace the original voice with your performance when the final audio track is completed.

In a video editing session, the producer may decide that portions of the audio need to be moved or *slid*. This might require a new track to be edited. It might be possible for the audio engineer to re-edit the spot using your original recording, or you may need to be called back in for a regular session. Just as for a demo session, your performance for a scratch track may be good enough for use in the final spot. You or your agent will know if the scratch track session is for a demo or a final commercial, and you will be paid accordingly. Of course, if you are doing the job freelance, your fee is whatever you are able to negotiate with the client.

REGULAR SESSION

This is a session for production of a final commercial. Many engineers refer to *regular sessions,* to differentiate them from demos, tags, scratch tracks and so on.

The only difference between this type of session and all the others is that it is for a complete commercial. You may do several reads of the copy in its entirety, or you may do the spot in pieces. Either way, when your voice tracks are recorded, the engineer will use the best parts of your performance to build the finished commercial.

DUBBING OR LOOPING SESSIONS

The term *looping* comes from the early days of film when a section of film was literally made into a loop and played back continuously. With each pass of the film, the performer duplicates his or her performance for a clean recording.

For some sessions, you may be reading your lines as you watch a video or film playback. The purpose of having the video playback is to enable you to hit very specific positions within the copy. The video will also give you a good idea of the attitude you should have as you deliver your lines.

A *dubbing session* is one at which you are replacing an existing audio track (similar to a scratch track session). For example, you might be hired to do the English version of a commercial that originated in France.

One form of a looping session is when you are replacing the voice of an on-camera performer. Looping sessions are also known in the business as *ADR* sessions or *dialogue replacement* sessions (the "A" stands for "automated" and refers to how the session is handled technically from an engineering standpoint). When possible, dialogue replacement is done by the original on-camera performer. However, in many cases (as with TV versions of movies or a foreign commercial), the original performer's voice may be replaced with yours.

A second type of looping session occurs when a small section of voice-over copy is repeatedly recorded in an attempt to achieve the perfect performance. This is also referred to as "over-dubbing."

Voice-over recording sessions can be for a variety of projects, including commercials for radio and TV, promos, tags, sales presentations, film narration, corporate or industrial video narration, animation, interactive CD-ROM, books on tape, and many others.

COMMERCIALS AND PROMOS

These are basically the same thing. The difference is that commercials typically sell a product or service and air on several stations, while promos sell a radio or TV station's programming and air only on that station. Promos can be of any length and include everything from the short "coming up next" tracks you hear over a TV show's credits, station IDs, 30-second spots for a specific show and longer image promos.

Commercials can stay current for years, while promos usually have a limited life span ranging from one day to several weeks. TV programming changes frequently and even if the program time slot stays the same, TV stations are constantly updating their visual graphics. Most of the time, changes in a program's time slot, or a station's image, will require production of new promos.

TAGS

Tags are used on both commercials and promos and are often referred to as the "sell." A tag is the last few seconds of the spot during which the final call for action is made. AFTRA defines a *tag* as an incomplete thought or sentence, which signifies a change of name, date, or time. For TV promos, it usually begins with a call to action, such as "don't miss," "watch," or "tonight at . . . ," followed by the name of the program, the time, and the station's call letters. The exact order of these elements may differ, but the general information is the same. A typical TV promo tag might be:

"Watch Jeopardy weeknights at 7 here on NBC 7-39."

Commercial tags are similar, except they tell the audience where to buy the product or how to contact the advertiser.

"Order your Super Chair today. Only $19.95. Call 1-800-555-7423."

If you are booked for a commercial tag session, you may do dozens of variations. Each tag may have a different address, phone number, or something unique. Each version you read must fit within a set period of time. AFTRA considers each tag to be a different commercial, so if you are doing a union session you are paid the tag rate for as many tags as you do, as well as the one-time session fee.

Types of Studio Setups and Script Formats

Recording sessions come in all shapes and sizes and with a variety of format styles. The following sections describe some of the setups you are likely to experience.

SINGLE SESSION

At a *single session*, you are the only person in the studio. There will be only one microphone, a music stand, a stool, and a pair of headsets. Many recording studios also have monitor speakers in the studio, so you can choose to wear the headset or not. Let the engineer make all adjustments to the mic. You can adjust the stool and music stand to your comfort.

For a single read, you are the only voice that is being recorded at the session. This does not necessarily mean that you are the only voice that will appear in the final project. Other performers, to be recorded at another time, may be scheduled for different sections of the project, or for the tag.

GROUP SESSION

Multiple-voice sessions are often the most fun of all types of sessions simply because of the ensemble. Dialogue copy is usually more creative than single-voice copy, and dialogue scripts frequently have a comedic premise where there needs to be an interaction between characters. In some cases, the principal actors and the tag announcer may all be in the studio at the same time — it can get cozy. Each performer normally has his or her own mic, music stand, and headset. Depending on the studio, two performers may be set up facing each other, working off the same mic, or on separate mics in different areas of the studio.

A group session is like a small play, only without sets. You will have an opportunity to rehearse your lines and get into character. Once the engineer starts recording, you're "on"! The producer or director may give direction to only one performer in the group, or to the group as a whole.

SCRIPT FORMATS

There are a variety of script formats used in the business of voice-over. Radio, television, film, multimedia, and corporate scripts all have slight differences. Regardless of the format, all scripts include the words you will be delivering and important clues you can use to uncover the three building blocks of any effective performance:

- Who is the audience?
- Who is your character?
- Why is your character speaking these words at this moment in time?

The scripts in Chapters 9 through 12 will give you a good idea of some of the script formats you can expect to see in the studio.

SESSION BASICS

All studio sessions are handled the same. Ideally, there are two soundproof rooms — the control room and the studio. These are separated by a wall of double glass and a sound lock with doors between the rooms. The studio is where you will be when you perform. Unless you are doing a group session, you will be the only person in the studio or "booth." In some cases, especially for sessions involving young children, the producer may also be in the studio. On the other end of the scale, there are many personal project studios that do not have ideal acoustics and offer much less than ideal recording conditions. One producer I know actually has his studio set up at the foot of his bed in his studio apartment.

Some sessions are done with a *phone patch*. For these sessions, some or all of the people involved with the session, including the recording engineer, may be hooked up by telephone. An engineer and performer may be the only people at the studio. Phone-patch sessions are also becoming increasingly popular with high-quality national voice-over talent.

With a phone patch, these performers can work from a studio at their home, and connect with producers around the world. They simply record their tracks to their computer or directly to digital media as the producer gives direction over the phone. The completed recording is then converted to a high-quality file in the format requested by the producer (usually a WAV, AIF, or an MP3 file), and delivered to the client via e-mail, FTP upload to a website, or shipped out that day for next day delivery.

Another variation of a phone-patch session uses ISDN (Integrated Services Digital Network) telephone lines. *ISDN* phone lines are special high-quality lines for transferring digital information in real-time. A studio with ISDN capabilities can connect with a performer on the other side of the world, and treat the session just as if the performer was in the studio, on the other side of the glass.

The producer will do most of the directing for the session. After all, it is his or her vision that you are attempting to create — and it is this person who is ultimately responsible for the project. If you are at a studio that does a lot of commercial production, the engineer may also be giving you direction. If you are on a phone patch, you may receive direction from the person on the phone, either relayed through the engineer or through your headset.

The Session: Step-by-Step

Let's walk through a session from the moment you enter the studio, until you walk out the door. Much of this is review from other parts of this book; however, this will give you a complete picture of a studio session. After reading this section, you will know what to expect and should be able to act as if you have done it all before. Although the studio session process is very consistent, there are many variables that may result in variations on the following scenario. Just "go with the flow" and you will be fine.

Once you enter the studio lobby, your first contact will be the receptionist. Introduce yourself, and tell her which session you are attending. If the studio is in an office building and you paid to park in the building's parking structure, don't forget to ask if the studio validates.

The receptionist will let the producer know you are there. You might be given your copy at this time, or you might have to wait until the producer comes out of the control room. Depending on how the session is going, you may have to wait awhile in the lobby, but it will be much shorter than the wait you had at the audition.

The producer or engineer will come out to get you when they are ready, or the receptionist will let you know that you can go back to the control room. Or, someone might come out to let you know that the session is running late. There are many things that can put a session behind schedule. Remember, this is a hurry-up-and-wait kind of business.

When you enter the control room, introduce yourself to the producer, the engineer, and anyone else in the room you have not yet met. You can be certain that anyone in the control room is important, so be friendly and polite.

If you did not receive the copy earlier, it will be given to you here. This is your opportunity to do a quick "woodshed," or script analysis, set your character and ask any questions you might have about the copy. Get as much information as you need now, because once you are in the studio, you will be expected to perform. Get a good idea of the target audience and correct pronunciation of the product's and client's names. Make notes as to attitude, mood, and key words. Mark your script to map your performance so that you will know what you are doing when you are in the studio. The producer or engineer may want you to read through the copy while in the control room for timing or to go over key points. When the engineer is ready, you will be escorted to the studio.

In the studio, you will usually find a music stand, a stool, and the microphone. Practice good studio etiquette and let the engineer handle any adjustments to the mic. Feel free to adjust the music stand to your comfort. If a stool is there, it is for your convenience, and you may choose not to use it if you feel more comfortable standing. Some studios will give you the option of performing without having to wear headphones, but for most you will need to wear them to hear the director. Wait until the engineer indicates that you can put your headphones on.

Occasionally, at the start of a session, the engineer records a reference tone for approximately 30 seconds. The reference tone is for setting playback levels later on, and can be very loud and annoying when listening on headphones. Most studios provide a volume control for your headphones that you can adjust, while others must adjust the volume from the control room.

If you wear a pager or carry a cellular phone, make sure they are on vibrate or turned off while you are in the studio. Better yet, leave them in the control room. The beeping or ringing might interrupt an otherwise perfect take and answering a call is disruptive to the session.

The microphone may have a *pop stopper* in front of it, or it may be covered with a foam *wind screen*. The purpose of both of these devices is to minimize popping sounds caused by your breath hitting the microphone. Popping can be a problem with words containing plosives such as "P," "B," "K," and "G." If the wind screen needs to be adjusted, let the engineer know.

When the engineer is ready to record, you will be asked for a *level* or to *read for levels*. He needs to set his audio controls for your voice. Consider this a rehearsal, so perform your lines exactly the way you intend to once recording begins. If you speak softly when reading for levels, and then speak much louder on your first take, your level will be too "hot" and your performance will have been wasted on an unusable recording. You may do several reads for levels, none of which will likely be recorded. However, the producer or engineer may give you some direction to get you on the right track once recording begins.

The engineer will *slate* each take as you go. You will hear all direction and slates in your headphones. This is not the same as slating your name for an audition. The engineer usually will slate, or identify the project or section you are working on, followed by "take 1," "take 2," and so on. Before or after the slate, you may receive some additional direction. You may also hear a low-frequency tone, or buzz, when the engineer is slating the track. This tone makes it easier for the engineer to locate the desired takes when he begins editing. The slate tone is used most commonly on analog tape recording sessions, and is not used as much on digital recordings.

Do not begin reading until the engineer has finished his slate and all direction is finished. You will know when you can start by listening for the sound of the control room mic being turned off. If you speak too soon, your first few words might be unusable. Wait a second or two after the slate, get a good supporting breath of air, then begin speaking.

As you are reading your lines, the engineer will be watching your level and listening to the sound of your voice. He will also be keeping a written log sheet of take numbers and will time each read with a stopwatch. He may also be discussing your delivery or possible copy changes with the producer or client.

COMMON DIRECTION CUES

After each take, you can expect to receive some direction from the producer. It may be that you read too slowly and need to speed up your delivery. Or, the producer might tell you that you have a few seconds "to play with." This means you read too fast, and can slow down a bit. Do not change your attitude or character, unless requested by the producer. Also, do not comment about things you feel you are doing wrong, or ask how you are doing. Let the producer guide you into the read he or she is after. Some of the other direction cues you might hear are:

- **"Pick up the pace"** — You need to read faster, but keep the same character and attitude.

- **"Split the difference"** — An earlier take was either too fast or too slow, and the last take was a bit the other direction. On this next take, adjust your pacing to something in between. The same direction applies to treatment of your character, or on your inflection or enunciation.

- **"Play with it . . ."** — The producer is giving you the opportunity to use your creativity to make the lines work better. Have some fun, modify your delivery, change your pace a bit, try a different inflection, and so on.

- **"Three in a row"** — You are being asked to read the same sentence or tag three times, back to back. Give each read in the set a slightly different treatment. The producer is looking for a read that will work best with the rest of the copy. You will frequently be asked for three in a row when doing tags.

- **"Add some smile"** — Literally, put a smile on your face as you read the copy. A smile changes the physical attitude of your body, your mental attitude, and comes through in your read. Smiling makes you sound more friendly, and adds energy to your delivery.

- **"More/less energy"** — Add some excitement to your read, or calm your delivery. Use your body and move your arms to increase energy. Relax and soften your body movement to reduce energy.

- **"Billboard a word"** — This is also referred to as *punching* a word or phrase. *Billboarding* simply means to give a word or phrase a little extra emphasis. The intent is to have that word stand out from the rest of the copy.

- **"Make it conversational"** — Take the reading out of your delivery. Pretend you are telling a story, or visualize yourself talking to your best friend. Talk *to* your audience, not *at* them. Everything you have been doing may be just right, but the illusion of realness may need a little help. Keep the pace and energy, maybe add some smile, and believe in what you are saying. Do this and you will make your delivery more natural.

- **"Warm it up a little"** — Make your delivery more friendly and more personal. Get a sense of what makes you feel warm and fuzzy and use that to shift your attitude to get a warmer delivery.

- **"Stay in character"** — You are drifting in and out of character. Your performance is inconsistent. Something in your delivery is not consistent from beginning to end. It could be an accent or speaking style, attitude, or even inconsistent volume. Try to keep your character the same as you read the copy from take to take.

- **"Do a pick-up"** — This means that the first part of a sentence or paragraph was fine, and that the director wants you to continue from a certain point in the copy. They will specify where they want you to "pick it up." When you do a pick-up, it's always a good idea to read into the pick-up line. Starting with the last few words before your pick-up will make the phrasing and flow natural, and the engineer's job of editing easier. It's also a good idea to read out after the line by continuing a few words into the next sentence.

- **"Wild line"** — The director or engineer is asking you to do a single line or phrase over. It's not uncommon to do several complete takes, then go back and do wild lines for certain parts of the copy. The director and engineer will be making notes as to which takes they think will work best when everything is edited together later.

- **"Do it again, but different"** — My personal favorite! This simply means that the producer is looking for something extra from your delivery, and he or she may not know how to describe what it is. When you get this direction, find a way to make your next take a little bit unique. Take it over the top, or underplay for a different effect.

- **"That's a buy"** — The three little words you've been waiting to hear! Good job, great take, you're done.

There are many other directions you will be given. Do your best to perform as the director requests. There is a reason why he or she is asking you to make adjustments, although that reason will sometimes not be clear to you.

You may think, and the director may tell you, that you have a perfect take. When the producer gets a good take, you may hear "do it again, just like that," or "one more time for protection." Then there may be several more takes. Each additional take may be slightly different from the one before, or the producer or director may ask for major adjustments, or even make changes to the copy. As you do many takes, you need to remember what you have done before. The producer may say he liked what you did three takes ago. You need to try to duplicate it, even if you don't remember what you did.

Producers usually have a clear idea of what they want, and may not be receptive to your suggestions. Find out what the producer is looking for when you first go through the script. Once in the studio, you should be pretty much on track for the entire session. However, if you get a great idea, or if it appears that the producer is having a hard time making a copy change, by all means speak up. You are part of a team, and part of your job is to help build an effective product. If your idea is not welcome, the producer will tell you.

Recording studio equipment sometimes has a mind of its own. There are times when the engineer may stop you in the middle of a take because of a technical problem, and you may have to wait awhile until it is corrected. Although not often, technical delays do happen. When they do, you need to be ready to pick up where you left off, with the same character and delivery, when the engineer is ready.

If you left your water in the control room, let the engineer know and it will be brought in for you. If you need to visit the restroom, let them know. If you need a pencil, let them know. If you need *anything*, let them know. Once your position is set in front of the microphone (on-mic), the engineer will prefer that you not leave the studio, or change your position. Even a small change relative to the microphone can make a big difference in the sound of your voice. This can be a problem when doing long scripts or lots of takes. If your mic position changes, you can sound very different on different takes, which can be a problem for the engineer if he needs to assemble several takes to build the final commercial. If you must move off-mic, try to keep your original mic position in mind when you return to the mic.

Keep your volume consistent throughout your session. Changes in dynamics may be useful for certain dramatic effects, but, generally, you will want to keep your voice at a constant volume or in a range that is consistent with your character. If your performance does call for sudden changes in volume, try to make sure they occur at the same place in the copy for each take. This becomes important later on, when the engineer edits different takes together. If your levels are erratic, the changes in volume may become noticeable in the final edit.

You know what the producer wants. You stay in character. Your timing and pacing are perfect. Your enunciation and inflection are on track. Your performance is wonderful. The producer is happy. The engineer is happy. And, most important, the client is happy. That's it! You're done, right?

Not quite.

Wrap It Up

Before leaving the studio, make sure you sign the contract for your services. If you are a union member, the producer will probably have a contract already filled out for you. Read the parts of the contract that apply to your session before signing. If you were booked for one commercial (spot announcement), and the producer had you do three spots plus tags, make sure the changes are made on the contract. Also make sure you call your agent and let him or her know about the changes. If you are unsure of anything on the contract, call your agent *before* signing the contract.

For union work, send your AFTRA form to the union within 48 hours of the session to avoid any penalties. The union form is the only way

AFTRA has of tracking your work, and making sure you are paid in a timely manner. If you are working freelance, make sure you are paid before you leave the studio, or that you have a signed invoice or deal memo. You've completed your part of the agreement, and you are entitled to be paid. It's up to you if you agree to have your payment sent to you, but keep in mind that you take a risk of delays or not being paid if you do this.

It's good form to thank the producer, engineer, client, and anyone else involved in the session before you leave. Keep the script for your files, if you like. If you think your performance was especially good, you can ask the producer for a copy of the spot when it is finished. Always ask for a DAT, a one-off CD, or a reel-to-reel copy, but don't argue if all you can get is a cassette. Audio cassettes and reel-to-reel copies will usually be sent to you or your agent, often at no cost. But there may be a charge for a DAT copy, CD, or videotape copies of a TV commercial. If distribution of a commercial is via audio tape, it's easy for the engineer to make an extra copy of your spot when making dubs for radio stations; however, sending tapes to performers is not a high priority. In this digital age, finished commercials are increasingly being distributed via ISDN networks directly from the studio's computer, e-mailed as MP3 files, uploaded to a website, or mailed as a one-off CD. The commercial you performed in may not leave the digital domain until it is aired and you may find yourself waiting several weeks, or even months, before you get your copy.

Once your session is over and the paperwork is done, you are free to leave. Your job is done, so don't stick around for the rest of the session or to talk. The producer and engineer have lots of work ahead of them and your presence can cause delays, costing time and money. After you are gone, the process of assembling all the pieces of the puzzle begins. It may take from several hours to several days before the final audio track is complete.

If your session is for a TV commercial, the completed audio will often be sent to a video post-production house where the video will be edited to your track to create a final TV spot. In some cases, just the opposite occurs — the video may have been edited to a scratch track, and the purpose of your session would have been to place your voice-over against the preproduced video. Once mastered, a number of copies are made and distributed to the radio and TV stations scheduled to air the spot.

Followup your session with a thank-you note to the producer. Thank him or her for good directing or mention something you talked about at the session. Be honest and sincere, but don't overdo it. A simple note or postcard is often all that's necessary to keep you in the mind of the producer or director and get you hired again. If you haven't already, be sure to add their names to your mailing list for future promotions you send out.

18

Tips, Tricks, & Studio Stories

This chapter is all about voice actors who are willing to help their fellow performers become better at their craft. Building a career in voice-over can be a daunting and seemingly overwhelming task at times. There are endless questions about technique, marketing, equipment, dealing with clients, setting rates, and so on. We are fortunate that so many professionals in this business are willing to share their experience and knowledge with those just beginning. The Internet offers a number of voice-over discussion boards where you can get answers to your questions from some of the top people in this business: **www.voiceartists.com**, **www.voicemodels.com,** **www.groups.yahoo.com/group/voiceactors,** and **www.flix.com** are only a few. You can get a lot of inside information about voice-over from these discussion boards.

As in any business, experienced professionals develop a special insight into the business, how they fit in, and what they can do to maximize their skills and market themselves. Many will develop a few special "tricks-of-the-trade" to make their job easier, while others might experience interesting or unusual situations during the course of their work. This chapter is a gift from some of the many professionals around the world I've come to know over the past few years. Please join me in thanking them for sharing their knowledge and use this chapter to learn from their experience.

NANCY WOLFSON (Los Angeles, CA) — www.braintracksaudio.com

Nancy is owner of Braintracks Audio and currently works in Los Angeles, California, as a Freelance Casting Director, a Commercial Voice-over Consultant, Voice-over Acting Coach/Demo CD Producer, and Freelance On-Air Promo Producer. Her specialty is helping actors "brand" their personal style from an aural, visual, cultural, and psychological perspective. Prior to going freelance, Nancy helmed the Voice-Over Department (Commercial, Animation & Celebrity) at Los Angeles talent agency Abrams-Rubaloff and Lawrence. Nancy definitely knows voice-over and she shares her insights from her vast experience in several different areas of the business:

> The academic in me has volumes of text analysis tricks to un-boggle the mind:
>
> - if a word repeats, don't emphasize it
> - if you're going to re-write the joke, put the funny word at the end of the sentence
> - work TV copy close mic as if you're relaying an urgent secret
> - hinge the comedic relief in a radio script with as much contrast as possible
>
> The cultural behaviorist in me has many lectures to give on the Death of Exuberance in Contemporary American Culture. Today, the slice of the consumer audience the advertisers care about most is a jaded generation who has no interest in hearing a commercial slathered with 1980's "sunshine" all over the read. (My 12 year old nephew, Justin, would say you sound like a liar — or worse, Cathy Lee Gifford — if you perk up your delivery with too much of a "stupid smile.") That "warm up the read" thing is about as much a thing of the past as the more commonly lambasted "bombastic 1950's trailer announcer."
>
> The music/acting coach in me has two basic tricks for jack-hammering announcer-ism out of a read: play the minor scales instead of the major ones and jazz up your tempo with a fresh sense of arrival.
>
> The Personal Marketing Consultant in me who specializes in chats about Branding and Personal Style could give you lots of metaphors about needing to figure out which crayon you are in the box/cereal on the shelf/broken toy in the chest before you ever hope to get a job.
>
> However, the best advice I think I can provide comes from the (former) Talent Agent in me: Any voice-over talent is best served to think of themselves as being involved in a service industry. Whether one is auditioning or in an actual recording session, it is the talent's primary job to be of service to the writer's intentions.
>
> The writer has endeavored to write copy that will service his or her client, and it is the actor's job to help the writer make those words sound like what they sounded like in the writer's head. Focusing on the grandeur of one's own genetic piping in the

midst of a performance will only obscure the intentions of the writer, servicing one's own ego more than the folks who have a widget to sell in Wisconsin.

1. Be available.
2. Be affable.
3. Be able.

In that order.

VIKTOR PAVEL (Berlin, Germany) — http://come.to/viktorpavel

Born in 1965 in the Czech Republic, Viktor's family fled to Germany in 1968 when the USSR and their allies crushed the democratic movement. He learned to speak German by watching TV. His is an interesting story of how someone can achieve their goals by learning their craft and being persistent. It also reveals that the voice-over business is very much the same in other countries as it is in the U.S. He shares many insights into the voice-over business that are usually only learned through experience. Viktor tells his story far better than I can, so here it is in his own words:

> After high school I had no clue what to do, but I knew office boredom and hard labor were not for me. I started working as an author (prose, drama), and recorded my first audio-book magazines at the age of 17 but with no intention to become a pro. I joined the West Berlin art scene, did performances, low and no budget film, readings, exhibitions, sung in a band, got some grants, publications, air play, hardly any money — the usual. For a living I was working in factories, I dropped out of university after 2 years (American studies and journalism) and got rather depressed. I had been living on a shoestring budget for a decade, my apartment was a dark, cold pit with no hot water, coal heating, and a toilet in the hallway. And I was heading for 30 with no proper career in sight.

> As I always had a rather deep voice (great to bullshit my way into discos at the age of 16) some guys recommended I should do something with my voice. So I did. Booking myself into a beginners voice training class at a private acting school I was very lucky. The teacher had had an East German training (much better than West German) and was great. So I took some private lessons with the guy. I realized I had potential and talent.

> My first job was reading the traffic news at a radio station. I was live on air for 12 times a shift, reading meaningless nonsense — what a great training!

The first years were hard. Okay, I was paid almost the same rate per job as today. But when you have only 2 jobs a month you're still on a compulsory diet. I must have called a hundred companies. And one guy said: "Hey, it's great you called. We just happen to need a voice-over talent for a documentary. Can you come this afternoon?" So that was that. I made sure they got the impression I had been doing this for years (why bother them with the information that this was my first job) and now I have. Which brings me to my philosophy (if you want to call it that): Make the client feel good! They want service not a diva. Throw in a joke or two (but never on the recording subject. I once recorded a corporate video and the family in the picture looked kinda nerdish to me — you know the inbreed type. So I wisecracked a cheap joke and the director said: "Buddy, that is my brother in law." Ouch!).

Give them the feeling you absolutely know what you are doing (as sometimes they do not and have to rely on your judgment and experience. Also these agency types can be hard to deal with).

Be a pro. The one and only goal is to achieve the best recording possible. The best is the one take that gets the client's message across perfectly well. So ask yourself: "What do these guys really want?" (It is not always what they say they want).

You need to learn different styles just like a good studio musician. In corporate videos, for example, the client wants to come across as the number 1 company, so you need sound relaxed and self-assured. Hard sell does not do the trick.
If there is something you are unsure of, ask. Stick to the sound engineer, these guys are always cool, friendly, and helpful. You can trust their judgment.

A big problem is flawed texts; be very careful with criticism, but do try to suggest improvements if you see a need for them. Some colleagues here in Berlin say they don't care about the text, if the client wants crap he gets it. That is not my philosophy, but I can tell you some companies dislike me for my criticism.

Sometimes the author of the text will be your director and nobody likes being told their text is not too great. Experience will help you to decide when to say something or when not to. You know what I think? When people with bad texts and unprofessional attitudes stop booking me I will end up working with the nice people only, which is great. Though I know it is not easy when you are a beginner with very few jobs.

Often, small things count. If you like the commercial tell them so, if you don't, keep your mouth shut. I have had recordings when the client was happy with the session whereas I was not. So I said I can do better and tried again. Or you'll have to stick around for a hour more waiting for some crucial phone call; it happens all the time. Don't grumble. Try to postpone your next date (especially if it's private). If they find out you have a private life, they will get jealous and dislike you. Again: these people work under awful stress and bear the burden of responsibility (unlike you!). Try to ease their tension, make them feel good. Offer help, bring them a coffee.

Don't be too modest. When I had to read awful translations (from English to German) I said: "I can do better, give me a book and you'll see." Since then I've translated about 80 documentaries for that company and after a while they asked me to work for them as a director, too. Had I kept my mouth shut I would have never gotten these great opportunities.

There are quite a few talented people out there, but there are very few people who have the talent AND the attitude AND run their business like a proper company. If you are one of them (and remember: you can work on at least two of these three prerequisites) you can make it big time! Good luck (that helps, too)!

I have never ever had regrets to have become a voice-over artist. I enjoy 4 out of 5 jobs, work with interesting people on new subjects every day, and make good money. I am long enough in the studio to be offered a coffee but never long enough to be exposed to possible internal company bull.

My warm up routine includes stretching and flexing my face muscles a lot. (Don't let anybody see this, you look like you just escaped from a loony asylum.)

Also I fight tenseness in my lips in the morning with releasing bilabial sounds like Bo, Boo, Bah. It is important to use one arm with this, pretending to throw something or chasing something away. Singing also is a great exercise. I try not to record too early in the morning as I need 2 hours to get going, which means that for an early session I gotta get up at 6 a.m. — yuck. (Voice-over work before 10 a.m. simply costs more.)

And of course: coffee is great in the morning, but is likely to ruin your sound as it makes your mouth dry producing annoying click sounds. No sparkling drinks either. You might feel alright, but once you start working with your diaphragm out comes a (in most cases rather inappropriate) BUURP!

I like carrot juice a lot, it moistens the throat but unlike orange juice it doesn't produce much saliva. Just like a dry mouth, spittle can be a real problem especially when you're reading live. Very quickly turn your head away from the mike when you swallow. This shouldn't take more time than inhaling for the next sentence.

Just 2 seconds before the take I make sure I have my mouth already open and have inhaled already (of course this works only when you have a time code or know when the take starts; otherwise your face turns red). Besides avoiding unwanted sounds this makes it easier for the engineer to edit the take. One of my weirdest and most difficult voice-over jobs was for a client in the US who wanted a hardcore Kraut accent. Now having studied American English at the university and doing VO work in English frequently I had to practice hard to sound like a friendly version of der fuehrer. So I rolled my "r's" and tried not to bring my tongue between the teeth for the "th," knowing that Germans often use an unvoiced "s" for a "th." Finally I managed to mingle fake Krautness with the South German dialect Swabian which is spoken in Baden-Wuerttemberg, the state I grew up in. I know for sure in some 20 years or so some fool is gonna dig up that recording making me look like a complete nitwit.

But, why didn't they take some regular Kraut in the first place? Good question. They wanted a pro, okay. But also they wanted to convey that this recording was done in Germany (which it was, in my studio in Berlin) by a German (that's me again, though I was born in the Czech Republic). Hmm, I just realized after all I might have been the perfect guy for that . . .

My guess is: as it was a corporate video about engineering someone might have come up with the brilliant idea of gaining extra credibility. You know: Germans — good beer, good engineering, bad English. Anyway, the job was well paid and my sound engineer had the recording session of his life collapsing with laughter (hey, he should have paid me for that).

Well, if you like absurdity, that is just one of the many good reasons to become a voice-over artist.

Hey, yesterday evening I heard myself on TV with my very first national campaign for Deutsche Bank. I kissed my girlfriend and said: "Finally I've joined the premiere league. Yippee!"

Best wishes from Berlin.

JON BEAUPRÉ (Los Angeles) — www.broadcastvoice.com

Jon is a well-known voice coach on the West coast, working mostly with radio and television broadcast journalists to help them improve their performance. He teaches in the Broadcast Communications program at California State University at Los Angeles, and conducts workshops and seminars with the Associated Press Radio and Television Association. Jon is also an award-winning radio producer and reporter and a frequent contributor to local and internationally syndicated programming on National Public Radio and the BBC.

The vast majority of my clients work in news and public affairs and not performers who work in commercial voice-over work, though much of what we do from a performance perspective is identical: we work from scripts, we have to connect the words on the page with feelings, and communicate those ideas to an audience.

Lesson one for my clients is based on the acronym "BATS," which is the encapsulation of the first couple of lessons we teach.

The "B" stands for "Breathing," which should be diaphragmatic, rather than in the upper chest. This seems counter-intuitive to novices, since we have spent so many of our years breathing from our upper chest. Breathing from the diaphragm, or lower stomach, is more efficient, more effective, and considerably more powerful once it becomes second nature.

"A" stands for "Audience." The idea here is that it is not terribly important what you as a performer feel or do. It is considerably more important what your AUDIENCE feels or does. In other words, while your intention may be one thing, you need to discover exactly what it is your audience is interpreting. Sorry, but you are not important, your audience is — at least in the context of voice performing.

"T" stands for "Three Part Rule," perhaps the most complicated part of the whole lesson. The three part rule is:

1. Settle (don't force your voice down, let it float).

2. Comfortable (to a natural, normal part of your own voice).

3. Lower (lower range, not lower note. It isn't fixed, it floats).

This is hard to figure out sometimes. It basically means to work in the lower part of your normal voice, not in a put-on voice at all, but as a natural lower range.

"S" stands for "set-up," which is a simple routine voice performers should get into the habit of doing before any rehearsal, performance, or recording. In short, the routine goes "relax toes, feet, legs, knees unlocked and relaxed, stomach relaxed, shoulders slumped, head and chin floating on the horizon, no tension or tightness; inhale and exhale. Inhale to prepare. Pause. Speak!" There is in fact much more to the set-up than this, but it's a good starting point.

So, there is no reason to let voice work drive you batty if you remember the acronym "BATS."

Keep breathing!

PAUL HECKMAN (Dallas, TX) — www.flixusa.com

Paul has been around the entertainment industry in one way or another since the 60's as an actor, writer, and night-club manager. He currently operates **www.FlixUSA.com**, a website which includes discussion boards, job opportunities, and lots of resources. Although most of Paul's work has been on-camera, the point of this story he shares is clear: It is not a good idea to eat before you do a voice-over session. Thanks for sharing, Paul.

We were shooting a commercial for Bonanza Steak Houses. It was around 1978 and they were premiering their new chicken finger dish.

We shot the actor's part first, where I was playing a young man who is proposing to his wife-to-be. As I handed her the ring, they wanted the camera to focus on the diamond ring which she was holding. It needed to be held at an exact angle to get the glint. At the same time, I was eating one of the chicken fingers. The Biz was fairly new to me, and I was actually eating the chicken fingers instead of spitting them out between takes. The girl opposite me could not get the ring in the position that the DP wanted, so they must have shot it about 25 times. Then I was supposed do the voice-over in a small room off to the side, but by this time, the 25 or so chicken fingers were starting to live a life of their own in my stomach. The soundman's speaker was directly in front of me, and then up came the chicken fingers! Needless to say the soundman wasn't thrilled and that was the last time I worked for them . . .

BOB JUMP (Norfolk, VA) — www.jumpworldwide.com

Bob is the voice behind Smucker's Jellies and Jams, Chevy Blazer, Arby's Roast Beef, and more. He's become an American brand name in voice-over — *and* one of the busiest voice-over talents performing today.

Bob's philosophy is refreshing: "What else allows you to be a road in Nebraska one day, an astronaut the next, a talking shrimp the day after; then become the voice of Smucker's on top of it all? And that's *just four days* out of the whole year. I love this business!"

The choice of many regional and national agencies worldwide, Bob's work airs throughout America, as well as campaigns running in New Zealand, Singapore, Australia, England, Italy, Scotland, Canada, and Ireland.

Bob's story illustrates the point that this business can at times be a bit fickle. It also makes the point that you just never know where a job might take you.

True story: Six months ago, a writer/producer of a large shop in Virginia Beach phoned me with a proposition. He explained that there is a fellow who's been voicing TV & Radio spots for a statewide furniture chain called Haynes for years. Haynes has used him over and over again because he has a unique style.

Anyway, the voice-over guy's name is John H——. The writer/ producer of this large shop *then* says "Bob, look . . . I want to rip off H——'s voice . . . *bigtime.* I <u>know</u> you "do" H—— —— do you have a problem with this?"

Well, being the "voicewhore" that I am, I said "no problemo!" So for the next six months, the Hampton Roads market was saturated with Bob Jump doing John H—— for Freedom Automotive. You could not escape this voice. It was everywhere. In fact, people were getting it in the fillings of their teeth it was so saturated. So *much* so, that *one day*, one of the creatives working with Haynes (Haynes being the store that had the original John H—— voice in the first place) called a local recording studio and asked them if they could find "the guy who's been doing all of the Freedom Automotive stuff for the last six months." The recording studio said "Find him? Hell, Bob Jump's on our talent roster! Why?" The reply was "Are you kiddin'? <u>*He's* gonna *be our new voice for Haynes!*</u>"

Tell me that this kind of story isn't what goes on daily in this industry. Ya gotta laugh.

PHIL GANYON (San Diego, CA)

Phil is Principal/Creative Director of *TGIF The Ganyon Idea Factory — Creative Advertising & Communication* — an award-winning San Diego–based ad agency founded in 1977. Phil has an extensive background in radio and television broadcasting and is a writer, comedian, actor, performer, emcee, and singer. He has produced, directed, and voiced hundreds of radio and television commercials and has recently translated into English a French book which proves, scientifically, the existence of the soul: *SPIRIT...The Stranger Inside Us* by Jean Emile Charon. Phil's fascination with words has led him to write a "fun-with-words" book entitled *Warped Worms...Naughty Plays on Words*. Following are some of Phil's experiences from his many years in broadcasting and advertising.

A booth VO announcement gave me tension sweats; it was for the annual Cherryfield Fair. The board engineer, with a twinkle in his eye, wouldn't let me pre-record it. Why? George was waiting for ME to spoonerize: "See the **B**ucking **F**ord!" F-F-Fortunately, I never did.

Tree Brand Pickles sponsored the M-F early evening news. I did live on-camera with product. Right before he cued me, cameraman Pete would whisper, "Pee-Trickles, Pee-Trickles, Pee-Trickles!" I never succumbed to the spooner-suggestion; but once, I did say they'd look really nice on your "**t**rellish **r**ay."

I was up at 4AM to go on the air at 5AM after only 3-4 hours of shut-eye. Remember the famous Bloopers record? Well, one never knows when the subconscious will trip you up. On that record was the classic Herbert Hoover flub: "Hoobert Heever." Wouldn't you know it . . . sleep deprivation made its move on that fateful morning when I got the bulletin: Former President, Herbert Hoover, had passed away. I hurried into the booth. The on-air jock hit the News Bulletin music, and I entoned: "Former President, Heebert Hoover . . . Ah, that's Former President, Hoobert Heever . . ." Yep it happened . . . I lost it. Completely LOST IT! I must have been on the floor, convulsing in helpless laughter for at least 5 minutes.

I was in a Salt Lake City recording studio doing a duet VO for Highland Dairy. After a particularly frustrating series of sibilant takes, the director pops onto the studio intercom and, through tightly clenched teeth, says: "Could somebody PLEASE call the President and have him take all the S's out of the English language?!"

DB COOPER (Boston, MA) — www.voxvobiscum.com

DB Cooper "got into radio" when she was 10 years old, as a daily feature on Granny Goose's afternoon radio show on KGMB in Honolulu, Hawaii. As "Little Friend" DB would call with a riddle every day. It wasn't long before she moved into theater as an actress and later producer/director/ owner of a small theater company. When called by a nearby radio station looking for actors to do character voice work for the station, she made the move into radio commercials. That was 1988, and she's been doing voice- over ever since as well as continuing her theatrical acting. According to DB, she's directed and/or acted in "about a million plays and musicals in New England regional theater." She's also been a popular radio disc jockey and traffic reporter in Boston. Here's how DB describes her career in voice- over: "The combination of mic skill and the ability to 'tell a story' has made voice acting a natural course to follow — oh what the heck; made it an easy path to take and a frustrating one to follow."

> I was voicing a number of 30-second spots for my local cable company and we ended up with one that was the proverbial 40 pounds of info in a 30-pound bag. I did all that I could, including my screamin' "motorcycles-for-sale" read (hardly appropriate, considering the client was a Bridal Salon), but it just wouldn't work so we alerted the Ad Exec that we needed to edit.

> Either not knowing or not caring that the control room had a mic that was always live, the ad exec huffed into the room with a withering glance at me through the window and asked the guys, "What's HER problem?" The producers explained that there was simply too much info for a 30-second spot (think of Salieri's suggestion of Mozart's "too many notes"). The AE retorted, "I can read it in 30 seconds." And she demonstrated.

> Consider, if you will, someone with no inflection reading a grocery list as quickly as possible and then add a terrific regional accent and that was her example. I offered to step aside, but the producers gently pushed for the edit instead, and as I recall the client was pleased with the results.

WARD FRANKLIN (New York, NY) — www.wardvoice.com

Wearing headphones when "in the booth" is common practice for voice- over. But as Ward points out, doing things the way they've always been done may not be the best way to get the results you want.

> I remember many years ago working with a production director and voicing a spot. I thought it had to be the traditional way, the

way it was always done. He broke it down and said "talk to me, take your headphones off and say . . ." Not knowing it, he was recording the session. After the so-called rehearsal, he said are you ready? I replied, Yes, and he said fine you're finished! I was shocked only to find out that he had recorded for regional distribution a Keating Ford radio spot. In the time that it took for me to reevaluate his direction, a phone patch was in place to the owner of one of the largest Ford dealers in Fairfield County. The spot ran and ran and I did numerous character bits as "Chipper" the expert who loved Fords. It was a hit, he got attention, and it made a return on everyone's investment. After that day the headphones came off for nearly everything I do and everything is a true performance.

JOHN MATTHEW (Los Angeles, CA) — www.johnmatthew.com

John is a professional voice actor with a long list of commercial voice-over credits. He has worked with major advertising agencies in Southern California, handled the voice work for numerous corporate projects, and provided looping VO for film and television. He shares a story that illustrates the "you never know — in the right place at the right time" aspect of the voice-over business.

I was at Different Drummer recently recording an industrial narration. While I was there, a recent client called to talk to the engineer about recording a scratch VO for some spec spots he was producing for a new client — right after my session. When he heard that I was there, he asked if I would do the scratch VO, and I agreed. After we finished the narration, we spent all of 5 minutes recording the scratch track, and I went home.

A week or so later, I was booked to record 3 spots (1 of which was lifted onto 3 more spots) for the client, who had approved my scratch VO. No audition, no nothing — it was just sheer luck that I had been at the studio that day! So it just goes to show you . . .

The moral of John's story is that you never know when that next booking will appear — or what it may lead to.

MELISSA REIZIAN FRANK (Lexington, KY) - www.melissavoiceover.com

Melissa is a freelance voice-over and on-camera actor. She left broadcast journalism after 10 years as a reporter/anchor/producer in order to have more flexible hours so she could spend more time with her three-year-old son, Jarod. Melissa's story points out both the simple joys and challenges of freelance voice-over work. As you will see, it can sometimes be an interesting session when you take your "fan club" with you.

> Working from home allows me to keep him home from daycare "just for the heck of it" occasionally. It never fails, however, that when I choose to do this, something comes up. One time, I was called in to do a messaging on hold session at the last minute, and had to bring Jarod with me. I impressed upon him that he'd have to be very good and very quiet while Mommy was working (as you know, 3-year-olds are known for their self-restraint!). He agreed, and did very well at first. This is a studio that has its talent record many scripts at a time, on their own, on individual mini discs. As Jarod saw me recording and stopping in a definite pattern, he must have decided he was an audience member at a performance, because right after I finished one take and began recording another, he began clapping wildly yelling, "Good job, Mommy!"

WILLIAM DUFRIS (Cumberland Center, ME)

William Dufris is a professional audio book narrator and producer with more than 300 projects to his credit. During his residency in London (13 years), he worked for the BBC (both radio and television — with Kathleen Turner, Stockard Channing, Sharon Gless, and many other well-known stars), as well as treading the boards in London and Frankfurt. During the latter part of his time there, William co-established a production company called the Story Circle (which has since received two Audie Awards — for Phillip Pullman's *The Golden Compass* and Jane Goodall's *A Reason For Hope*). William returned to the States in 1999, living in Seattle for two years, before settling back in his home state of Maine. He is now continuing with audio book producing and narrating, as well as organizing a Radio Theatre Troupe and performs the voice of "Bob" in the popular animated series on Nickelodeon Jr., *BOB the Builder*. William also teaches workshops on how to effectively voice an audio book and was kind enough to contribute an extensive series of "tips for audio book narration" that can be found in Chapter 12. He offers this rather humorous story about a session he was doing in London.

> This session was for a rather long and dull narration with extremely dry copy. The recording complex was one with several studios, each of which had a window in the door that provided a clear view of the control room to anyone looking in.

We were well into our session, without any breaks, when an engineer from one of the other studios happened to walk down the hall and glance into our studio. He was expecting to see our session busy at work, but what he saw when he looked through that window completely took him by surprise! As he peered through the glass, cupping his hands around his eyes to block the glare from the hallway lights, there was no one to be seen — the control room appeared to be completely empty. Yet there, across the room, the reels continued to turn on the tape recorder. A most unusual sight.

Curious, the engineer quietly opened the door and entered the control room. Walking slowly up the ramp to the audio console, he carefully perused first the control room, and then turned to look through the large double-glass windows into the studio. It took no time at all to realize what had happened.

There, slumped over the audio desk in the control room was the producer/engineer — sound asleep. And in the studio, there I was, still sitting on my stool — also sound asleep. Apparently, the session engineer had fallen asleep before I did, and the tape just kept on rolling.

We eventually finished that narration, but following our "nap" we did take breaks far more frequently.

BRUCE HAYWARD (Toronto, Canada) — www.brucehayward.com

Bruce was on the air for 6½ years at 5 radio stations in Ontario and made the move to professional voice-over in 1987. He pursued a variety of other types of work finally getting back to voice-over on a full-time basis in 1998. From 1987 to 1998, Bruce was actively doing voice work, but he was not marketing his talent. He has a versatile style and can do anything from soft-sell to hard-sell to character voice work.

What follows is excerpted from numerous e-mails Bruce has sent to people who have asked for his help and advice. He's a goldmine of valuable information and offers his thoughts from the point of view as a non-union voice actor in Canada.

On home recording:

This involves a microphone, sound card, and digital audio recording and editing software. Combined with a website, anyone in the world with access to the web and a desire for voice talent becomes a potential client. Scripts and direction are emailed to you. Recorded and edited voice (not produced/final versions normally) are emailed back. And you trust the agreed upon fee will be sent to you unless you have a merchant email account and accept credit cards. Most people are honest. If they're not, you're only out a little time and you never work with/for them again and black list and bad mouth them every chance you get. Plus, a home studio is also an excellent way to get the practice you need.

I should warn you that these days, with the plummeting prices for home recording, the same thing is happening in audio that happened in graphic arts and printing with the advent of cheap desktop publishing. Everyone and anyone now considers themselves able to either do voice or audio production or both. I don't say this to discourage you, only to make you aware that there is a lot of competition in the business at the moment and for the foreseeable future. What should happen is that people begin to realize they only get what they pay for and become more discriminating when casting a project. When and if this will actually happen is anybody's guess.

On rates:

I usually try to be just a little more than fair. My minimum charge is normally $100, but I've worked for a lot less, sometimes for reciprocal services such as recording and editing, sometimes because the project was a demo or spec for that person/business to get more business — which, hopefully, means more business for me. My rates are not carved in stone, they're flexible and negotiable. I usually try to work within a given client's budget. Under these "rules" if the current client has a small budget, you take less and when a client has more budget, you get more. While I have worked for no money many times I never advocate working for free. You are providing a service for which you should get paid — either in money, quid pro quo, or future work.

This business is cyclical — this means slow periods and busy periods. While this means little or no income in a slow period, it also means a chance to catch up on other things. Right now I'm getting a chance to complete my own home studio, which should be finished and "open" for business soon. Hopefully it will pay for itself over time, although I must confess, I really wanted the gear whether it ever pays for itself or not.

My best advice is to find a way to practice, practice, practice, get a professionally produced demo, and then market, market, market and be available. I would also suggest you have other sources of income because there are not a lot of people in the business who make substantial money over time.

On marketing:

When you are marketing, don't expect more than a 5% — yes that's five percent — acknowledgement and/or request for CD from an email or letter campaign. Studies of Direct Mail programs in other industries cite 6% as a great response rate. You must also take into consideration that even those people who do respond to your marketing and say they will use you may not or at least not for some time. Six months seems to be the median time. Remember, they already have talent that they use and they don't necessarily have projects on the go or ones which your talent would fit. They usually call when they have an emergency — their regular person is not available and they can't wait — and/or they want a change of voice on a project or they think your voice fits the project.

The big money resides with the big agencies who have the big clients. These agencies use the big producers who hire the big time talent — a nice little circle. Except for the clients — all you need is money to get in — the rest of the circle is a very tight clique. It's very, very hard to become a part of the circle — and if you fall out — very, very, very hard to get back in. I can only speak for Toronto, but I'm sure every other major advertising center has the same kind of circle. Because of ISDN — a digital hook-up between studios — the circle is becoming a little larger since talent doesn't even have to be flown in — they go to a studio with ISDN where they are and are recorded at a studio with ISDN where the producer is — just as if they were all in the same studio. Costly, but the big boys have a lot of money to burn. Even at this level work is cyclical.

Sometimes there's a lull and then you're back, sometimes you're just never called back. There was a performer named Steve Weston who was on every other commercial going it seemed. He then disappeared from view. He described it this way, "Who's Steve Weston . . . Let's try Steve Weston . . . Get me Steve Weston . . . Get me somebody who sounds like Steve Weston . . . Who's Steve Weston?"

I also once worked with a gentleman who used to be in the magic circle. He told me he was making $750,000 a year as a producer and arranger as part of the clique. Through a series of problems, some medical, he fell out of the circle and now cannot get back in no matter what he does or how hard he tries. I guess it's like a pyramid — there's all of us at the bottom and as you move up there's less and less people making more and more money. Getting to the top isn't easy and if you fall off you rarely get a second chance at climbing back up. Such is life.

And as you move up the pyramid so to speak there's normally less and less call for versatility. It's much like radio where in a small station you get to do everything and in a major market they have the money to hire "specialists" and plug them in where they need them. "It's nice you're an announcer who can write copy, but we have four award-winning copywriters on staff." The big producers hire people who do one, maybe two things very well with their voice and cast the people who fit the performance required perfectly. However, down at the bottom layers of the pyramid, versatility can be a good thing and will probably get you more work.

Also, the farther up the pyramid you go, the less tolerant they are of inexperience. Again, it's like radio. Small markets are where you go to make your mistakes and learn your craft. In a major market you're plugged in and expected to perform, not learn. At the prices the big boys pay for studio and talent, they don't have the time to help you improve. At the bottom of the pyramid the rates are much lower and some inexperience is usually excused, although I know everyone down here at the bottom likes to work with a professional.

ISDN to a small extent, but mostly digital audio recording, the Internet and MP3, have now opened up literally a world full of potential clients. This, however, has also raised the level of competition and vastly increased the number of competitors. I don't say this to discourage you, only to present the playing field realistically. With talent, availability and marketing, and by following the four "P's" — Practice, Patience, Perseverance, and Professionalism — you should be able to at least get a toehold in the voice business.

On getting voice-over work:

If you want to work on a reasonably steady basis do as much of everything and anything as you possibly can. It keeps you in "shape," is a pretty good income and being versatile — at least on the bottom levels of the pyramid — is a very good thing because it means you'll be working. It may not be as ego gratifying, but the bills get paid and food shows up on the table — which is a good thing.

In other words, don't be self-limiting in what you'll do — that just restricts the type of work you're willing to do and, therefore, your income. Let the people who are auditioning/hiring the talent worry about whether you fit their project or not. Then, once you're hired, all you have to worry about is doing the best job you can and making sure the client gets what they're looking for.